Total Quality Management Blueprint

Barrie Dale and Heather Bunney

LIVERPOOL
JOHN MOORES UNIVERSITY
AVRIL ROBARTS LRC
TITHEBARN STREET
LIVERPOOL L2 2ER
TEL. 0151 231 4022

Copyright © Barrie Dale and Heather Bunney 1999

The right of Barrie Dale and Heather Bunney to be identified as authors of this work has been asserted in accordance with the Copyright, Designs and Patents Act 1988.

First published 1999

2 4 6 8 10 9 7 5 3 1

Blackwell Publishers Ltd
108 Cowley Road
Oxford OX4 1JF
UK

Blackwell Publishers Inc.
350 Main Street
Malden, Massachusetts 02148
USA

All rights reserved. Except for the quotation of short passages for the purposes of criticism and review, no part of this publication may be reproduced, stored in a retrieval system, or transmitted, in any form or by any means, electronic, mechanical, photocopying, recording or otherwise, without the prior permission of the publisher.

Except in the United States of America, this book is sold subject to the condition that it shall not, by way of trade or otherwise, be lent, re-sold, hired out, or otherwise circulated without the publisher's prior consent in any form of binding or cover other than that in which it is published and without a similar condition including this condition being imposed on the subsequent purchaser.

British Library Cataloguing in Publication Data

A CIP catalogue record for this book is available from the British Library.

Library of Congress Cataloging-in-Publication Data has been applied for

ISBN 0-631-21664-2 (hbk)
ISBN 0-631-19577-7 (pbk)

Typeset in 11 on 13 pt Palatino by Ace Filmsetting Ltd, Frome, Somerset
Printed in Great Britain by TJ International, Padstow, Cornwall

This book is printed on acid-free paper

Contents

List of figures

List of tables

Preface

The focus of this Blueprint is Total Quality Management (TQM). The main objective is to provide basic guidance in easy to understand language to those people who wish to increase their knowledge and appreciation of TQM.

It will prove useful to both second and third year undergraduates taking business, management, engineering and science degrees and also to postgraduate students studying for specialist Master's degrees and MBAs. People studying for professional examinations which involve considerations of TQM should also benefit from reading the book. The book will give helpful advice to those managers initiating TQM and those wishing to develop and advance the concept. We believe that management at all levels of the organization hierarchy will find something of value in the text.

In a book of this size, format and price it is not easy to decide the detail and depth of the text, what is to be put in and what is to be left out. Whilst there is nothing particularly radical in the book it does cover some of the main concepts and issues currently being debated and considered by business leaders in organizations throughout the world. We believe that an appropriate balance has been struck.

We hope readers will study the complete book to gain a full understanding of TQM. However, most of the chapters can be used in standalone studies and readers may be selective in order to learn more about a particular topic.

The initiative for the book has arisen from the academic-industrial collaboration enjoyed by the authors during the last eight or so years, firstly at Betz Dearborn, then at United Utilities and more recently at Fielden-Cegos Bex Ltd. The sharing of ideas between theory and practice has helped to develop the authors' understanding of TQM. The evidence and material on which the book is based comes both from practical cases and experience and empirical research which has been conducted by Barrie Dale at UMIST since 1981. We have learned a lot from each other and hope that this knowledge is transmitted to the readers.

Barrie Dale
Manchester School of Management
UMIST
Manchester
and
Heather Bunney
Fielden-Cegos Bex Ltd
Manchester

Glossary of terms

AQAP	Allied Quality Assurance Publications
AQL	Acceptable Quality Level
AQP	Advanced Quality Planning
AQ+	Aeroquip Quality Plus
ASQ	American Society for Quality
ASQC	American Society for Quality Control
BCS	British Calibration Service
BPM	Business Process Management
BPR	Business Process Re-engineering
BQG	Business Quality Group
BSI	British Standards Institution
CANDO	Cleanliness, Arrangement, Neatness, Discipline and Orderliness
CBI	Continuous Business Improvement
CEN	European Committee for Standardization
CENELEC	European Committee for Electrotechnical Standardization
CEO	Chief Executive Officer
C_p	Process Potential Capability Index
C_{pk}	Process Capability Index
CSG	Customer Steering Group
CWQC	Company-Wide Quality Control
DPA	Departmental Purpose Analysis
DTI	Department of Trade and Industry
EC	European Community
EDI	Electronic Data Interchange
EFQM	European Foundation for Quality Management
EOQ	European Organization for Quality
EQA	European Quality Award
FMEA	Failure Mode and Effects Analysis
FTA	Fault Tree Analysis
GM	General Motors

HMSO	Her Majesty's Stationery Office
HPWT	High-Performance Work teams
IIP	Investors in People
ISO	International Organization for Standardization
IT	Information Technology
JIT	Just-in-Time
JUSE	Japanese Union of Scientists and Engineers
KT	Kawakita Jiro
LCL	Lower Control Limit
MBNQA	Malcolm Baldrige National Quality Award
MD	Managing Director
MoD	Ministry of Defence
NACCB	National Accreditation Council for Certification Bodies
NAMAS	National Measurement Accreditation Service
NASA	National Aeronautics and Space Administration
NATLAS	National Testing Laboratory Accreditation Service
NATO	North Atlantic Treaty Organization
NEDO	National Economic Development Office
NIST	National Institute of Technology
NWW	North West Water
PDCA	Plan, Do, Check, Act
PDPC	Process Decision Program Chart
PERT	Programme Evaluation and Review Technique
PIMS	Profit Impact of Market Strategy
PMP	Project Management Process
POC	Price of Conformance
PONC	Price of Non-Conformance
PPM	Parts per Million
Ppk	Preliminary Process Capability
QA	Quality Assurance
QCs	Quality Circles
QCCs	Quality Control Circles
QCD	Quality, Cost, Delivery
QFD	Quality Function Deployment
QSG	Quality Steering Group
RPN	Risk Priority Number
RPQ	Relative Perceived Quality
SLA	Service Level Agreement
SMEs	Small and Medium Sized Enterprises
SMED	Single Minute Exchange of Die
SMMT	Society of Motor Manufacturers and Traders
SPC	Statistical Process Control

SQA	Supplier Quality Assurance
TC	Technical Committee
UCL	Upper Control Limit
TPM	Total Productive Maintenance
TQC	Total Quality Control
TQI	Total Quality Improvement
TQM	Total Quality Management
TQSG	Total Quality Steering Group
UCL	Upper Control Limit
UK	United Kingdom
UKAS	UK Accreditation Service
UMIST	University of Manchester Institute of Science and Technology
US	United States
YITs	Yield Improvement Teams

1

Total Quality Management: an introduction

INTRODUCTION

In today's global competitive marketplace the demands of customers are forever increasing as they require improved quality of products and services but are prepared to pay less for their requirements. Continuous improvement in total business activities with a focus on excellence and the customer throughout the entire organization is one of the main means by which companies meet these demands. This is why quality and its management, the focus of this chapter, is looked upon by many organizations as the means by which they can gain and maintain a competitive edge over their rivals. The chapter introduces the reader to Total Quality Management (TQM). Many of the themes outlined here are explored later in the book.

The chapter opens by examining the different interpretations which are placed on the word 'quality'. It then goes on to outline why quality has grown in importance during the last decade or so. The evolution of quality management is described through the stages of inspection, quality control, quality assurance and to TQM. In presenting this evolution the drawbacks of a detection based approach to quality are compared to the recommended approach of prevention. The elements of TQM are explored along with its perceived benefits from a senior management perspective.

WHAT IS QUALITY?

'Quality' is now a familiar word. However, there are a variety of interpretations placed on its use and meaning. Today and in a variety of situations it is perhaps an overused word. For example, when a case is being made for extra funding and resources, preventing a reduction in funding, keeping a unit in operation and trying to emphasize excellence, just count the number of times the word 'quality' is used in the ensuring argument/ presentation.

Many people say they know what is meant by quality; they typically claim 'I know it when I see it', (i.e. quality by feel, taste, instinct and/or smell). This simple statement and the interpretations of quality made by lay people mask the need to define quality in an operational manner. In fact, quality as a concept is quite difficult for many people to grasp and understand, and much confusion and myth surrounds it.

In a linguistic sense, quality originates from the Latin word 'qualis' which means 'such as the thing really is'. There is an international definition of quality 'totality of characteristics of an entity that bear on its ability to satisfy stated and implied needs' (BS EN ISO 8402 1995).

In today's business world there is no single accepted definition of quality. However, irrespective of the context in which it is used, it is usually meant to distinguish one organization, institution, event, product, service, process, person, result, action, communication, from another. For the word to have the desired effect as intended by the user and to prevent any form of misunderstanding in the communication, the following points need to be considered:

- The person using the word must have a clear and full understanding of its meaning.
- The people/audience to whom the communication is directed should have a similar understanding of quality to the person making the communication.
- Within an organization, to prevent confusion and ensure that everyone in each department and function is focused on the same objectives, there should be an agreed definition of quality. For example, Betz Dearborn Ltd define quality as: 'That which gives complete customer satisfaction', Rank Xerox (UK) as 'Providing our customers, internal and external, with products and services that fully satisfy their negotiated requirements'. The Utility Division of United Utilities use the term business quality and define this as:

    Understanding and then satisfying customer requirements in order to improve our business results.

    Continuously improving our behaviour and attitudes as well as our processes, products and services.

    Ensuring that a customer focus is visible in all that we do.

There are a number of ways or senses in which quality may be defined, some being broader than others. These different definitions are now examined.

Qualitative

When used in this way, it is usual in a non-technical situation (BS EN ISO 8402 1995) to refer to it as relative quality where products or services are ranked on a relative basis in the 'degree of excellence' or 'comparative sense'. The following are some examples of this:

- in advertising slogans to assist in building an image: Esso – Quality at Work; Hayfield Textiles – Committed to Quality; Kenco – Superior Quality; Philips Whirlpool – Brings Quality to Life; Thompson Tour Operations – Thompson Quality Makes the World of Difference;
- by television and radio commentators (a quality player, a quality goal, a quality try);
- by directors and managers (quality performance, quality of communications); and
- by people, in general (quality product, top quality, high quality, original quality, quality time, quality of communications, quality person, loss of quality, German quality and 100% quality).

It is frequently found that in such cases the context in which the word quality is used is highly subjective and in its strictest sense is being misused. For example, there is more than one high street shop who trade under the name of 'Quality Seconds' and there is even a shop which advertises under the banner of 'Top Quality Seconds'. A van was recently spotted with the advertising slogan 'Quality Part Worn Tyres'.

Quantitative

The traditional quantitative term which is still used in some situations is Acceptable Quality Level (AQL). This is defined in BS 4778: Part 2 (1991) as: 'When a continuing series of lots is considered, a quality level which for the purposes of sampling inspection is the limit of a satisfactory process'. This is when the product quality and/or production quality is paradoxically defined in terms of non-conforming parts per hundred (i.e. some defined degree of imperfection).

An AQL is often imposed by a customer on its supplier in relation to a particular contract. In this type of situation they will then inspect the incoming batch according to the appropriate sampling scheme. If more than the allowed number of defects is found in the sample the entire batch is returned to the supplier or the supplier can, on the request of the customer, sort out the conforming from non-conforming product on the customer's site. The employment of an AQL is also used by some companies under the mistaken belief that trying to eliminate all defects is too costly.

The setting of an AQL by a company can work against a 'right first time' mentality in its people as it appears to condone the production and delivery of non-conforming parts or services, suggesting that errors are acceptable to the organization. It is tantamount to planning for failure. For example, take a final product which is made up of 3,000 parts, if the standard set is a 1 per cent AQL, this would mean that the product is planned to contain 30 non-conforming parts. In all reality it is likely to be many more because of the vagaries of the sampling used in the plan or scheme, whereby acceptance or rejection of the batch of product is decided. This is clearly an unacceptable situation in today's business environment and represents a non-survival performance.

Table 1.1   OFWAT levels of service performance 1995–6

Comparative measure	Grade	Billing queries: % answered within 5 days	Written complaints: % answered within 10 days	Billing metered customers: % read minus % unread
Well above average	A	>95	>98	>99.4
Above average	B	92–95	96–98	98.5–99.4
Average	C	89–92	94–96	96.0–98.4
Below average	D	86–89	92–94	93.0–95.9
Well below average	E	<86	<92	<93.0

Another example of a quantitative measure of quality are levels of service performance requirements, see the data in table 1.1 below from OFWAT's Levels of Service Report, 1995/1996.

Uniformity of the product characteristics or delivery of a service around a nominal or target value

In a manufacturing situation if a product or service dimensions are within the design specification or tolerance limits this is considered acceptable and conversely, if outside the specification this is not acceptable, see figure 1.1. The difference between what is considered to be just inside or just outside the specification is marginal. It may also be questioned whether

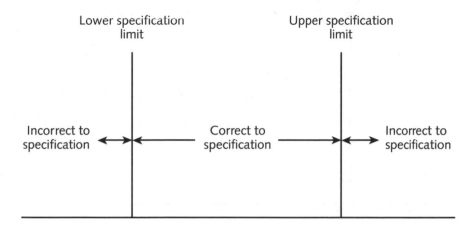

Figure 1.1 The inside/outside specification dilemma.

this step change between pass and fail has any scientific basis and validity.

Designers often establish specification limits without sufficient knowledge of the process by which the product and/or service is to be produced/delivered and its capability. It is often the case that designers cannot agree amongst themselves about the tolerances/specification to be allocated and it is not uncommon to find outdated reasoning being used. They also tend to define and establish a tighter tolerance than is justified to provide safeguards and protect themselves, taking the view that operational personnel will find the tolerance too tight and the part difficult to make and will request that the tolerance be increased. In many situations there is inadequate communication on this matter between the design and manufacturing functions. Fortunately, this is changing with the increasing use of simultaneous or concurrent engineering.

The problem with working to the specification limits is that it frequently leads to tolerance stack-up and parts not fitting together correctly at the assembly stage. This is especially the case when one part which is just inside the lower specification limit is assembled to one which is just inside the upper specification. If the process is controlled such that a part is produced around the nominal or a target dimension, see figure 1.2, this problem does not occur and the goodness of fit and smooth operation of the final assembly and/or end product is enhanced.

The idea of reducing the variation of part characteristics and process parameters so that they are centred around a target value can be attributed to Taguchi (1986). He writes that 'The quality of a product is the (minimum) loss imparted by the product to the society from the time the product is shipped'. This is defined by a quadratic loss curve. Among the losses

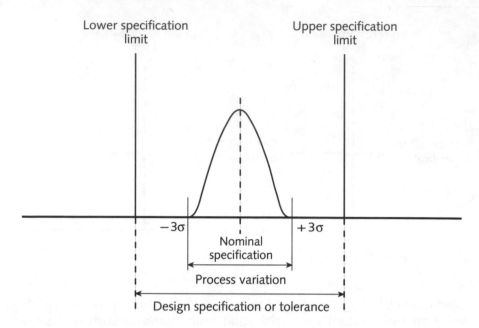

Figure 1.2 Design tolerance and process variation relationship.

he includes consumers' dissatisfaction, warranty costs, loss of reputation and, ultimately, loss of market share.

The relationship of design specification and variation of the manufacturing and/or production process can be quantified by a capability index, for example, Cp which is a process potential capability index:

$$\text{Cp} = \frac{\text{Total specification width}}{\text{Process variation width}}$$

Conformance to agreed and fully understood requirements

This definition is attributed to Crosby (1979). He believes that quality is not comparative and there is no such thing as high quality or low quality, or quality in terms of goodness, feel, excellence and luxury. A product or service either conforms to requirements or it does not. In other words, quality is an attribute (a characteristic which, by comparison to a standard or reference point, is judged to be correct or incorrect) not a variable (a characteristic which is measurable). Crosby makes the point that the requirements are all the actions required to produce a product and/or deliver a service that meets the customer's expectations, and that it is management's responsibility to ensure that adequate requirements are created and specified within the organization.

This is a useful definition to use in the development of service level agreements (SLAs) in an internal customer-supplier relationship. For example the purpose and scope of SLA between the Regional Engineering Managers and Distribution Finance of Norweb Distribution is detailed below:

> This agreement specifies the services to be provided by Distribution Finance to Regional Engineering Managers for the period 1st July 1995 to 30th June, 1996. The agreement covers the following services:

- Management accounts
- Revenue and capital forecasting, commentary, budgeting and monitoring
- Business modelling
- Auditing
- Capital appraisal
- Administration of financial aspects of capital projects
- Overtime monitoring
- Financial aspects of strategic and business planning
- Ad hoc professional financial advice and invetigations

- Control account reconciliation
- Capital and revenue costing
- Financial policy
- Corporate financial and taxation returns
- Cashiering services
- Rechargeable billing, disputed accounts and sales ledger facilities
- Retention of records
- Administration of financial aspects of fault projects

Some products are highly sophisticated in terms of their design but are poor in terms of conformance to requirements. On the other hand, some products are simple in terms of their design but exhibit high levels of conformance to requirements. The 'quality of design' (the degree to which the design of the product and/or service achieves its purpose) can be confused with the 'quality of conformance' (how well the product and/or service conforms to the design). Stemming from this confusion about design and conformance there can be a tendency to believe that 'better' quality means higher costs. This view results from the confusion between quality and grade. Grade represents the addition of features and characteristics to satisfy the additional needs of customers and this clearly requires extra monies, but grade is different to quality.

Fitness for purpose/use

This is a standard definition of quality first used by Juran (1988). Juran classifies 'fitness for purpose/use' into the categories of: quality of design, quality of conformance, abilities and field service. Focusing on fitness for use helps to prevent the overspecification of products. Overspecification can add greatly to the manufacturing costs and tends to militate against a right first time performance. How fit a product or service is for use has obviously to be judged by the purchaser, customer or user.

Satisfying customer expectations and understanding their needs and future requirements

A typical definition which reflects this sentiment is: 'The attributes of a product and/or service which, as perceived by the customer, makes the product/service attractive to them and gives them satisfaction'. The focus of the definition is adding-value to the product and/or service.

This is the crux of TQM, which concerns itself with effective and efficient management and having customers who are totally satisfied and who come back for more of the same product and/or service. The customer is the major reason for an organization's existence and customer loyalty and retention is perhaps the only measure of organizational success. In most situations customers have a choice; they need not place future orders with a supplier who does not perform as they expect. They will certainly not jeopardize their own business interest out of loyalty to a supplier whose products and service fail to perform properly. The aim of the superior performing companies is to become the supplier of choice of their customers' and to 'lock themselves' into their customers' mode of operation by becoming the sole supplier and adding value to their customers' businesses by process improvement and cost down activities.

The process of continuous improvement is all about customer orientation and many company missions are based entirely on satisfying customer perceptions. The superior performing organizations go beyond satisfying their customers; they emphasize the need to delight customers by giving them more than what is required in the contract; they also now talk about winning customers and becoming infatuated with their customers. The wisdom of this can be clearly understood when we consider a situation in which a customer receives more than expected from a supplier (e.g. an extra glass of wine on an aircraft, a sales assistant going out of their way to be courteous, helpful and providing very detailed information) and the warm feelings conveyed by this type of action.

A customer focused organization also places considerable effort in anticipating the future expectations of its customer and by working with them in long-term relationships helps them to define their future needs and expectations. These organizations listen very closely to their customers and 'real' users of the product/service, in order to gain a clearer perspective of customer experiences. They aim to build quality into the product, service, system and/or process as much upstream as is practicable. Those companies intent on satisfying their customer needs and expectations will have in place a mechanism for facilitating a continuous two way flow of information between themselves and their customers. This is essential to the process of continuous improvement. There are a variety of means available to companies for them to assess issues such as:

- how well they are meeting customer expectations
- what are the customers' chief causes of concern
- what are the main complaints
- what suggestions the customers might have for improvements
- how they might add value to the product and/or service
- how well they act on what the customer says
- the best means of differentiating themselves in the marketplace

The trend is for increasing the level of contact with the customer. These 'moments of truth' (Carlzon 1987) occur far more frequently in commerce, public organizations, the civil service and service type situations than in manufacturing organizations. The means, include:

- customer workshops
- panels and clinics
- using 'test' consumers and mystery shoppers
- focus groups
- customer interviews
- market research
- dealer information
- questionnaire surveys
- product reports
- trailing the service and/or product
- trade shows

Having listened to 'customer voices' an organization should put into place appropriate strategy and actions for making the necessary changes and improvements. It is also important to clarify and identify the elements and characteristics of the product and service which the customer finds attractive. The SERVQUAL questionnaire developed by Parasuraman et al. (1988) may be used to track these kind of issues. The leading companies are obsessed with service excellence, which they use to:

1.   Be different.
2.   Increase productivity.
3.   Earn customers' loyalty.
4.   Generate positive, word-of-mouth advertising.
5.   Protect themselves against cut-price competition.

Service excellence pays richly and everyone (customers, employees, management, shareholders and the community) wins. Leadership plays a central role in delivering excellent service: managing is not enough. Service work can be difficult and demoralizing. Customers can be rude. Policies can be suffocating. Sheer numbers of customers can serve to be overwhelming. End-of-day fatigue can be desensitizing. Over time, many service employees become less effective with customers, even as they gain technical experience that should produce the opposite results.

People in service work need a vision in which they can believe, an achievement culture that challenges them to be the best they can be, a sense of team that nurtures and supports them, and role models that show them the way. This is the stuff of leadership. Too many service workers are overmanaged and underled.

Service leaders have four characteristics:

1.   Service vision: such leaders see service as integral to the organization's future, and they believe fundamentally that superior service is a winning strategy.
2.   High standards.
3.   In-the-field leadership.
4.   Integrity: such leaders recognize the impossibility of building a service-minded attitude in an organization whose management lacks integrity.

Improving service in the eyes of customers is what pays off. When service improvement investments lead to perceived service improvement, quality becomes a profit strategy, as demonstrated by the database produced under the PIMS ((Profit Impact of Market Strategy) – see section called 'Quality leads to better performance in the marketplace' below).

The customers' view of service quality

From previous works on the subject, three main points become apparent.

1.   Service quality is more difficult for customers to evaluate than the

quality of goods. The criteria which customers use to judge service quality may be difficult for the marketer to evaluate.

2. Customers do not evaluate the quality of a service solely on the outcome. They also consider the process of service delivery and the personal interactions.
3. Only customers can judge quality; the judgements of others are essentially irrelevant.

Zeithmal et al. (1990) conducted a series of focus-group interviews with respondents who had engaged on one or more transactions with particular service companies within the previous 3 months. The services in question were: retail banking; credit cards; securities brokerage; and product repair and maintenance. The findings from the interviews were as follows.

1. Definition: the respondents all supported the notion that service quality is meeting or exceeding what customers expect from the service. Whether service quality is high or low depends upon the extent of the discrepancy between customers' expectations or desires and their perceptions.
2. Factors influencing expectations:

    (a) word-of-mouth communications from other customers;
    (b) the personal needs of each individual customer;
    (c) the customer's past experience of the service; and
    (d) external communications by the supplier – the expressed and implied messages in advertisements, brochures and the like.

Underlying these factors is the question of price; there seems to be a link between price levels and expectation levels.

In addition to the factors mentioned above, Zeithmal et al. (1990) initially identified ten dimensions of service quality – general criteria by which all the respondents in the focus-groups judged the quality of a service. These are listed below.

1. Tangibles: appearance of physical facilities, equipment, personnel, and communication materials.
2. Reliability: ability to perform the promised service dependably and accurately.
3. Responsiveness: willingness to help customers and provide prompt service.
4. Competence: possession of the required skills and knowledge to perform the service.
5. Courtesy: politeness, respect, consideration and friendliness of

LIVERPOOL
JOHN MOORES UNIVERSITY
AVRIL ROBARTS LRC
TITHEBARN STREET
LIVERPOOL

contact personnel.
6. Credibility: trustworthiness, believability and honesty of the service provider.
7. Security: freedom from danger, risk or doubt.
8. Access: approachability and ease of contact.
9. Communication: keeping customers informed in language they can understand and listening to them.
10. Understanding the customer: making the effort to know customers and their needs.

Zeithmal et al. (1990) recognized that these ten dimensions were not necessarily independent of one another, and that they could overlap. Indeed, when they developed SERVQUAL – a questionnaire to identify the expectations and the perceptions of customers – they were able to reduce the ten dimensions to five. Thus:

1. Tangibles	1. Tangibles
2. Reliability	2. Reliability
3. Responsiveness	3. Responsiveness
4. Competence	4. Assurance
5. Courtesy	5. Empathy
6. Credability	
7. Security	
8. Access	
9. Communication	
10. Understanding the customer	

Their final definitions were:

1. Tangibles: appearance of physical facilities, equipment, personnel and communication materials.
2. Reliability: ability to perform the promised service dependably and accurately.
3. Responsiveness: willingness to help customers and provide prompt service.
4. Assurance: knowledge and courtesy of employees and their ability to convey trust and confidence.
5. Empathy: caring, individualized attention which the firm provides to its customers.

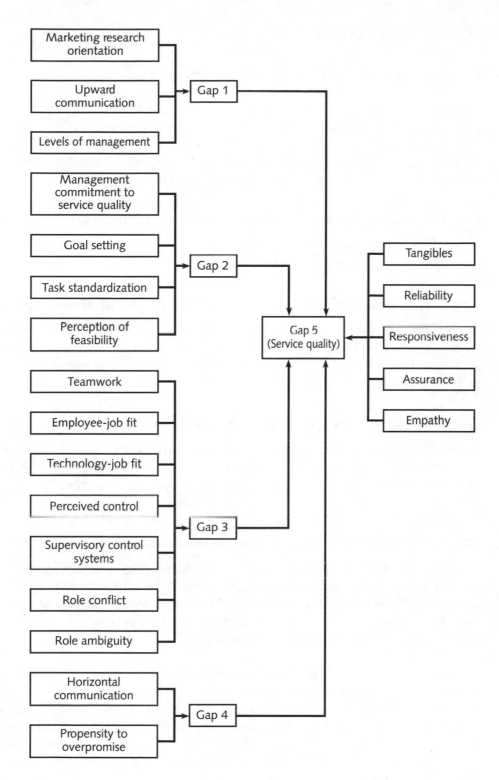

Figure 1.3 Service model (Zeithmal et al. (1990)).

Potential causes of service-quality shortfalls

Where there is a gap between the customer's expectation and perception (hereinafter called 'Gap 5'), the fault may be traced ultimately to one of four shortfalls, or a combination of them, within the company itself, this is specified in some detail by Zeithmal et al. (1990). By closing the internal Gaps 1, 2, 3 or 4 it may be possible to close Gap 5 (see figure 1.3).

Gap 1 Customers' expectations/management-perceptions gap

There is a discrepancy between the customers' expectations, and what management perceive those expectations to be.

Gap 2 Management's perceptions/service-quality specifications gap

Even where management correctly identify the customers' expectations, management may fail to translate their knowledge into concrete perform-ance standards. Such failure probably stems from the absence of whole-hearted management commitment to service quality.

Gap 3 Service-quality specifications/service-delivery gap

Even where management set the kind of standards which satisfy custom-ers, companies' employees may fail to meet those standards because man-agement fail to provide adequate and appropriate resources (people, systems, technology).

Gap 4 Service-delivery/external communications gap

This gap would be caused by broken promises. Also, less obviously, it could be caused by a failure to explain internal procedures which are fol-lowed for the benefit of the customers. In short, external communications can affect not only customers' expectations about a service but also cus-tomers' perceptions of the delivered service.

The root cause of deficient service quality is not inadequate structures, systems or research, but insufficient leadership. Improvements in service are thwarted because senior managers, middle managers, and first-line providers lack the will, knowledge and/or skills to play their part in mov-ing the organization forward. Moreover, the process of continuous im-provements is a slow one. Managers can become disheartened at the length of time it takes. Quality service is a 'slow fix'.

The quality required by customers (i.e. their wants) should be translated into the language of internal needs and driven back through all levels in the organizational hierarchy. It is important that the requirements are put into terms that are measurable, realistic and achievable. The use of Quality Function Deployment (QFD) is useful in this respect. This is central to the issue of total customer satisfaction. Customers' needs and requirements are forever changing and organizations have to live up to their customers' expectations and they are never satisfied even though the supplying organization may think they are.

WHY IS QUALITY IMPORTANT?

To answer this question just consider the unsatisfactory examples of product and/or quality service that you the reader have experienced, the bad feelings it gave, the resulting actions taken and the people you told about the experience and the outcome. The following customer service information (CMC Partnership Ltd 1991) provides some quantitative facts about this:

*Customer Service Facts – Did You Know That . . .

1. If 20 customers are dissatisfied with your service, 19 won't tell you. Fourteen of the 20 will take their business elsewhere.
2. Dissatisfied customers tell an average of ten other people about their bad experience; 12 per cent tell up to 20 people.
3. Satisfied customers will tell an average of five people about their positive experience.
4. It costs five times more money to attract a new customer than to keep an existing one.
5. Up to 90 per cent of dissatisfied customers will not buy from you again, and they won't tell you why.
6. In many industries, quality of service is one of the few variables that can distinguish a business from its competition.
7. Providing high quality service can save your business money. The same skills that lead to increased customer satisfaction also lead to increased employee productivity.
8. Customers are willing to pay more to receive better service.
9. Ninety-five per cent of dissatisfied customers will become loyal customers again if their complaints are handled well and quickly.

* *Sources: statistics compiled by Mattson & Associates from service sector companies in the USA. CMC Partnership Ltd (1991).*

The following are examples of survey data which have focused on the perceived importance of product and service quality.

1. Public perceptions of product and service quality

In 1988 the then American Society for Quality Control (ASQC), now the American Society for Quality (ASQ), commissioned the Gallup Organization to survey public perceptions on a variety of quality-related issues. This survey was the fourth in a series which began in 1985; the 1985 and 1988 surveys focused on US consumers and the 1986 and 1987 studies surveyed attitudes of company executives. The 1988 study was done by conducting telephone interviews with 1,005 adults in the United States during the Summer of 1988. A selection of results, as reported by Ryan (1988) and Hutchens (1989), is outlined below:

- The following is a ranking of factors that people consider important when they purchase a product:

    - performance
    - durability
    - ease of repair, service availability, warranty, and ease of use (these four factors were ranked about the same)
    - price
    - appearance
    - brand name

- People will pay a premium to get what they perceive to be higher quality
- Consumers are willing to pay substantially more for better intrinsic quality in a product
- According to the respondents, the following are the factors what make for 'higher' quality in services:

    - courtesy
    - promptness
    - a basic sense that one's needs are being satisfied
    - attitudes of the service provider

- When consumers do experience a problem with the product, they appear reluctant to take positive action with the manufacturer. The 1987 survey revealed that executives regard customer complaints, suggestions and enquiries, as key indicators of product and service quality. This feedback gap clearly needs to be bridged.

An ASQC/Gallup survey was conducted in 1991 (Gallup Organisation Inc 1991) to survey the attitudes and opinions of consumers in Japan, West Germany and the United States in relation to questions such as 'What does quality really mean to them? How do they define it and does it influence their buying behaviour? What is their perception of the quality from other parts of the world? and What are the dynamics underlying a consumer's reasons for buying or not buying something produced in a foreign country?' On a number of issues, this survey updates American attitudes expressed in the 1988 survey. Over 1,000 people in each country were questioned. A selection of summary highlights from the report (Gallup Organisation Inc 1992) are outlined below:

- 'Consumers in the US, Japan and West Germany in many respects are alike in terms of the attributes they consider important in determining the quality of the products they buy. For example, approximately one in five look to the brand name of a product. Durability is also important to at least 10% of the consumers in each of the countries surveyed'.
- 'Asked what factors are most important in influencing their decision to buy a product, price is the leading response in West Germany (64%) and in the US (31%). Performance (40%) is most important among Japanese consumers, followed by price (36%)'.
- 'Compared to the 1988 survey, US consumers are now more likely to rate American-made products higher for quality (55% rating them an "8", "9" or "10" versus 48% who do so in 1988)'.
- 'A majority (61%) of US consumers believe it is very important to US workers to produce high quality products or service'.
- 'Price and quality are the reasons given most frequently by American consumers for buying a product made in Japan or Germany'.

2. Views and roles of senior management

(a) In 1992 ASQC commissioned the Gallup Organisation to study the nature of leadership for quality within American business organizations by surveying opinions of senior management in both large and small organizations. The objective was to explore their views concerning quality improvement and the role of directors with regard to quality. Some 684 executives were interviewed. The following is a summary of the main findings extracted from Gallup Organisation Inc (1992).

  - 'At least six in ten executives report that they have a great deal of personal leadership impact on customer focus and satisfaction, strategic quality planning, quality and operational results and financial results.'

- 'On average, executives rate American-made products 7.0 on a ten-point scale for quality. Thirty three per cent give American products a rating of "8" or better.'
- 'Most executives believe management plays a greater role than the board in determining quality policy within their company.'
- 'More than four in ten (45%) report their board does discuss quality frequently.'
- 'Four in ten (43%) executives report their board reports on consumer satisfaction frequently, and almost as many (38%) report the board reviews reports on customer retention or loyalty frequently.'

(b) The European Foundation for Quality Management (EFQM) contracted McKinsey and Company to survey the CEOs (Chief Executive Officers) of the top 500 Western European corporations in relation to quality performance and the management of quality; 150 CEOs responded to the survey. The following are some of the main findings as reported by McKinsey & Company (1989).

- 'Over 90% of CEOs consider quality performance to be "critical" for their Corporation.'
- 60% of CEOs said that quality performance had become a lot more important than before (late 70s)
- 'The four main reasons why quality is perceived to be important are:
  - primary buying argument for the ultimate customer
  - major means of reducing costs
  - major means for improving flexibility/responsiveness
  - major means for reducing throughput time.'
- 'The feasible improvement in gross margin on sales through improved quality performance was rated at an average of 17%.'
- 'More than 85% of the leading CEOs in Europe consider the management of quality to be one of the top priorities for their corporations.'

(c) Lascelles and Dale (1990) reporting on a survey they carried out of 74 UK CEOs say that 'Almost all the respondents believe that product and service quality is an important factor in international competitiveness. More than half have come to this conclusion within the past four years.'

(d) One of the findings of a survey on the subject of Business Excellence by Total Research in association with Manchester Business School of senior directors of 60 leading European companies is reported (Anon 1997) as:

Incidence of total or near total success against objectives	1–3 years	4+ years
Higher employee productivity	10%	43%
Reduction in employee turnover	0%	33%
Better service quality	29%	56%
Improved customer satisfaction	21%	49%
Greater shareholder value/improved stock market performance	0%	27%
Higher rating within the financial community	6%	31%
Enhanced profit margins	0%	21%
Reduced costs	11%	31%

Quality is not negotiable

An order, contract or customer which is lost on the grounds of non-conforming product and/or service quality is much harder to regain than one lost on price or delivery terms. In a number of cases the customer could be lost forever; in simple terms the organization has been outsold by the competition.

If you have any doubt about the truth of this statement just consider the number of organizations who have gone out of business or lost a significant share of a market, and consider the reported reasons for them getting into the position. Quality is one of the factors which is not negotiable; in today's business world the penalties for unsatisfactory product quality and poor service are likely to be punitive.

Quality is all pervasive

There are a number of single focus business initiatives which an organization may deploy to increase profit. However, with the improvements made by companies of their mode of operation, reduction in monopolies, government legislation, deregulation, changes in market share, mergers, takeovers and collaborative joint ventures, there is less distinction between companies than there was some years ago. TQM is a much broader concept than previous initiatives, encompassing not only product, service and process improvements but those relating to costs and productivity and people involvement and development. It also has the added advantage that it is

LIVERPOOL
JOHN MOORES UNIVERSITY
AVRIL ROBARTS LRC
TITHEBARN STREET
LIVERPOOL L2 2ER
TEL. 0151 231 4022

totally focused on satisfying customer needs, something with which few people can disagree with.

A related issue is that organizations are often willing to pay more for what they perceive as a quality product; see the results of the ASQC oblique Gallup Survey (Gallup Organisation Inc 1992), as outlined below.

Industry type	Number of customers willing to pay more for a quality product	Number of customers unwilling to pay extra for better quality
Clothing/textiles	135	5
Furniture	74	4
TV/audio	66	6
Home	55	4
Automotive	36	10

Quality increases productivity

Cost, productivity and quality improvements are complementary and not alternative objectives. Managers sometimes say that they do not have the time and resources to ensure that product and/or service quality is right the first time. They go on to argue that if their people concentrate on planning for quality then they will be losing valuable production and operating time, and as a consequence output will be lost and costs will rise. Despite this argument, management and their staff will make the time to rework the product and service a second or even a third time, spend considerable time and organizational resources on corrective action, and placating customers who have been affected by the non-conformances. Remember 'Murphy's Law': 'There is never time to do it right but always time to do it once more.'

Quality leads to better performance in the marketplace

The Profit Impact of Market Strategy (PIMS), conducted under the Strategic Planning Institute in Cambridge, (Massachusetts), have a database which contains over 3,000 records of detailed business performance. The Institute is a co-operative run by its members. The data base allows a detailed analysis of the parameters which influence business performance. A key PIMS concept is that of Relative Perceived Quality (RPQ); this is the product and service offering as perceived by the customer. PIMS data are often used to model options before adapting a change initiative and to assess how improvements translate into improved profits and enhanced customer loyalty. It has been established that the factors having most leverage on return on investment are RPQ and relative market share and that companies with large market shares are those whose quality is relatively high, whereas companies with small market shares are those whose quality is relatively low (see Buzzell and Gale 1987). Another key finding is 'that businesses who know and understand customers priorities for quality improvements can achieve a three fold increase in profitability' (Roberts 1996).

Quality means improved business performance

Kano et al. (1983) have carried out an examination of 26 companies which won the Deming Application Prize (this is a prize awarded to companies for their effective implementation of company-wide quality control – for details see chapter 8, section called 'Award models') between 1961 and 1980. Kano et al. found that financial performance of these 26 companies in terms of earning rate, productivity, growth rate, liquidity, and net worth was above the average for their industries.

A report published by the US General Accounts Office (1991) focused on the top 20 scorers of the Malcolm Baldrige National Quality Award (MBNQA) in the period 1988–9. Using a combination of questionnaire and interview methods, the companies were asked to provide information on four broad classes of performance measures – employee related indicators, operating indicators, customer satisfaction indicators and business performance indicators. Improvements were claimed in all these indicators (e.g. market share, sales per employee, return on assets, and return on sales). Useful information on financial performance was obtained from 15 of the 20 companies who experienced the following annual average increases:

- market share, 13.7%
- sales per employee, 8.6%
- return on assets, 1.3%
- return on sales, 0.4%

Larry (1993) reports on a study carried out on the winners of the MBNQA and found that they 'Yielded a cumulative 89% gain, whereas the same investment in the Standard and Poor 500- Stock Index delivered only 33.1%.' Wisner and Eakins (1994) also carried out an operation and financial review of the MBNQA winners, 1988 to 1993. One of the conclusions reached was that the winners appear to be performing financially as well or better than their competitors.

The 'Baldrige Index' is made up of publicly-traded US companies that have won the MBNQA during the years 1996–7. The National Institute of Technology (NIST) invested a hypothetical $1,000 in each of the six whole company MBNQA winners. The NIST also made the same investment in the Standard and Poors 500 at the same time. The investments have been tracked from the first business day in April of the year they won the Award to December 1998. NIST have found, (NIST, 1999), that these six companies outperformed the Standard and Poors 500 by more than 2.6 achieving a 460% return on investment compared to a 175% return for the S & P 500. NIST also tracked a similar hypothetical investment in a group made up of the six whole company winners and the parent companies of 17 subsidiary winners. This group of 23 companies out-performed the S & P 500 by 2.5 to 1, a 426% return on investment compared to a 173% return for the S & P 500. The 'Baldrige Index' has for the fifth time in a row, outperformed the Standard and Poors 500 (NIST, 1999).

The Aeroquip Corporation, which is a Trinova company, involved in aerospace, automotive and industrial markets, have 9,000 employees in 12 countries and on 40 manufacturing sites. It has developed its own version of the MBNQA called Aeroquip Quality Plus (AQ+). Each of its operating sites is required to obtain a score of 700 out of 1,000 points to attain an AQ+ award. The following are the details of the 1994 performance of the nine sites who have attained the award compared to those sites who are still working towards it:

- 64% of Aeroquip operating income is generated from 31% of sales
- 15.1% return on sales against 3.9% for remainder of the Aeroquip companies
- 21% sales growth against 5.0% for the remainder of the Aeroquip companies
- 31% income growth against a 3.2% decrease for the remainder of the Aeroquip companies

A study (The Bradford Study – Letz et al. 1997) carried out at the University of Bradford Management Centre identified 29 companies within the UK which display characteristics associated with TQM. The study was first carried out over the period 1987 to 1991 and has been repeated for the period 1991 to 1995. Nine measures have been used by the study team to compare company performance with the median for the particular industry. The second study reveals the following:

- 81% of companies are above the industry median for turnover per employee

- 81% of the companies provide a higher salary to turnover ratio than their peers
- 74% of the organizations remunerate their employees above the median for the industry
- 65% of the organizations produce above median profit per employee for their industry
- 62% of the organizations have a higher net asset turnover than their peer group

The authors also go on to say that 'Four of the nine measures are marginally below the median for their industry but this is to be expected as quality becomes institutionalised and more widespread.'

A survey published in 1996 by the PA Consulting Group surveyed 687 European companies. The findings show that organizations using a TQM approach achieve better results and improve customer and employee satisfaction.

The cost of non-quality is high

Based on a variety of companies, industries and situations, the cost of quality (or to be more precise the cost of not getting it right the first time) ranges from 5 to 25% of an organization's annual sales turnover in manufacturing or annual operating costs: services (see chapter 4, section called Quality costing and Dale and Plunkett (1999) for details). An organization should compare its profit to sales turnover ratio to that of its quality costs to sales turnover ratio, in order to gain an indication of the importance of product and service quality to corporate profitability.

Product liability

The 1987 Consumer Protection Act and the 1988 legislation on strict product liability has resulted in:

- CEOs and senior managers becoming more aware of the importance of having a recognized quality system which meets the requirements of the ISO 9000 series of quality management system standards. Registration to this series of standards is seen by many executives as some defence against any product liability claims.
- Organizations being able to trace batches of work which have been

produced, sometime in the past, keeping detailed records of actions taken, and engaging in advanced quality planning using techniques such as Failure Mode and Effects Analysis (FMEA) to pinpoint, early on in the planning of the design and operating processes, potential modes of failure.

Customer is king

In today's markets, customer requirements are becoming increasingly more rigorous and their expectations of the product and/or service in terms of conformance, reliability, dependability, durability, interchangeability, performance, features, appearance, serviceability, user-friendliness, safety, and environment-friendliness, is also increasing. These days many superior performing companies talk in terms of being 'customer obsessed'. At the same time, it is likely that the competition will also be improving and, in addition, new and low cost competitors may emerge in the marketplace, consequently there is a need for the process of improvement to be continuous and involve everyone in the company. The organization who claims that it has achieved TQM will be overtaken by the competition. Once the process of continuous improvement has been halted, under the mistaken belief that TQM has been achieved, it is much harder to re-start and gain the initiative on the competition, (see figure 1.4). This is why TQM should always be referred to as a process and not a programme. Those people who frequently refer to TQM as a programme do not understand the

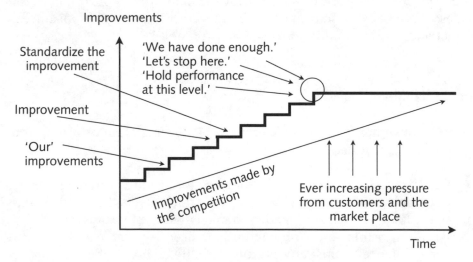

Figure 1.4 Quality improvement is a continuous process.

fundamentals of continuous improvement. It is reported (Anon 1995) that 'Britain's businesses are serving their customers better than five years ago, but the battle for top customer care is still far from over. Three out of four people surveyed in a recent NOP poll said they had cause to make complaints to businesses over the past 12 months.' The report went on to say 'there is comforting evidence that their customers are recognising real efforts to improve service'.

Quality is a way of life

Quality is a way of organizational and everyday life. It is a way of doing business, living and conducting one's personal affairs. In whatever each person does, and in whatever situation, the task(s) must be undertaken in a quality conscious way. Quality is driven by a person's own internal mechanisms – 'heart and soul', 'personal beliefs'. It can be likened to those people who follow a religious faith.

An organization committed to quality needs quality of working life of its people in terms of participation, involvement and development and quality of its systems, processes and products.

THE EVOLUTION OF QUALITY MANAGEMENT

Systems for improving and managing quality have evolved rapidly in recent years. During the last two decades or so simple inspection activities have been replaced or supplemented by quality control, quality assurance has been developed and refined, and now most companies are working towards TQM. In this progression, four fairly discrete stages can be identified: inspection; quality control; quality assurance and Total Quality Management, see figure 1.5 from Dale (1999). International Organization for Standardization definitions of these terms are given to provide the reader with some understanding of the general meaning, but the discussion and examination is not restricted by these definitions.

Inspection

This is defined as 'Activity such as measuring, examining, testing or gauging one or more characteristic of an entity and comparing the results with specified requirements in order to establish whether conformity is achieved for each characteristic' (BS EN ISO 8402 1995).

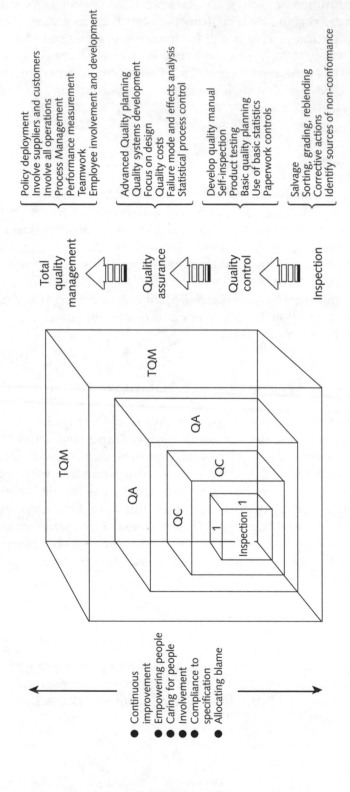

Policy deployment
Involve suppliers and customers
Involve all operations
Process Management
Performance measurement
Teamwork
Employee involvement and development

Advanced Quality planning
Quality systems development
Focus on design
Quality costs
Failure mode and effects analysis
Statistical process control

Develop quality manual
Self-inspection
Product testing
Basic quality planning
Use of basic statistics
Paperwork controls

Salvage
Sorting, grading, reblending
Corrective actions
Identify sources of non-conformance

Total
quality
management

Quality
assurance

Quality
control

Inspection

TQM

TQM

QA

QA

QC

QC

1

Inspection 1

Continuous
improvement
Empowering people
Caring for people
Involvement
Compliance to
specification
Allocating blame

Figure 1.5   The four levels in the evolution of Total Quality Management.
Source: Developed from Dale (1994)

At one time inspection was thought to be the only way of ensuring quality. Under a simple inspection-based system, one or more characteristics of a product, service or activity are examined, measured, tested, or assessed and compared with specified requirements to assess conformity. In a manufacturing environment the system is applied to incoming goods, manufactured components and assemblies at appropriate points in the process and before passing finished goods into the warehouse. In service and commercial type situations the system is also applied at key points, sometimes called appraisal points, in the producing and delivery processes. The inspection activity can be carried out by staff employed specifically for the purpose or by self-inspection of those responsible for a process. Materials, components, paperwork, forms, products and goods which do not conform to specification may be scrapped, reworked, modified or passed on concession. In some cases inspection is used to grade the finished product. The system is an after-the-event screening process with no prevention content other than, perhaps, identification of suppliers, operations, or workers, who are producing non-conforming products/services. Simple inspection-based systems are usually wholly in-house and do not directly involve suppliers or customers in the activity.

Quality control

This is defined as 'Operational techniques and activities that are used to fulfil requirements for quality' (BS EN ISO 8402 1995).

Under a system of quality control one might expect, for example, to find in place a paperwork and procedures control system, raw material and intermediate stage product testing, logging of elementary process performance data, and feedback of process information to appropriate personnel. With quality control there will have been some development from the basic inspection activity in terms of sophistication of methods and systems and the tools and techniques which are employed. Whilst the main mechanism for preventing off-specification products and services from being delivered to a customer is again screening inspection, quality control measures lead to greater process control and fewer incidence of non-conformances.

Those organizations whose approach to the management of product and service quality is based on inspection and quality control are operating in a detection type mode (i.e. finding and fixing mistakes).

Quality assurance

Finding and solving a problem after a non-conformance has been created is not an effective route towards eliminating the root cause of a problem. A lasting and continuous improvement in quality can only be achieved by directing organizational efforts towards planning and preventing problems occurring at source. This concept leads to the third stage of quality management development which is quality assurance. This is defined as 'All the planned and systematic activities implemented within the quality system and demonstrated as needed to provide adequate confidence that an entity will fulfil requirements for quality' (BS EN ISO 8402 1995).

Examples of additional features acquired when progressing from quality control to quality assurance are, for example: a comprehensive quality management system to increase uniformity and conformity; use of the seven quality control tools (e.g. histogram, check sheet, Pareto analysis, cause and effect diagram, graphs, scatter diagram and control chart); Statistical Process Control (SPC); FMEA; and the gathering and use of quality costs. Above all one would expect to see a shift in emphasis from mere detection towards prevention of non-conformances. In short, more emphasis is placed on advanced quality planning, improving the design of the product, process and services, improving control over the process, and involving and motivating people.

Total Quality Management

The fourth and highest level that of TQM involves the application of quality management principles to all aspects of the business, including customers and suppliers.

Total Quality Management requires that the principles of quality management should be applied in every branch and at every level in the organization. It is a company-wide approach to quality, with improvements undertaken on a continuous basis by everyone in the organization. Individual systems, procedures and requirements may be no higher than for a quality assurance level of quality management, but they will pervade every person, activity and function of the organization. It will, however, require a broadening of outlook and skills and an increase in creative activities from that required at the quality assurance level. The spread of the TQM philosophy would also be expected to be accompanied by greater sophistication in the application of tools and techniques and increased emphasis on people. The process will also extend beyond the organization to include partnerships with suppliers and customers. Activities will be reorientated to focus on the customer, internal and external.

There are many interpretations and definitions of TQM, the following is the definition given in BS EN ISO 8402 (1995):

> Management approach of an organization, centred on quality, based on the participation of all its members and aiming at long-term success through customer satisfaction, and benefits to all members of the organization and to society.

Put simply, TQM is the mutual co-operation of everyone in an organization and associated business processes to produce products and services which meet the needs and expectations of customers. TQM is both a philosophy and a set of guiding principles for managing an organization.

PREVENTION VERSUS DETECTION

In tracing the development of quality management from inspection to TQM it was said that inspection and quality control are basically detection type activities whilst quality assurance and TQM are prevention-based. The point was made of the need to switch resources from detection to prevention. The key differences between detection and prevention are now examined.

In a detection or 'firefighting' environment, the emphasis is on the product, procedures and/or service deliverables and the downstream producing and delivery processes. Considerable effort is expended on after-the-event inspecting, checking, screening and testing of the product and/or service and providing reactive 'quick fixes' in a bid to ensure that only conforming products and services are delivered to the customer. In this approach, there is a lack of creative and systematic work activities with planning and improvements being neglected. Detection will not improve product and service quality but only highlight when it is not present, and sometimes it does not even manage to do this. Problems in the process are not removed, but contained. Inspection is the primary means of control in a 'policeman' or 'goalkeeper' type role and thereby a 'producing' versus 'checking' situation is encouraged, leading to confusion over people's responsibilities for quality – 'Can I, the producer, get my deliverables past the checker?' It leads to the belief that non-conformances are due to the product/service not being inspected enough and also that operators are the sole cause of the problem, not the system. A question which organizations operating in this mode must answer is 'Does the checking of work by

LIVERPOOL
JOHN MOORES UNIVERSITY
AVRIL ROBARTS LRC
TITHEBARN STREET
LIVERPOOL L2 2ER
TEL. 0151 231 4022

inspectors affect an operator's pride in the job and responsibility for their own quality assurance?' The production-inspection relationship is described in some detail by McKenzie (1989).

With a detection approach to quality, non-conforming 'products' (products are considered in their widest sense) are culled, sorted and graded, and decisions made on concessions, rework, reblending, repair, downgrading, scrap, and disposal. It is not unusual to find products going through this cycle more than once. Whilst a detection type system may prevent non-conforming products, services and paperwork being delivered to the customer (internal or external), it does not stop them being made. Indeed, it is questionable whether such a system does in fact cull out all the non-conforming products and services. Physical and mental fatigue decreases the efficiency of inspection and it is commonly claimed that, at best, 100 per cent inspection is only 80 per cent effective. It is often found that with a detection approach the customer also inspects the incoming product/service, thus the customer becomes a part of the organization's quality control system.

In this type of approach a non-conforming product must be made and a service delivered before the process can be adjusted and this is inherently inefficient in that it creates waste in all its various forms; all the action is 'after-the-event' and backward looking. The emphasis is on 'today's events', with little attempt to learn from the lessons of the current problem or crisis. It should not be forgotten that the scrap, rework, retesting and reblending

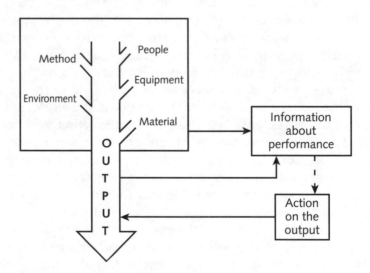

Figure 1.6   A detection-based quality system.
Source: Ford Motor Company (1985)

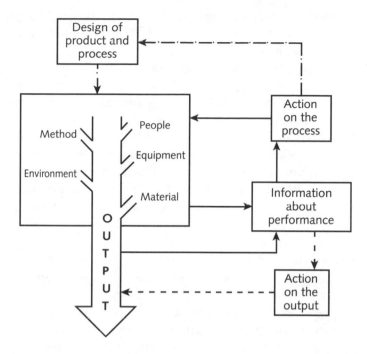

Figure 1.7 A prevention-based quality system.
Source: Ford Motor Company (1985)

are extra efforts, and represent costs over and above what has been budgeted and which ultimately will result in a reduction of profit. Figure 1.6 taken from the Ford Motor Company (1985) three-day SPC course notes is a schematic illustration of a detection type system.

An environment in which the emphasis is on making good the non-conformance rather than preventing it arising in the first place, is not ideal for engendering team spirit, co-operation and effective climate for work. The focus tends to be on switching the blame to others, people making themselves 'fireproof', not being prepared to accept responsibility and ownership and taking disciplinary action against people who make mistakes. In general, this behaviour and attitude emanates from middle management and quickly spreads downwards through all levels of the organizational hierarchy.

Quality Assurance (QA) is a prevention-based system which improves product and service quality, and increases productivity by placing the emphasis on product, service and process design. By concentrating on source activities, it stops non-conforming products being produced or non-conforming services being delivered. This is a proactive approach compared with detection, which is reactive. There is a clear change of emphasis from downstream to the upstream processes and from product to process, see figure 1.7 (Ford Motor Company 1985). This change of emphasis can also be considered in terms of the Plan, Do, Check, Act (PDCA) cycle. In the detection approach the Act part of the cycle is limited, resulting in an incomplete cycle. Whereas with prevention it is an essential part of individuals and teams striving for continuous improvement as part of their everyday work activities.

Quality is created in the design stage and not in the control stage. The majority of quality-related problems are caused by poor or unsuitable designs of products and processes. In the prevention approach, there is a recognition of the process as defined by its input of people, machines, materials, method, management and environment. It also brings a clearer and deeper sense of responsibility for quality to those actually producing and delivering the product and/or service.

Changing from detection to prevention requires not just the use of a set of tools and techniques, but the development of a new operating philosophy and approach which requires a change in management style and way of thinking. It requires the various departments and functions to work and act together in cross-functional teams to discover the root cause of problems and pursue their elimination. Quality planning and improvement truly begins when top management includes prevention as opposed to detection in its organizational policy and objectives and starts to integrate the improvement efforts of various departments together.

THE KEY ELEMENTS OF TOTAL QUALITY MANAGEMENT

Despite the divergence of views on what constitutes TQM, there are a number of key elements in the various definitions which are now summarized. Other chapters will provide more detail of these elements.

Commitment and leadership of senior management

Without the total commitment of the CEO and his/her immediate executives and other senior managers, nothing much will happen and anything that does will not be permanent. They have to take charge personally, provide direction, and exercise forceful leadership. However, whilst some specific actions are required to give it a focus, as quickly as possible it must be seen as the natural way of operating a business.

Planning and organization

This features in a number of facets of a continuous improvement process including:

- Developing a clear long-term approach for TQM which is integrated with other strategies such as information technology, production/operations and human resources and the business plans of the organization.
- Building product and service quality into designs and processes.
- Developing prevention-based activities (e.g. mistake proofing devices).
- Putting quality assurance procedures into place which facilitate closed loop corrective action.
- Planning the approach to be taken for the effective use of quality systems, procedures and tools and techniques, in the context of the overall strategy.
- Developing the organization and infrastructure to support the improvement activities. Whilst it is recommended to set-up some form of steering committee and make people responsible for co-ordinating and facilitating improvement, the infrastructure should not be seen as separate from the management structure.
- Pursuing standardization, systematization and simplification of work instructions, procedures and systems.

Using quality management tools and techniques

To support and develop a process of continuous improvement an organization will need to use a selection of tools and techniques. Without the effective employment and mix of tools and techniques it will be difficult to solve problems. The tools and techniques should be used to facilitate improvement and be integrated into the routine operation of the business. The organization should develop a route map for the tools and techniques which it intends to apply. The use of tools and techniques helps to get the process of improvement started: employees using them feel that they are involved and making a contribution; quality awareness is enhanced; behaviour and attitude change starts to happen; and projects are brought to a successful conclusion.

Education and training

Employees should be provided with the right level of education and training to ensure that their general awareness of quality management concepts, skills and attitudes is appropriate and suited to the continuous improvement philosophy. The right level of education and training also provides a common language throughout the business. A formal programme of education and training needs to be planned and provided on a timely and regular basis to enable people to cope with increasingly complex problems. It should suit the operational conditions of the business: i.e. is training done in a cascade mode (everyone is given the same basic training within a set time frame) or is an infusion mode (training by team/function on a gradual progression basis) more suitable? The training programme should be viewed as an investment in developing the ability and knowledge of people and helping them realize their potential. Without training it is difficult to solve problems and without education people's behaviour and attitude will not change. The training programme must also focus on helping managers think through what improvements are achievable in their areas of responsibility. It also has to be recognized that not all employees will have received and acquired adequate levels of education. The structure of the training programme may incorporate some updating of basic educational skills in numeracy and literacy, but it must promote continuing education and self-development. In this way, the latent potential of many employees will be released.

Involvement

There must be a commitment to the development of employees, with recognition that they are an asset which will appreciate over time. All available means from suggestion schemes to various forms of teamwork must be considered for achieving broad employee interest, participation and contribution in the continuous improvement process. To facilitate this, management must be prepared to share some of their powers and responsibilities. This also involves seeking and listening carefully to the views of employees and acting upon their suggestions. Part of the approach of TQM is to ensure that everyone has a clear understanding of what is required of them and how their processes relate to the business as a whole. The more people who understand the business and what is going on around them, the greater the role they can play in continuous improvement. People have got to be encouraged to control, manage and improve the processes which are within their sphere of responsibility.

Teamwork

Teamwork needs to be practised in a number of forms. Consideration needs to be given to the operating characteristics of the teams employed, how they fit into the organizational structure, and the roles of member, team leader, sponsor and facilitator. Teamwork is one of the key features of involvement and without teamwork it will be difficult to gain the commitment and participation of people throughout the organization.

There is also a need to recognize positive performance and achievement and celebrate and reward success. People must see the results of their activities and that the improvements made really do count. This needs to be constantly encouraged through active communication. If TQM is to be successful it is essential that communication must be effective and widespread. Sometimes managers are good talkers but poor communicators.

Measurement and feedback

Measurement needs to be made continually against a series of key results or performance indicators – internal and external. The latter are the most important as they relate to customer perceptions of product and/or service improvement. The indicators should be developed from existing business measures, external (competitive, functional and generic) and internal benchmarking, as well as customer surveys and other means of external input. This enables progress and feedback to be assessed against a roadmap or checkpoints. From these measurements, action plans must be developed to meet objectives and bridge gaps.

Working together

It is necessary to create an organizational environment which is conducive to continuous improvement and in which everyone can participate and work together. Quality assurance also needs to be integrated into all of an organization's processes and functions. This requires changing people's behaviour, attitudes and working practices in a number of ways. For example:

- Everyone in the organization must be involved in 'improving' the processes under their control on a continuous basis and take personal responsibility for their own quality assurance.

- Employees must inspect their own work.
- Defects must not be passed, in whatever form, to the next process. The internal customer supplier relationship (everyone for whom you perform a task, service or provide information is a customer) must be recognized.
- Each person must be committed to satisfying their customers, both internal and external.
- External suppliers and customers must be integrated into the improvement process.
- Mistakes must be viewed as an improvement opportunity. In the words of the Japanese – every mistake is a pearl to be cherished.
- Honesty, sincerity and care must be an integral part of daily business life.

Changing people's behaviour and attitudes is one of the most difficult tasks facing management, requiring considerable powers and skills of motivation and persuasion. Considerable thought needs to be given to facilitating and managing these types of change.

WHAT ARE THE BENEFITS OF TOTAL QUALITY MANAGEMENT?

The various benefits of TQM are mentioned by most of those writing on the subject. Indeed, in the early discussion of the importance of quality some of the benefits have been aired. In drawing to a close this introductory chapter on Total Quality Management, the benefits of TQM, as outlined in different ways by four executives from diverse business situations and with differing lengths of TQM experiences, are now summarized.

> **Case study: John McAndrew, Deputy Managing Director, RHP Bearings Ltd**
>
> The company is a European manufacturer of bearings to the general industrial, automotive, machine tool and aerospace industries.
> Total quality has been the major catalyst which has united the management and workforce in the common pursuit of profitable growth of the company. The key areas of success have been:

People involvement
In 1992 teamwork was virtually non-existent and only given lip service by management. By 1998 approximately 50% of the workforce was involved regularly in teamworking activities tackling such issues as:

- Scrap – dramatic reduction (90 per cent reduction in 3 years at one factory).
- Lead times – in one factory down from 2 weeks to 2 days.
- Arrears – dramatic and ongoing improvements now measured in hours and minutes rather than days and weeks.
- Cost reductions approximately 10 per cent of turnover as cost savings through teamwork activities in one year
- Customer complaints – dramatically reduced, now at ⅕ of the level they were at in 1992, despite a large turnover and more discerning customers.
- Development of a learning culture evidenced through a significantly increased number of employees undertaking further education.
- Employee surveys have indicated substantial improvement of employee satisfaction and morale?
- A flatter organization plus a more participative, less autocratic management style.

Customer satisfaction
Customer surveys: in 1994 when we started surveying our industrial customers RHP were seen as better than the competition in five out of ten most critical requirements; in 1998 this had improved to being better in all ten of the most critical requirements.

Environmental issues
We have greatly reduced our adverse impact on the environment and have achieved two environmental awards and an award for our environmental report. We have a greater involvement in our local communities.

Better results
In 1995 RHP returned to profit after 3 years of loss, a result of 3 consecutive years of improvement. There was a 20 per cent improvement in productivity in both 1994 and 1995.

In recent years the company achievements have been recognized by the following:

- Perkins Quality Award
- IIP Award
- QS 9000
- Michelin Award
- ISO 14001
- North West Quality Award

Case study: Derek Green – Chief Executive of United Utilities plc

The company is a multi-utility involved with electricity, water and waste-water services

Our actions to improve the services we deliver to our customers, and each other, have had a significant positive impact on our business. We have used our business improvement process to provide an objective view on where, and in what way, to focus our attention. This focus has enabled us to improve what we do and how we do it. This in turn has led to major bottom line benefits. In the past year:

- We have saved over £1m from just one of our critical process benchmarking projects.
- We have ensured that over half of our entire workforce have been involved in business improvement activity that has enabled us to reduce our operating costs by 1 per cent.
- We have implemented innovative programmes of investment that are targeted at 'delighting' our customers (and differentiating ourselves within the utility sector).
- We have increased the number of employees who believe that we are a quality company from 40 per cent to 70 per cent.
- We have increased the proportion of the public who think that we meet or exceed community expectations of a leading company from 54 per cent to 71 per cent.
- We have been voted the second most admired company in the North West by the business community.
- Our plant maintenance facility has won the North West Quality Award.

This process of improvement has also aided our ability to respond to changing operating conditions, a tough economic environment and the Windfall Tax:

- We have improved everyone's understanding of what we are doing and why we are doing it.
- We have improved everyone's awareness of the wider context within which our business has to operate.

Overall we believe that a quality approach to doing business will be a cornerstone of our drive to maintain our 'licence to operate' in what can only be described as turbulent times.

Case study: Hugh Grainger, Managing Director, Rexam Corrugated, Heavy Duty

The company is a supplier of heavy duty corrugated board.

In our company we have been travelling the TQ road for over 10 years. The landscape in that time has evolved from one of Total Quality Performance to Total Quality Management thereafter to Continuous Business Improvement and now on into Self-Assessment against the EFQM model.

The consistent underlying themes throughout this journey have been 'training' and 'communication'. They have reached into every corner of the company's activity. Most significantly they have helped us to work better as a team, to take our individual responsibilities, to be more aware both of others' problems and, above all, of the overriding imperative of customer satisfaction. This happens on the good days!

We can point with momentary satisfaction to a more than doubling of sales and profit, expansion into Continental Europe, industry design awards, ISO 9000 (1 and 2) standards at all plant and average productivity increases of 10 per cent per annum. In all these areas the quality concept has played its part, engendering clearer thought, greater understanding by everyone of the 'what?' and the 'why?' and the 'how?'.

And yet we can truly say that the more you progress the further there is to go. TQ inspiration like the wind can blow hard and soft. At present, after a brief lull we are all now getting to grips with better customer care, developing our common culture and attaining continuous improvement in all sectors of activity.

This should keep us occupied for at least another 10 years . . . .

Case study: Roy Polson, Managing Director, Via-Systems (Midlands)

The company is a supplier of advanced technology printed circuits to the defence and aerospace industry.

TQM has brought into sharp focus the ultimate importance of customer satisfaction as it is consistently and ruthlessly measured in the areas of delivery performance, internal remakes and customer returns. Whilst our performance remains the subject of continual improvement, we are getting better and most importantly it is being recognized by our customers. This is of vital importance in the relationship with our blue chip customer base. Recognition of the company's progress has been in the form of:

- costs down
- Smiths Industries Quality Award (Bronze)
- ship to stock status with GEC-Marconi
- operational benefits
- formal collaboration partnership with British Aerospace Defence

SUMMARY

This chapter has explored the various ways in which quality is defined. In relation to this the point is made that an organization must develop for itself its own definition of quality, which everyone in the organization can understand and identify with. The importance of quality in today's business environment is explored and it is concluded that despite the various surveys which are less than enthusiastic about TQM, the experience from the business world is that a process of continuous improvement is vital to take cost out of the organization in order to become more efficient and to meet the needs of customers. These organizations are ignoring the noise and are continuing to increase the velocity of their improvement process. The views from a number of CEOs at the end of the chapter on the benefits of TQM provide an insight into this. The chapter has also traced the development of quality management from inspection, quality control, quality assurance to TQM. The drawbacks of a detection-based approach is outlined and the need for a more preventative-based approach is emphasized.

REFERENCES

Anon 1995: 'Customers Unimpressed by Empty Smiles and Promises', *Customer Service Management Ltd*, December.
Anon 1997: 'Does Business Excellence Work?' *Organizational Excellence*, February, 1–7.
BS. 4778: Quality Vocabulary, Part 2 1991: *Quality Concepts and Related Definitions*, British Standards Institution, London.
BS EN ISO 8402 1995: *Quality Management and Quality Assurance*, British Standards Institution, London.
Buzzell R. D. and Gale B. T. 1987: *The Profit Impact of Marketing Strategy: Linking Strategy to Performance*, The Free Press, New York.
Carlzon, J. 1987: *Moments of Truth*, Ballinger, New York.
CMC Partnerships Ltd, 1991: *Attitudes Within British Business to Quality*

Management Systems, The CMC Partnership, Buckingham.

Crosby P. B. 1979: *Quality is Free*, McGraw Hill, New York.

Dale B. G. and Plunkett J. J. 1999: *Quality Costing*, (Third Edition), Gower Press, Hants.

Dale B. G. (ed.) 1994: *Managing Quality*, (Second Edition), Prentice Hall, Hertfordshire.

Ford Motor Company 1985: *Three-day Statistical Process Control Notes*, Ford Motor Company, Brentwood, Essex.

Gallup Organization Inc. 1991: *An International Survey of Consumers' Perceptions of Product and Service Quality*, American Society for Quality Control, Milwaukee.

Gallup Organization Inc. 1992: *An ASQC/Gallup Survey on Quality Leadership Roles of Corporate Executives and Directors*, American Society for Quality Control, Milwaukee.

Hutchens S. 1989: What Customers Want: Results of ASQC/Gallup Survey, *Quality Progress*, February, 33–6.

Juran J. M. (ed.) 1988: *Quality Control Handbook*, (Fourth Edition), McGraw Hill, New York.

Kano N., Tanaka H. and Yamaga Y. 1983: *The TQC Activity of Deming Prize Recipients and its Economic Impact*, Union of Japanese Scientists and Engineers, Tokyo.

Kosko J. 1998: *Baldrige Index Outperforms S and P 500 for Fourth Year*, http://www.nist.gov/public., February, 9.

Larry L. 1993: 'Betting to Win on the Baldrige Winners', *Business Week*, 18, October 16–17.

Lascelles D. M. and Dale B. G. 1990: Quality Management: the Chief Executive's Perception and Role, *European Management Journal*, 8 (1), 67–75.

Letz S. R., Zairi M. and Whymark J. 1997: TQM – *Fad or Tool for Sustainable Competitive Advantage: an Empirical Study of the Impact of TQM on Bottom Line Business Results*, University of Bradford Management Centre, Bradford.

McKenzie R. M. 1989: *The Production-Inspection Relationship*, Scottish Academic Press, Edinburgh and London.

McKinsey & Company 1989: 'Management of Quality: the Single Most Important Challenge for Europe', *European Quality Management Forum*, 19, October, Montreux, Switzerland.

National Institute of Technology 1999, *NIST Stock Study of Malcolm Baldrige National Quality Award Recipients*, http://www.nist.you/publicaffairs/stockstudy.htm.

OFWAT Levels of Service Report 1995/1996, HMSO, London.

Parasuraman A., Zeithamal V. A. and Berry L. L. 1998: 'SERVQUAL: a Multiple Item Scale for Measuring Consumer Perceptions of Service

Quality', *Journal of Retailing*, 64 (1), 14–40.

Roberts K. 1996: 'Viewpoint – Customer Value and Market-Driven Quality Management', *Strategic Insights into Quality*, 4 (2), 3.

Ryan J. 1988: 'Consumers See Little Change in Product Quality', *Quality Progress*, December, 16–20.

Taguchi G. 1986: *Introduction to Quality Engineering*, Asian Productivity Organization, Dearborn, Michigan.

Wisner J. D. and Eakins S. G. 1994: 'Competitive Assessment of the Baldrige Winners', *International Journal of Quality and Reliability Management*, 11 (2), 8–25.

Zeithmal V. A., Parasuraman A, and Berry L. L 1990: *Delivering Quality Service: Balancing Customer Perceptions and Expectations*, The Free Press, New York.

2

The received wisdom on Total Quality Management

INTRODUCTION

The purpose of this chapter is to introduce the reader to what the leading exponents of TQM have to say on the subject and explore, in brief, their teachings and advice.

In the Western world the four best known quality management experts are all Americans – Crosby (1979), Deming (1982), Feigenbaum (1983) and Juran (1988). These four men have had a considerable influence in the development of TQM in organizations throughout the world. In addition to the approaches and philosophies of these four experts the Japanese quality management culture is also widely publicized. In recent times the work and ideas of a number of Japanese quality experts have been published in English. They include Imai (1986), Ishikawa (1985), Mizuno (1988), Nemoto (1987), Ozeki and Askaka (1990), Shingo (1986) and Taguchi (1986). The ideas of these Japanese experts are all being applied in the West but perhaps it is the work of Imai, Ishikawa, Shingo and Taguchi which are the best known. For this reason their work is briefly reviewed before reviewing some of the familiar concepts associated with how Japanese companies manage a process of continuous improvement.

CROSBY

Philip Crosby's audience is primarily top management. He sells his approach to top management and stresses increasing profitability through quality improvement. His argument is that higher quality reduces costs and raises profits. He defines quality as conformance to requirements. Crosby's programme has 14 steps (Crosby 1979) that focus on how to change the organization and tend to be specific action plans for implementation:

Crosby's 14-step quality improvement programme

1. management commitment
2. quality improvement team
3. quality measurement
4. cost of quality evaluation
5. quality awareness
6. corrective action
7. establish an ad hoc committee for the zero defects programme
8. supervisor training
9. zero defects day
10. goal setting
11. error cause removal
12. recognition
13. quality councils
14. do it over again

Crosby's approach is based on four absolutes of quality management:

1. quality means conformance, not elegance
2. it is always cheaper to do the job right the first time
3. the only performance indicator is the cost of quality
4. the only performance standard is zero defects

Crosby also has produced a 'Quality Vaccine' comprising 21 areas divided into the five categories of integrity, systems, communications, operations and policies which he treats as preventive medicine for poor quality.

Crosby does not accept the optimal quality level concept because he believes that higher quality always reduces costs and raises profit. Cost of quality is used as a tool to help achieve that goal. Regarding cost of quality, he produced the first serious alternative to the prevention, appraisal and failure categorization for quality costs and introduced the price of conformance and price of non-conformance model. In terms of employee roles, Crosby allocates a moderate amount of responsibility to the quality professional. Top management has an important role, and the hourly workforce has a role which is limited to reporting problems to management. One way that Crosby measures quality achievement is with a matrix, the quality management maturity grid, that charts the stages that management goes through from ignorance to enlightenment.

In summary, Crosby is acknowledged as a great motivator of senior management in helping to get the improvement process started. His approach is generally regarded as simple and easy to follow, this leads his critics to claim he lacks substance in giving detailed guidance on how to apply quality management principles, tools, techniques and systems.

DEMING

W. Edwards Deming's argument is that quality through a reduction in statistical variation improves productivity and competitive position. He defines quality in terms of quality of design, quality of conformance, and quality of the sales and service function. Deming aims to improve quality and productivity, jobs, ensure the long-term survival of the firm, and improve competitive position. He does not accept the trade-off shown in the 'economic cost of quality' models and says there is no way to calculate the cost of delivering defective products to customers, which he believes is the major quality cost.

Deming advocates the measurement of quality by direct statistical measures of manufacturing performance against specification. While all production processes exhibit variation, the goal of quality improvement is to reduce variation. Deming's approach is highly statistical and he believes that every employee should be trained in statistical quality techniques. A 14–point approach (Deming 1986) summarizes his management philosophy for improving quality:

Deming's 14 points for management

1. Create constancy of purpose towards improvement of product and service, with the aim to become competitive, stay in business, and to provide jobs.
2. Adopt the new philosophy – we are in a new economic age. Western management must awaken to the challenge, learn responsibilities and take on leadership for future change.
3. Cease dependence on inspection to achieve quality. Eliminate the need for inspection on a mass basis by building quality into the product in the first place.
4. End the practice of awarding business on the basis of price tag. Instead, minimize total cost. Move toward a single supplier for any one item with a long-term relationship of loyalty and trust.
5. Constantly improve the system of production and service, to improve quality and productivity, and thus constantly decrease costs.
6. Institute training on the job.
7. Institute leadership (see point 12). The aim of supervision should

be to help people, machines and gadgets to do a better job. Supervision of management, as well as supervision of production workers, is in need of overhaul.

8. Drive out fear, so that everyone may work effectively for the company.

9. Break down barriers between departments. People in research, design, sales and production must work as a team, to foresee problems of production and problems in use that may be encountered with the product or service.

10. Eliminate slogans, exhortations and targets for the workforce that ask for zero defects and new levels of productivity. Such exhortations only create adverse relationships, as the bulk of the causes of low quality and low productivity belong to the system and thus lie beyond the power of the workforce.

11. (a) Eliminate work standards (quotas) on the factory floor. Substitute leadership instead.
     (b) Eliminate management by objectives, by numbers and by numerical goals. Substitute leadership instead.

12. (a) Remove barriers that rob the hourly worker of his or her right to pride of workmanship. The responsibility of supervisors must be changed from sheer numbers to quality.
     (b) Remove barriers that rob people in management and in engineering of their right to pride of workmanship. This means, *inter alia*, abolishment of the annual or merit rating, and of management by objectives.

13. Institute a vigorous programme of education and self-improvement.

14. Put everybody in the company to work to accomplish the transformation. The transformation is everybody's job.

Deming's view is that quality management and improvement is the responsibility of all the firm's employees. Top management must adopt the 'new religion' of quality, lead the drive for improvement and be involved in all stages of the process. Hourly workers should be trained and encouraged to prevent defects and improve quality, and be given challenging and rewarding jobs. Quality professionals should educate other managers in statistical techniques and concentrate on improving the methods of defect prevention. Finally, statisticians should consult with all areas of the company.

Other contributions from Deming include the PDCA cycle of continuous improvement, which Deming himself termed the Shewhart cycle after the Father of statistical quality control. Deming also pinpointed the seven

'Deadly Diseases': (i) lack of consistency of purpose; (ii) emphasis on short-term profits; (iii) evaluation of performance, merit rating, or annual review; (iv) mobility of management; (v) running a company on visible figures alone; (vi) excessive medical costs and; (vii) excessive cost of liability. He used these 'Deadly Diseases' to criticize Western management and organization practices.

In summary, Deming expects the managers to change – to develop a partnership with those at the operating level of the business and to manage quality with direct statistical measures without cost-of-quality measures. Deming's approach, particularly his insistence on the need for management to change the organizational culture, is closely aligned with Japanese practice. This is not surprising in view of the assistance he gave to the Japanese after the Second World War.

A number of Deming User Groups and Associations have been formed which are dedicated to facilitating awareness and understanding of his work and helping companies introduce his ideas. Also a number of authors (e.g. Aguayo 1990, Kilian 1992, Scherkenbach 1991 and Yoshida 1995) have produced books explaining Deming's approach and ideas.

FEIGENBAUM

Armand V. Feigenbaum was General Electric's world-wide chief of manufacturing operations for a decade until the late 1960s. He is now president of an engineering consultancy firm, General Systems Co., that designs and installs operational systems in corporations around the world. Feigenbaum was the originator of the term 'Total Quality Control', defined in 1961 in his first edition of *Total Quality Control* as:

> Total Quality Control is an effective system for integrating the quality-development, quality-maintenance, and quality-improvement efforts of the various groups in an organization so as to enable marketing, engineering, production, and service at the most economical levels which allow for full customer satisfaction.

Feigenbaum does not try so much to create managerial awareness of quality as to help a plant or company design its own system. To him, quality is a way of managing a business organization. Significant quality improvement can only be achieved in a company through the participation of everyone in the workforce, who must, therefore, have a good understanding of what management is trying to do. Fire-fighting quality problems has to be replaced with a very clear, customer-oriented quality management process that people can understand and commit themselves to.

Senior management's understanding of the issues surrounding quality improvement and commitment to incorporating quality into its management practice is crucial to the successful installation of Feigenbaum's total quality system. They must abandon short-term motivational programmes that yield no long-lasting improvement. Management must also realize that quality doesn't mean only that customer problems have to be fixed faster. Quality leadership is essential to a company's success in the marketplace.

Feigenbaum takes a very serious financial approach to the management of quality. He believes that the effective installation and management of a quality improvement process represent the best return-on-investment opportunity for many companies in today's competitive environment. His major contribution to the subject of cost of quality was the recognition that quality costs must be categorized if they are to be managed. He identified three major categories: appraisal costs, prevention costs and failure costs (Feigenbaum 1956). Total quality cost is the sum of these costs. He was also the first of the international experts to identify the folly of regarding quality professionals as being solely responsible for an organization's quality activities.

According to Feigenbaum the goal of quality improvement is to reduce the total cost of quality from the often quoted 25 to 30 per cent of annual sales or cost of operations to as low a percentage as possible. Therefore, developing cost-of-quality data and tracking these data on an ongoing basis is an integral part of the process.

Feigenbaum says that management must commit itself to:

- strengthening the quality improvement process itself
- making sure that quality improvement becomes a habit
- managing quality and cost as complementary objectives

In summary, though Feigenbaum does not espouse 14 points or steps like Deming or Crosby, it is obvious his approach is not significantly different; it simply boils down to managerial know-how. He does, however, identify ten benchmarks for success with TQM:

Feigenbaum's ten benchmarks for Total Quality Success

1. quality is a company-wide process
2. quality is what the customer says it is
3. quality and cost are a sum, not a difference

4. quality requires both individual and team zealotry
5. quality is a way of managing
6. quality and innovation are mutually dependent
7. quality is an ethic
8. quality requires continuous improvement
9. quality is the most cost-effective, least capital-intensive route to productivity
10. quality is implemented with a total system connected with customers and suppliers

JURAN

Joseph Juran has made perhaps a greater contribution to the quality management literature than any other quality professional. Like Deming, he has had an influence in the development of quality management in Japanese companies. Whilst Deming provided advice on statistical methods to technical specialists from the late 1940s onwards, Juran in the mid-1950s focused on the role of senior people in quality management.

Part of his argument is that companies must reduce the cost of quality. This is dramatically different from Deming. Deming ignores the cost of quality while Juran, like Crosby and Feigenbaum, claim that reducing it is a key objective of any business. A ten-point plan summarizes his approach:

The Juran method

1. build awareness of the need and opportunity for improvement
2. set goals for improvement
3. organise to reach the goals
4. provide training
5. carry out projects to solve problems
6. report progress
7. give recognition
8. communicate results
9. keep the score
10. maintain momentum by making annual improvement part of the regular system and processes of the company

Juran defines quality as 'fitness for use', which he breaks into quality of design, quality of conformance, availability, and field service. The goals of Juran's approach to quality improvement are increased conformance and decreased cost of quality, and yearly goals are set in the objective-setting phase of the programme. He developed a quality trilogy comprising of quality planning, quality control and quality improvement. Basically, his approach focuses on three segments: a programme to attack sporadic problems; one to attack chronic problems; and an annual quality programme, in which top management participates, to develop or refine policies. Juran defines two major kinds of quality management: breakthrough (encouraging the occurrence of good things) that attacks chronic problems; and control (preventing the occurrence of bad things) that attacks sporadic problems. He views the improvement process as taking two journeys: from symptom to cause (diagnosis); and cause to remedy (diagnosis to solution).

Diff ←   Juran also allocates responsibility among the workforce differently from Deming. He puts the primary responsibility to quality professionals (who serve as consultants to top management and employees). The quality professionals design and develop the programme, and do most of the work. While granting the importance of top management support, Juran places more of the quality leadership responsibility on middle management and quality professionals. The role of the workforce is mainly to be involved in quality improvement teams.

In summary, Juran emphasizes the cost of quality, because the language of top management is money, and he recommends cost of quality for identifying quality improvement projects and opportunities and developing a quality cost scoreboard to measure quality costs. Juran's approach is more consistent with American management practices – he takes the existing management culture as a starting point and builds a quality improvement process from that baseline.

IMAI

Imai (1986) and (1997) is the person accredited with bringing together the various management philosophies, theories, techniques and tools which have assisted Japanese companies over the last four or so decades to improve their efficiency. The published evidence indicates that the impact of Kaizen in Japanese companies has been considerable.

In simple terms Kaizen is the process of incremental, systematic and continuous improvement that uses the best of all techniques, tools, systems and concepts (e.g. TPM, JIT, SMED, quality circles and the PDCA cycle). From this it is clear that Kaizen is generic in its application. The improvements taking place in steady planned steps are contrasted with the usual methods of Western organizations of large step innovation of efforts. A good idea of what is encompassed in Kaizen is given by the

Glossary of Kaizen terminology and concepts at the front end of Imai's book (1986).

The aim of Kaizen is to ensure that everyone in an organization is of the frame of mind to pursue naturally continuous improvement in whatever they do. It also encourages people to accept continuing change. Running through the concept are a number of basic principles such as:

- continuous focus on improvement
- everyone in the company should be involved
- delighting the customer
- everything should be considered from a total system standpoint

The key elements of Kaizen are:

- adaptability of both people and equipment
- use of existing technology to optimize capacity
- creative involvement of all employees
- 'make it a little better each day' attitude

ISHIKAWA

Ishikawa's contribution is in three main areas: (i) the simplification and widespread use of the seven basic quality control tools, (ii) the company-wide quality movement and; (iii) quality circles.

An underlying theme throughout Ishikawa's work (i.e. Ishikawa 1979, 1985 and 1991) was that people at all levels of the organization should use simple methods and work together to solve problems, thereby removing barriers to improvement, co-operation and education and developing a culture which is conducive to continuous improvement.

Ishikawa developed the cause and effect diagram and was also responsible for bringing together the selection of tools which are now known as the seven basic quality control tools. His argument was that these seven tools, when used together, could help solve most problems.

Ishikawa was an original member of the quality control research group of the Japanese Union of Scientists and Engineers (JUSE). In this activity he became involved in the teaching of JUSE Total Quality Control (TQC) courses and was involved in this activity until his death in 1989. In Japan, if a company wants to start TQC it is usual for the senior management to attend a course organised by JUSE. This type of course is run by three teachers known fondly as 'the Big three', Ishikawa was one of these three. As part of his work with this research group he was involved in studying

American methods and helping Japanese companies adapt and develop them for their own environment, and operating conditions. He was renown for working in harmony with his academic colleagues.

Ishikawa is regarded as the 'Father of Quality Control Circles'. This was because he was on the editorial staff of the JUSE publication *Genba to QC* which when it was launched in April 1962 called for the formation of quality circles. Subsequently JUSE started to register the quality circles which then formed in manufacturing organizations. From this start Ishikawa played a great role in the development of quality circles in Japan and assisted with world-wide spread of the concept. Dale (1993) quoting Dr Noguchi (Executive Director of JUSE) makes the point that Ishikawa claimed quality circles are effective in solving 30 to 35 per cent of an organization's quality problems.

SHINGO

Shingo has had a number of books (e.g. Shingo 1985, 1986 and 1989) translated into English. He is best known for his work on Single Minute Exchange of Die (SMED), mistake proofing (poka-yoke) defect prevention system and in conjunction with Ohno the development of the Toyota production system. He liked to be known as 'Dr Improvement' and is renown for his work on improving manufacturing processes.

Shingo advocates the use of the poka-yoke system to reduce and eliminate defects. Shingo classifies poka-yoke systems into two types – regulatory functions and setting functions. Two main functions are performed by the regulatory devices: (i) control methods which when abnormalities are detected shut down the machine, thus preventing the occurrence of further non-conformities and; (ii) warning methods which signal, by means of noise and/or light devices, the occurrence of an abnormality. There are three main types of poka-yoke setting functions: (i) contact methods in which sensing devices detect abnormalities; (ii) fixed-value methods in which abnormalities are detected by counting devices and; (iii) motion-step methods where abnormalities are detected by failure to follow a predetermined motion or routine.

The term SMED refers to the theory and technique for performing set-up operations in under 10 minutes. It is a fundamental approach to continuous improvement, bringing benefits in terms of stock reduction, productivity improvements, flexibility, reduction in set-up errors and defects and improved tool management. The concept of SMED and quick change-over advanced by Shingo challenges traditional wisdom (e.g. economic batch sizes, set-up always take a long time, and the skills required for set-up changes can only be acquired through long-term practice and experience). Shingo identifies three main stages of improvement through SMED:

1. Differentiate and separate internal set-up (which can only be performed when a machine is shut down) from external set-up (which can be done while the machine is running).
2. Shift internal set-up elements to external set-up.
3. Improve the methods involved in both internal and external set-ups.

The contribution Shingo made to the development of the Toyota Production System is legendary and his written work outlines a number of methods (e.g. JIT, scheduling, workplace layout, stock control SMED, mistake proofing) for improving quality and productivity.

TAGUCHI

Genichi Taguchi is a statistician and electrical engineer who was involved in rebuilding the Japanese telephone system. He was contracted to provide statistical assistance and design of experiment support. Taguchi rejected the classical approach to design of experiments as being too impractical for industrial situations and revised these methods to develop his own approach to design of experiments. He has been applying Taguchi design of experiments in the Japanese electronics industry for over 30 years. His ideas fall into two principal and related areas known as 'the loss function' and 'off-line quality control'.

In his ideas about the loss function Taguchi (1986) defines quality as 'The quality of a product is the loss imparted to society from the time the product is shipped.' Among the losses he includes consumers' dissatisfaction, warranty costs, loss of reputation and, ultimately, loss of market share. Taguchi maintains that a product does not start causing losses just when it is out of specification, but also when there is any deviation from the target value. Further, in most cases the loss to society can be represented by a quadratic function, i.e. the loss increases as the square of the deviation from the target value. This leads to the important conclusion that quality (as defined by Taguchi) is most economically achieved by minimizing variance, rather than by strict conformance to specification.

This conclusion provides the basis for Taguchi's ideas for off-line quality control. Off-line quality control means optimizing production process and product parameters in such a way as to minimize item to item variations in the product and its performance. Clearly this focuses attention on the design process. Taguchi promotes three distinct stages of designing-in quality:

1. System design – the basic configuration of the system is developed This involves the selection of parts and materials and the use of feasibility studies and prototyping. In system design technical knowledge and scientific skills are paramount.
2. Parameter design – the numerical values for the system variables (product and process parameters which are called factors) are chosen so that the system performs well, no matter what disturbances or noises (i.e. uncontrollable variables) are encountered by the system (i.e. robustness). The objective is to identify optimum levels for these control factors so that the product and/or process is least sensitive to the effect in changes of noise factors and the changes that they make. The experimentation pinpoints this combination of product/process parameter levels. The emphasis in parameter design is on using low-cost materials and processes in the production of the system. It is the key stage of designing-in quality.
3. Tolerance design – if the system is not satisfactory, tolerance design is then used to improve performance by tightening the tolerances.

When seeking to optimize production process and product or service parameters it is frequently necessary to determine experimentally the effects of varying the parameter values. This can be a very expensive and time consuming process which may produce a lot of redundant information. By using fractional factorial experiments, which Taguchi calls orthogonal arrays, the number of experiments required can be reduced

	Gap	Straw unwind	Gaylord heater	Fluting shower	Liner wrap	Small P/heat	Roll pressure	Strength	Variation
Set 1	6	Off	On	Off	Off	Off	40	58.73	6.93
Set 2	6	Off	On	On	On	On	60	76.27	7.18
Set 3	6	On	Off	Off	Off	On	60	63.26	6.29
Set 4	6	On	Off	On	On	Off	40	67.07	7.53
Set 5	9	Off	Off	Off	On	Off	60	61.65	4.51
Set 6	9	Off	Off	On	Off	On	40	61.19	4.90
Set 7	9	On	On	Off	On	On	40	65.56	4.57
Set 8	9	On	On	On	Off	Off	60	62.73	5.41

Figure 2.1 Design of experiments: liner bond strength.
Source: Rexam Corrugated South West Ltd.

drastically. An orthogonal array from a design of experiment carried out on the corrugator at Rexam Corrugated South West Ltd is shown in figure 2.1.

The attention given to what are commonly termed, 'Taguchi methods' has been largely responsible for organizations examining the usefulness of experimental design in making improvements. Quite apart from the successes derived from using his methods, the level of awareness he has promoted in design of experiments is an achievement in itself. However, it should not be overlooked that a number of other people have made significant improvements with other approaches to experimental design.

JAPANESE STYLE TQC

The Japanese define their goal as continual improvement towards perfection. They allocate responsibility for quality management among all employees. The workers are primarily responsible for maintaining the system although they have some responsibility for improving it. Higher up, managers do less maintaining and more improving. At the highest levels, the emphasis is on breakthrough and on teamwork throughout the organization.

There are a number of now-familiar concepts associated with Japanese style TQM or Total Quality Control (TQC) or Company-Wide Quality Control (CWQC) as they term it. CWQC is defined by JUSE The Deming Prize Committee (1996) as:

> CWQC is a set of systematic activities carried out by the entire organization to effectively and efficiently achieve company objectives and provide products and services within a level of quality that satisfies customers, at the appropriate time and price.

Earlier work tried to make a distinction between TQC and CWQC, but in Japanese companies today they appear to be one and the same. These concepts include:

- total commitment to improvement
- perfection and defect analysis
- continuous change
- taking personal responsibility for the quality assurance of one's own processes
- insistence on compliance
- correcting one's own errors
- adherence to disciplines
- orderliness and cleanliness

Various practices facilitate continuous improvement in Japanese companies, including:

- policy deployment of targets for improvement
- use of statistical methods
- housekeeping
- daily machine and equipment checking
- successive and self-check systems
- visual management
- mistake-proofing
- detailed quality assurance procedures
- visual standards

- the concept that the next person or process is the customer
- improvement followed by standardization
- the Just-In-Time philosophy
- total productive maintenance
- quality circles
- suggestion schemes
- treating suppliers as part of the family

SUMMARY

The published writings and philosophies of the eminent people mentioned in this chapter can provide the necessary inspiration and guidance to organizations in introducing and developing a process of continuous improvement. Whilst the slavish following of a guru's teachings is no guarantee of success, despite the propaganda, it would be a brave manager who can afford not to learn from the collective wisdom of the eminent people mentioned in this chapter. Managers should, however, be prepared to adapt and develop their teachings to suit their operating conditions and available resources.

REFERENCES

Aguayo R. 1990: *Dr. Deming: The American who Taught the Japanese about Quality*, Simon and Schuster, New York.

Crosby P. B. 1979: *Quality is Free*, McGraw Hill, New York.

Dale B. G. 1993: 'The Key Features of Japanese Total Quality Control', *Quality and Reliability Engineering, International*, 9 (1), 169–78.

Deming W. E. 1982: *Quality, Productivity and Competitive Position*, Massachusetts Institute of Technology, Massachusetts.

Deming W. E. 1986: *Out of the Crisis*, Massachusetts Institute of Technology, Centre of Advanced Engineering Study, Cambridge, Massachusetts.

Feigenbaum A. V. 1956: 'Total Quality Control', *Harvard Business Review*, vol. 34, no. 6, 93–101.

Feigenbaum A. V. 1983: *Total Quality Control*, McGraw Hill, New York.

Imai M. 1986: *Kaizen the Key to Japan's Competitive Success*, Random House Business Division, New York.

Imai M. 1997: *Gemba Kaizen: A Commonsense Low Cost Approach to Management*, ASQC Quality Press, Milwaukee.

Ishikawa K. 1979: *Guide to Quality Control*, Asian Productivity Organization, Tokyo.

Ishikawa K. 1985 (translated by Lu D. J.): *What is Total Quality Control? The Japanese Way*, Prentice Hall, Englewood Cliffs, New Jersey.

Ishikawa K. 1991: *Introduction to Quality Control*, Chapman and Hall, Tokyo.

Juran J. M. (Editor-in-Chief) 1988: *Quality Control Handbook*, (Fourth Edition), McGraw Hill, New York.

JUSE, The Deming Prize Committee 1996: *The Japan Quality Medal Guide for Overseas Companies*, Japanese Union of Scientists and Engineers, Tokyo.

Kilian C. S. 1992: *The World of W. Edwards Deming*, SPC Press Inc, New York.

Mizuno S. 1988: *Company-Wide Total Quality Control*, Asian Productivity Organization, Tokyo.

Nemoto M. 1987: *Total Quality Control for Management*, Prentice Hall Englewood Cliffs, New Jersey.

Ozeki K. and Asaka T. 1990: *Handbook of Quality Tools*, Productivity Europe, Buckinghamshire.

Scherkenbach W. W. 1991: *The Deming Route to Quality and Productivity: Road Maps and Roadblocks*, ASQC Quality Press, Milwaukee.

Shingo S. 1985: *A Revolution in Manufacturing: the SMED System*, Productivity Press, Massachusetts.

Shingo S. 1986: *Zero Quality Control: Source Inspection and the Poka-Yoke System*, Productivity Press, Cambridge, MA.

Shingo S. 1989: *A Study of the Toyota Production System from an Industrial Engineering Viewpoint*, Productivity Press, Massachusetts.

Taguchi G. 1986: *Introduction to Quality Engineering*, Asian Productivity Organization, New York.

Yoshida K. 1995: 'Revisiting Deming's 14 Points in Light of Japanese Business Practice', *Quality Management Journal*, 3 (1), 14–30.

3

The role of management in Total Quality Management

INTRODUCTION

In introducing this chapter on the role of management in TQM the reader may be interested to know that more than one director has commented that the word quality should be removed from the term Total Quality Management. The reasoning for this argument is TQM is all about good management behaviour and practice. It is an integral and natural part of the management of an organization, its structure and business processes. Can any current or would be executive who wishes to improve his/her management skills and abilities afford not to understand more about the subject and get involved with its introduction and development?

This chapter outlines the main reasons why it is important that senior managers should become personally involved in TQM. It examines what they need to know about TQM and what they should do in terms of positive actions. It then goes on to discuss the role which middle management and first-line management need to play in introducing and putting the principles of TQM into place in their organizations.

WHY SENIOR EXECUTIVES SHOULD BECOME INVOLVED IN TQM

The decision to introduce TQM can only be taken by the Chief Executive Officer (CEO) and his/her senior management team. Developing and deploying organizational vision, mission, values, objectives and plans and communicating the reason for their existence is the province of senior management. This is why they have to become personally involved in TQM and the improvement process, and demonstrate visible commitment to it by leading this way of thinking and managing the business. They have got to empower a total corporate commitment to improve every aspect of the business. This not only requires their personal commitment and confidence but a significant investment of their time.

The responsibility for quality lies with the CEO and his/her senior management team. Everyone in the organization has a role to play in continuous improvement but this effort is likely to be disjointed and spasmodic if the senior management team has not made the organizational requirements for quality and route map to excellence crystal clear. If the senior management team does not get involved, it is likely that the improvement process will stagnate and employees will experience disillusionment.

McKinsey and Company (1989) reporting on a survey of the CEOs of the top 500 European corporations in relation to the key requirements for success in TQM, found the following:

- top management attention   95% agreement
- people development   85% agreement
- corporate team spirit   82% agreement
- quality performance information   73% agreement
- top management capability building   70% agreement
- sense of urgency   60% agreement

Lascelles and Dale (1990) reporting on their research into what triggers the need to introduce TQM also make the point that 'the CEO is the primary internal change agent for quality improvement'. They go on to say that in this capacity he/she has two key roles: 'shaping organizational values, and establishing a managerial infrastructure to actually bring about change'.

Senior management commitment and involvement in TQM is vital to gain credibility for the concept within the organization, assure continuity and establish longevity. The CEO, supported by the senior management team, is the only person in the organization who can make quality the number one organizational priority and the top item on the management agenda. He/she must have faith in the long-term plan for TQM and not expect immediate financial benefits. Ultimately, he/she is responsible for the organizational environment, behaviour, values, climate and style of management in which TQM will either flourish or wither. The CEO and his/her senior managers need to create and promote an environment in which, for example:

- people can work together as a team
- teams work with teams
- mistakes are freely admitted without recriminations and that any that occur are perceived as an improvement opportunity (i.e. a 'blame free' culture)

- people are involved in the business through decision making
- people are not afraid to step out of their comfort zones
- people improve on a continuous basis the processes under their control
- people direct their attention to identifying, satisfying and delighting and winning over customers, whether they be internal or external
- ideas are actively sought from everyone
- development of people is a priority
- employee involvement is worked at continually
- permanent solutions are found to problems
- departmental boundaries between functions are non-existent
- effective two-way communication is in place
- recognition is given for improvement activities
- status symbols are removed

Change is not something that any department and individual takes to easily, and administering changes in organizational practices has to be considered with care. Senior managers should also bear in mind that some people, albeit a minority, will be 100 per cent negative to the concept and principles of TQM. These people should be identified and worked upon to encourage a more positive perception. Senior management should not underestimate the impact they can have on these people. However, if these people are not prepared to change their behaviour and attitudes, harsh decisions will be required. To quote the Personnel Director of a blue chip UK conglomerate ' "neutral" (those employees who do their day-to-day work effectively but do not wish to get involved in improvement activities) can be tolerated but "blockers" (those employees who exert a negative influence on continuous improvement) should be removed'. In response to such employees a CEO of an American automotive components manufacturer uses the term 'change the people or change the people'.

In the majority of Western organizations, people have witnessed the latest fads and 'flavours of the month' which have come and gone. They have become accustomed to senior managers talking a lot about a topic or issue, but failing to demonstrate visible commitment to what they are saying. Typical of the comments made by people are 'He is at it again, lets humour him' and 'TQM will go the way of all other fads and fancies'. It is only the CEO and his/her senior managers who can break down this cynicism, influence the indifference and persuade people that the organization is serious about TQM. It is they who have got to communicate in person to their people why the organization is setting out on the journey to excellence.

The senior management team has got to demonstrate that it really cares about quality. This can be done by getting involved in activities such as:

- setting-up and chairing a TQM Steering Committee or ensuring that TQM becomes an agenda item at all Board and management meetings
- identifying the major quality issues facing the organization and becoming personally involved in investigating the issues, as a leader, member, mentor or sponsor to an improvement team
- getting involved in quality planning, audit and improvement meetings and housekeeping and playing an active part in team competitions and quality award events
- leading and/or attending quality training courses
- chairing individual sessions with operatives about the importance of following procedures and carrying out the appropriate checks
- organizing and chairing defect review boards
- instigating and carrying out regular audits and self-assessment of the progress being made with continuous improvement
- dealing with customer complaints and visiting customers and suppliers
- leading customer workshops and panels
- visiting, on a regular basis, all areas and functions of the business, and discussing improvement issues
- developing, communicating and then following a personal improvement action plan
- communicating as never before on TQM, for example, carrying out team briefs, preparing personal 'thank you' notes to teams and writing articles for the TQM newsletter
- chairing employee forums and taking responsibility for improvement actions
- removing status symbols such as reserved car parking and directors' dining rooms

In this way, the senior management team leads, teaches and learns by example and, consequently, everyone in the organization starts to share the same value system and develop a sense of company loyalty. It is only by getting personally involved that a full understanding of the philosophy underlying continuous improvement can be developed. It is also helpful if the senior management team has a charismatic leadership style, and makes a deliberate attempt to create some organizational folklore relating to the lengths it has gone to in terms of commitment to TQM, satisfying customers and ensuring a right first time performance. In other words, senior managers need to become TQM heroes, TQM giants, 'captain marvels' and legends in their own right. Once this commitment and leadership has been demonstrated, ideas, innovations and improvements will start to feed through from the lower levels of the organizational hierarchy. At this stage of the development of TQM the CEO must also be aware that some employees will be complying through fear and have no real commitment or belief.

The continuous improvement process is a roller-coaster of troughs and peaks (see figure 3.1). At certain points in the process, it will become apparent that although a considerable amount of organizational resources is being devoted to continuous improvement there is little progress being made. When the process is at one of these low points, it is not uncommon for some middle and first-line managers and functional specialists to claim that TQM is not working and start to ask questions such as 'Why are we doing this?' 'Are we seeing real improvements?', 'What are the benefits?' and 'Such and such a concept would be a better bet'. Consequently, they will switch their attention to what they claim are more pressing matters (this is a natural tendency for people wanting to be associated with success). If the senior management team is personally involved in TQM, people are much less likely to express this type of view. The team has a key role to play in helping to get employees through this crisis of confidence.

In most Western organizations, a few key people are usually vital to the development and advancement of an organization's improvement process and if one of these key people leaves it can leave a major gap in the man-

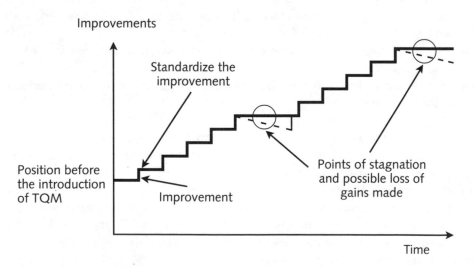

Figure 3.1   The continuous improvement process.

agement team. In the case of organizational changes, the CEO plays a major role in developing the TQM understanding and diffusing beliefs to new managers and technical and business specialists. When key people leave the organization and the improvement process continues without interruption and improvement teams continue to meet this is an indication that an environment which is conducive to TQM is firmly in place.

Organizations are not usually experienced in holding the gains made in TQM. In addition to leadership and organizational changes, factors such as take-overs, industrial relations problems, short-time working, redundancies, cost cutting, downsizing, streamlining, no salary increases, growth of the business, and pursuit of policies which conflict with TQM in terms of resources, can all have an adverse effect on the gains made. People will be looking to senior management to provide continuity and leadership in such circumstances. It is highly likely that there will be some middle management resistance to TQM, in particular, from those managers with long service this is more likely than from staff and operatives. The senior management team can break down this resistance by explaining its own role uncertainties in relation to TQM, the mistakes made, how it got over the stumbling blocks and overcame the crisis of confidence. They are the main route for demonstrating and communicating the TQM message and are able, through the role of insight, to carry a message to their reportees. It is important that top and middle management have unified thinking on TQM.

WHAT SENIOR EXECUTIVES NEED TO KNOW ABOUT TQM

The first thing they must accept from the outset is that TQM is a long-term commitment and an arduous process. There are no:

- quick fixes
- easy solutions
- universal panacea
- quality management tool or technique and/or system which will provide all the answers
- ready made packages which can be plugged-in and guarantee success.

In addition, senior executives must understand that TQM is not the responsibility of the quality function and managers/employees will be in no hurry to change to this way of working.

The planning horizon to put the elements of TQM into place is at least

10 years. The Japanese manufacturing companies typically work on 16 years made up of four 4 year cycles: introduction; promotion into non-manufacturing areas; development/expansion; and fostering advancement (see Dale and Asher 1989). Consequently, executives have got to practise and communicate the message of patience, tolerance and tenacity. Having said this, there will be achievable benefits in the short term, providing that the introduction of TQM is soundly based.

In spite of the claims made in some quarters, senior management must recognize there is no single or best way of introducing and developing TQM. There are, however, common strands and principles which do apply in all organizations. Every organization is different in terms of its people, culture, history, customs, prejudices, structure, products, services, technology and processes and operating environment. What works successfully in one organization and/or situation will not necessarily work in another.

A good example of what works and what does not work is quality awareness training. Quality awareness training should, as a minimum consist of the following approaches:

- why quality?
- current status.

- what is quality?
- next steps

Other possibilities for inclusion in quality awareness training are:

- principles/philosophies at the organization
- current programme of events
- quality tools

- case study/application exercise
- support available

There are two main approaches to quality awareness training: (i) cascade (sheep dip) in which training is given to everyone over a relatively short time frame and; (ii) infusion where people are trained on a need-to-know basis. The authors know of organizations who have been successful with both methods and, on the other hand, organizations in which both methods have been a dismal failure. This is why executives need to be wary of the people selling 'TQM packages' and prescriptive approaches.

The way of launching an approach to TQM matters little. What really is critical is that senior managers demonstrate long-term commitment and leadership to TQM and the improvement process is cost effective. Senior management must be prepared to think out the issues for itself and test out ideas, modify them and adapt, as appropriate to the operating environment and prevailing culture of the business. The key point is to learn from the experience. If mistakes are openly admitted and explanations given, employees are usually forgiving of management.

Senior managers need to commit time in order to develop their own personal understanding of the subject. He/she needs to read books, attend conferences and courses, visit the best practices in terms of TQM and talk to as many people as possible. The self-assessment criteria of the Malcolm Baldrige National Quality Award (MBNQA), the EFQM Model for Business Excellence, the Deming Application Prize for overseas companies, can assist in developing this overall understanding. In this way they will avoid the false trails laid down by their own staff and outside influences. Flaws in thinking are often a result of a person's lack of understanding of the subject. For example, it must be recognized that whilst quality management systems and procedures and tools and techniques are important features of TQM it is people who make TQM a reality and a success. People must also have the confidence/expertise to make full use of tools and techniques. This understanding of TQM will also assist the CEO in deciding, together with senior managers and other key staff, how the organization is going to introduce TQM. For example: what method of training is required?; how many and what type of improvement teams will be introduced?; how many teams can be effectively supported?; and what form should a TQM Steering Committee take – should it be the management committee, should it meet separately or should TQM be the top item on the management agenda, what should be its meeting frequency, what is its role? It is important that the quality process has a close fit with the business planning approach of the organization. The key to any organization 'institutionalizing' total quality is the successful integration of the business planning process and the quality improvement process. This is readily achieved by many organizations utilizing a Business Planning Process. Figure 3.2 shows how this is done by the Utility Division of United Utilities.

The issue of getting started on TQM is not an easy one. Most organizations will have already undertaken a number of improvement initiatives and a key issue is how to bring together and consolidate these initiatives. A number of elements of TQM are nebulous and senior managers often have some difficulty in seeing how they might operate in their organization. It is important that the more nebulous elements are combined with the readily understood aspects such as quality systems and practices, teamwork, and tools and techniques. As part of the getting started process the CEO and his/her senior managers must also be involved in diagnosing the organization's strengths and weaknesses in relation to the management of quality. This typically takes the form of: an internal assessment of employees' views and perceptions (internal and group assessments and questionnaire surveys); a systems audit; and a cost of quality analysis and obtaining the views of customers (including those accounts who have been lost) about

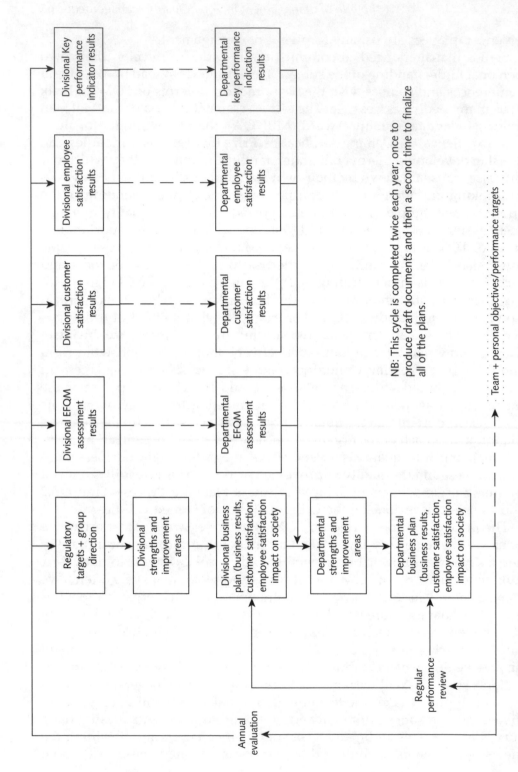

Figure 3.2 The business planning process.
Source: United Utilities

the organization's performance in terms of product, service, people, administrative, innovation and strengths and weaknesses. This type of internal and external assessment of perspectives should be carried out on a regular basis to gauge the progress being made towards TQM and help decide the next steps. An increasing number of organizations are using the criteria of the MBNQA and the EFQM models to undertake this activity. However, there are risks of utilizing self-assessment at this early stage of the quality journey, including:

- overcomplexity
- emphasis on scoring and scores and not improvement actions
- award seeking rather than a business improvement focus
- no formal business planning process to handle and action the improvement areas identified

The CEO and his/her senior management team need to develop a company vision and mission statement. This should include developing an organizational definition of quality. It is important that every company employee can relate to the vision and mission statement and that progress towards its achievement can be measured using key performance indicators.

WHAT SENIOR EXECUTIVES NEED TO DO ABOUT TQM

Senior management needs to decide the actions it is going to take in relation to TQM. Senior management needs to allocate time and commitment to:

- communicate its views on TQM; it should take every opportunity to talk and act in a manner consistent with the principles of TQM
- decide how the company will approach the introduction of TQM
- assess the improvements made
- get personally involved in improvement activities
- become involved in benchmarking as this will enable it to see, for example, what superior performing organizations have achieved and the discrepancies with its organization's performance for the processes in which the benchmarking study is being undertaken

Executives should consider how they are going to demonstrate to people from all levels of the organization hierarchy their commitment to TQM. They need to visit every area of the organization to see what is happening in relation to TQM, ask about results and problems, give advice, and create good practice through leadership. In relation to this latter point executives should take the lead in organizational housekeeping with the objective of seeing that all aspects of the site (manufacturing and office areas) are a model of cleanliness and tidiness. The five Ss (i.e. Seri (organization) – separating out what is required from that which is not, Seiton (neatness) – arranging the required items in a tidy manner and in a clearly defined place, Seiso (cleaning) – keeping the surrounding area and equipment clean and tidy, Seiketsu (standardization) – clean the machinery and equipment according to laid down standards in order to identify deterioration and Shitsuke (discipline) – follow the procedures which have been laid down) or CANDO – Cleanliness, Arrangement, Neatness, Discipline and Orderliness is often used to provide the framework for this type of assessment.

The following are some of the issues of role model behaviour of executives:

- remove status symbols (e.g. reserved car parking spaces, management restaurants)
- make realistic but challenging demands
- give recognition
- reprimand without discouraging
- be open to criticism
- create the right environment

There are considerable demands on senior managers' time and a vast number of projects and matters seeking their attention; one CEO of a small high technology printed circuit board manufacturing company uses the term 'spinning like a top' to describe this situation. However, if TQM is to be successfully introduced it has got to take precedence over all other activities. The CEO should plan his/her diary so that some time each week is devoted to TQM activities. The experience from the superior performing companies is once the process is bedded in, the time devoted by the CEO to TQM can be reduced and he/she can focus on maintenance issues and the promotion of new themes.

It is the responsibility of senior managers to ensure that everyone in the organization knows why the organization is adopting the concept of TQM and that people are aware of its potential in their area, department and or process. The commitment of the senior management team must filter down through all levels of the organizational hierarchy. It is important that all employees feel they can demonstrate initiative and have the responsibility to put into place changes in their own area of work.

The senior management team needs to commit resources to TQM. For example, release people for improvement activities and ensure that key decision makers are made available to spend time on TQM issues. The CEO needs to delegate responsibility for improvement to people within the organization. Some organizations appoint a total quality facilitator/ manager/ co-ordinator to act as a catalyst or change agent. The role of this person must be clearly defined and his/her relationship with the CEO understood by all levels of management. Ideally this person should have the following attributes:

- understand the business from an internal stand-point but especially with respect to the external customer
- very good interpersonal and communications skills
- should want to and be able to champion the cause of continuous improvement and business excellence throughout the organization
- should have, or be able to rapidly gain, credibility throughout the organization
- should have the ability to absorb and develop new ideas and approaches for application throughout the organization

From the vision and mission statements a long-term plan needs to be drawn-up which sets-out the direction of the company in terms of its development and management targets. This plan should be based on the corporate philosophy, sales forecast, current status, previous achievements against plan and improvement objectives. From this long-term plan an annual policy should be compiled, and plans, policies, actions, and improvement objectives established for each factory, division, department and section. Middle managers and first-line supervisors should, at the appropriate point, participate in the formulation of these plans, targets and improvement objectives. This ensures that the policies initiated by the senior management team are cascaded down through the organizational hierarchy so that all employees in each function of the business can carry out their activities with the aim of achieving common goals and improvement targets.

The process of policy deployment ensures that the quality policies, targets and improvement objectives are aligned with the organization's business goals. The ideal situation in policy deployment is for the senior person at each level of the organizational hierarchy to make a presentation to his/ her staff on the plan, targets and improvements. This ensures the penetration and communication of policies, objectives and improvements, on a step-by-step basis throughout the organization, with general objectives being converted into specific objectives and improvement targets. It is a primary communications vehicle. Lee and Dale (1998) provide details of a useful model which helps to facilitate policy deployment.

As part of this policy deployment some organizations formulate, every year, a plan which focuses on a different improvement theme. There must also be some form of audit at each level to check whether or not targets and

Customer

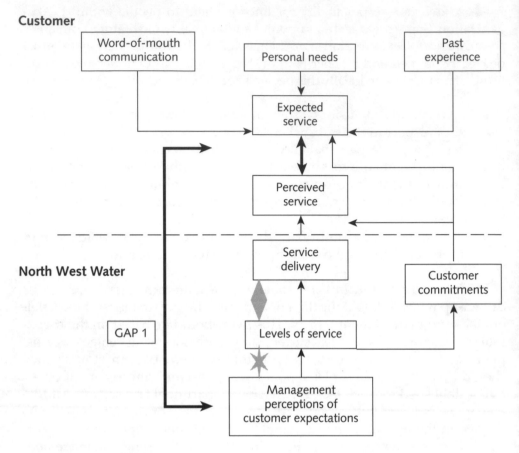

Figure 3.3 Service gap model.
Source: Developed from SERVQUAL–Zeithmal, et al. (1990)

improvement objectives are being achieved, and the progress being made with specific improvement projects. The EFQM business excellence model provides a method for organizations to self-assess both their capabilities and the results they achieve. It is increasingly being used by organizations to validate internal improvement processes and compare themselves against other organizations. This commitment to quality and the targets and improvements made should be communicated to customers and suppliers. Some organizations use seminars to explain these policies and strategies. The respective reporting and control systems must be designed and operated in such a manner which will ensure that all managers co-operate in continuous improvement activities.

The CEO must ensure that his/her organization really listens to what its customers are saying, and what they truly need and their concerns. This is more easily said than done; none of us like criticism and we have a tendency to think we know best. This customer information is the starting point of improvement planning. Executives must ensure that they do not disguise things from the customer; honesty is the byword in TQM. If it does resort to elaborate camouflage measures, then the organization will be, to use a navy term, 'dead in the water'. The CEO must be aware of the ways in which customer expectations are developed and how the organization can ensure that these expectations are perceived as being satisfied, see figure 3.3 from the UK Utility Division of United Utilities and based on SERVQUAL, Zeithamal et al. (1990).

Senior managers should ensure their organizations take every opportunity to join the customers and suppliers improvement processes; mutual improvement activities can strengthen existing partnerships and build good working relationships. Senior managers must ensure that corrective action procedures and defect analysis are pursued vigorously and a closed-loop system operated to prevent repetition of mistakes.

It is important that the CEO ensures that his/her organization has positive quantifiable measures of quality as seen by the customers. This enables the CEOs to keep an outward focus on the market in terms of customer needs and future expectations. These typical performance measures include:

- field failure statistics
- reliability performance statistics
- customer returns
- customer complaints
- customer satisfaction levels
- 'things gone wrong' data
- adverse customer quality communications
- customer surveys
- lost business
- non-accepted tenders
- prospect to customer conversion rate

The CEOs also need to develop internal measures to assess if the improvement process is advancing and the gains are being held, such as:

- non-conformance levels
- quality audit results
- yield results
- quality costs
- employee satisfaction
- employee involvement
- service level achievements
- score achieved against the EFQM or MBNQA models
- percentage of employees satisfied that the organization is customer focused and the organization is a quality company

It is usually necessary to evaluate the current internal and external performance measures to assess their value.

A measurement system to monitor the progress of an improvement process is a key necessity;, without it improvement will be more difficult. In the words of Scharp (President and CEO of A B Electrolux) (1989) 'What gets measured gets done'. Consequently people will focus on those actions necessary to achieve the targeted improvements. All the evidence from the Japanese companies (Dale 1999) indicates that improvement targets act as key motivators.

Senior managers should never overlook the fact that people want to be informed on how the improvement process is progressing and its effect in the marketplace. They need to put into place a two-way process of communication for ongoing feedback and dialogue; this helps to close the loop. Communications up and down the organizational hierarchy are one of the most important features of the relationships between directors, managers and staff. Regular feedback needs to be made regarding any concerns raised by employees through, for example, Quality Action Days and Key Issues Conferences. Feedback will help to stimulate further involvement and is a useful means for every employee to communicate with the CEO.

The Balanced Scorecard was developed to improve performance measurement systems. The Balanced Scorecard concept retains financial measures, such as return-on-capital-employed and supplements these with new measures such as: value creation for customers; enhancement of internal processes, including innovation, to deliver desired value propositions to targeted customers; and the creation of capabilities in employees and system.

Innovative companies today are using their Balanced Scorecards to:

1. gain consensus and clarity about their strategic objectives;
2. communicate strategic objectives to business units, departments, teams and individuals;
3. align strategic planning, resource allocation and budgeting processes;
4. obtain feedback and learn about the effectiveness of their strategic plan and its implementation.

The senior management team should be prepared to learn about statistical methods, use them in decision-making processes, and demonstrate an active interest and involvement in techniques such as SPC. This ensures that knowledge and decisions are based on fact not opinion. For example, when passing through manufacturing and office areas senior managers should get into the habit of looking at the control charts, which are on display and direct questions to the people responsible for charting and analysing the data. They can also learn, from the data portrayed on the charts, of any problem which the 'operator' is experiencing with the process. The control chart is a communication to senior management on the condition of the process – it is a 'window' on the operating world of processes. Ignoring the message will only cause frustration amongst those involved with SPC and will hinder the process of continuous improvement. It should also not be forgotten that SPC teaches people to ask questions about the process.

Continuous improvement can be facilitated by the rapid diffusion of information to all parts of the organization. A visible management system and a storyboard style presentation in which a variety of information is collected and displayed is a very useful means of aiding this diffusion. The CEO needs to consider seriously this form of transparent system.

Senior managers need to understand that TQM is not a campaign, nor a programme, it is a process which is company-wide and continuous. The CEO and his/her senior management team must never become satisfied and complacent with the progress the organization has made in TQM. They must strive continually to achieve improvements in the product, service and associated processes. They need to adopt the philosophy and mindset that there is no ideal situation and the current state can always be improved upon. Areas of organizational waste and non-value adding activity need to be identified and attacked in a ruthless manner.

THE ROLE OF MIDDLE MANAGEMENT

Middle managers have a vital part to play in the introduction and development of TQM; they are the implementors of improvement initiatives. They will only be effective, however, if they are committed to it as a concept. The middle manager's role typically involves:

- developing specific improvement plans for the departments and processes for which they are responsible;
- ensuring that the objectives, values, policies and improvement initiatives of their departments are aligned with the company's business goals, TQM strategy, and quality management system;
- communicating the company's approach to TQM in common sense and jargon-free language to first-line managers and other employees;
- acting as TQM coach and counsellor to the employees for whom he/ she is responsible;

- ensuring that first-line managers are individually trained in the use of tools and techniques and that they are used effectively;
- acting as a 'guardian, or sponsor or mentor' to improvement teams and securing the means to reward employees;
- providing top management with considered views on how to manage the continuing implementation of TQM, taking into account feedback from first-line managers and employees on potential difficulties or obstacles.

THE ROLE OF FIRST-LINE MANAGEMENT

First-line managers and supervisors are at the forefront of TQM. They have the key role of encouraging its implementation in the workplace, and are especially important because of the numbers of people they influence and lead. If first-line managers lack commitment, training, appropriate resources and a supportive management system and culture then the TQM cascade will fail at its most critical level. They are directly responsible for:

- analysing the individual procedures and processes for which they are responsible in order to identify areas where improvements might be initiated;
- encouraging individual employees to contribute improvement ideas, and ensuring that good ideas and efforts are acknowledged and rewarded by middle and top management;
- ensuring that any quality concerns reported by employees are analysed and resolved through permanent long-term preventative action;
- participating in improvement teams in their own and in related work areas;
- providing workplace training in the use of specific tools and techniques to capture improvement data;
- communicating the results of improvement activities effectively to middle managers;
- providing the data and responses required by the company's formal quality management system, including where applicable the requirements of the appropriate part of the ISO 9000 series;
- providing the data for self-assessment against a recognized model, for example, the MBNQA and EFQM models;
- representing the people and processes they supervise in management discussions about TQM resources and strategies.

SUMMARY

This chapter has examined the role which senior management is required to take and the leadership and commitment they need to display if TQM is to be successful. Senior management will often ask what it needs to do to demonstrate its commitment to TQM. The chapter has outlined some of the things it needs to get involved with, including chairing the TQM Steering Committee, organizing and chairing defect review boards, self-assessment of progress and developing and following a personal improvement action plan. It has also summarized in brief what senior management needs to know about TQM and what it needs to do to ensure TQM is successful. This chapter also pointed out that middle managers and first-line managers have a vital role in putting the principles of TQM in place at the cutting edge of the business and looked at the typical activities which they need to get involved with.

REFERENCES

Dale B. G. (ed.) 1994: *Managing Quality*, (Second Edition), Prentice Hall, Hertfordshire.
Dale B. G. and Asher J. M. 1989: 'Total Quality Control: the Lessons European Executives can Learn from Japanese Companies', *European Management Journal*, 7 (4), 493–503.
Lascelles D. M. and Dale B. G. 1990: 'Quality Management: the Chief Executives' Perception and Role', *European Management Journal*, 8 (1), 67–75.
Lee R. and Dale B. G. 1998. 'Policy Deployment: an examination of the Theory', *International Journal of Quality and Reliability Management*, 15 (4), 521–40.
McKinsey and Company 1989: *Management of Quality: The Single Major Important Challenge for Europe*, European Quality Management Forum, 19 October, Montreux, Switzerland.
Scharp A. 1989: *What Gets Measured Gets Done: The Electrolux Way to Improve Quality*, European Quality Management Forum, 19 October, Montreux, Switzerland.
Zeithamal V. A., Parasuraman A. and Berry L. L. 1990: *Delivery Quality Service: Balancing Customer Perceptions and Expectations*, The Free Press, New York.

4

Business Process Management

INTRODUCTION

Many terms are used for the study of processes, including process simplification, process improvement and process re-engineering and quality costing. A number of authors (e.g. DeToro and McCabe 1997 and Elzinga et al. 1995), put forward the view that this area of improvement is Business Process Management (BPM) and is taking over from Business Process Re-engineering (BPR), which is claimed not to have delivered the results it promised (e.g. Deakin and Makgill 1997 and Caldwell 1994). With process management there is of course considerable synergy with TQM, see Macdonald (1995). Zairi (1997) describes BPM as:

> A structured approach to analyse and continually improve fundamental activities such as manufacturing, marketing, communications and other major elements of a company's operations.

He goes on to say:

> BPM is concerned with the main aspects of business operations where there is high leverage and a big proportion of added value. BPM has to be governed by the following rules:

- Major activities have to be properly mapped and documented.
- BPM creates a focus on customers through horizontal linkages between key activities.
- BPM relies on systems and documented procedures to ensure discipline, consistency and repeatability of quality performance.
- BPM relies on measurement activity to assess the performance of each individual process, set targets and deliver output levels which can meet corporate objectives.
- BPM has to be based on a continuous approach to optimisation through problem-solving and reaping out extra benefits.

- BPM has to be inspired by best practices to ensure that superior competitiveness is achieved.
- BPM is an approach for culture change and does not result simply through having good systems and the right structure in place.

Most organizations have a combination of live initiatives in the generic field of process management. These initiatives will typically focus on areas of process mapping, process modelling, process redesign, business modelling, business process re-engineering, business process improvement and benchmarking. However, the approach of organizations to process management is often fragmented and disparate. It is usual to find that a loose alliance has evolved between all the various people who are actively working on the different pieces of this jigsaw. However, taken across the organization there can be a lack of consistency and common direction. Figure 4.1 illustrates some of the problems with this lack of co-ordination.

Whilst operating within functional confines, areas of conflict can be minimized. However, as soon as responsibility passes to another function within the business or overlaps with another function occur, then there is ample opportunity for confusion and conflict to arise.

In these types of organizations it is common to find that many different functions have the same requirement for access to a small group of individuals who are expert in the area of process management. It is not unusual to find that a company's strategy and development function requires assistance in the area of strategic development projects as well as major process design and that the key service delivery and production functions require support for the roll-out of improvements which are driven by the implementation of cost down initiatives. All this type of activity must be

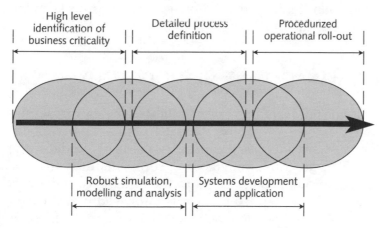

Figure 4.1   End-to-end process management – overlapping responsibilities.

5 = <u>Optimizing</u>
Continuous process improvement from feedback.

4 = <u>Managed</u>
Detailed measurements collected for processes and product quality.

3 = <u>Defined</u>
Documented, standardized processes integrated into organization-wide processes.

2 = <u>Repeatable</u>
Tracking and reporting of costs, schedules and requirements.

1 = <u>Ad hoc</u>
Semi-chaotic process. No formal management or development process.

Figure 4.2   Process improvement capability maturity model.

co-ordinated and focused so as to make optimum use of people, resources and tools and techniques, as well as complementing key internal initiatives.

This chapter opens by providing the details of a methodology for tackling process management. It goes on to discuss process ownership and strategic process thinking and quality costing.

PROCESS MANAGEMENT METHODOLOGY

There are a considerable number of methodologies surrounding process management each of which has its good points, as described by Povey (1998). Figure 4.2 is a five step capability maturity model for process improvement. This describes five steps of process maturity from *ad hoc* methods where no formal process exists to the other end of the continuum of optimizing where the defined process is improved year on year.

An organization somewhere between steps 1 and 2 will exhibit the following type of characteristics:

- non-process orientated
- employees are still thinking and acting in functional terms
- no process management in place
- measurements internally performance focused

There is a need for such organizations to examine the cross-functional value adding processes both to the customer and internal to the organization. They will usually find that current processes are not formally owned and consequently are unmanaged and chaotic. Processes will not be formalized and so users are unaware of how they operate and do not understand the reasons for what they do. This can lead to misuse of the process and inefficiency in terms of process operation. Quality is compromised and any process improvement offers only minor benefits over the long term. It is also likely that any ongoing process improvement activity will occur disparately and there will be duplication of effort. Another feature in such organizations is that no tools and techniques are used to first understand the process and then improve it.

The methodology shown in figure 4.3 is used by several organizations and builds on the process maturity model given in figure 4.2. This method

Step 1	Key business processes are **identified**.
Step 2	**Ownership** of them has been established.
Step 3	They are formally **flowcharted/documented**.
Step 4	Appropriate **measures** are used to **monitor** the process and to enable **learning**.
Step 5	**Feedback** from customers, suppliers and employees is used as the basis for improvement.
Step 6	An **improvement** and **review** mechanism is in place with **targets** for improvement.
Step 7	The processes are **systematically** managed for **continuous** improvement and **learning** is shared.
Step 8	The processes are **benchmarked** against best practice.
Step 9	The processes are regularly **challenged** and re-engineered if required.
Step 10	The processes are **role models** for other organizations.

Figure 4.3   Process management model.

can be applied to both internal processes and the critical customer-facing processes used to provide a service to customers.

PROCESS OWNERSHIP

In the development of process management there needs to be 'global' agreement as to what process ownership means and in particular the roles and responsibilities of process sponsor, process champion and process team members.

Process Sponsor

- Documentation of the process to an appropriate level – as a minimum a top level flowchart of the end-to-end process should be created.
- The creation and sponsorship of a process improvement plan.
- The management reporting of process performance, based on appropriate business measures and metrics.
- Inspection of the process to ensure that the process is being correctly implemented.
- Appropriate two way communication of process performance and requirements to all those employees who play a part in the operation of the process.
- Process problem escalation both internal and external.
- Owner and guardian of appropriate intellectual property rights.

Process Champion

- To advise and guide the process sponsor on the creation and execution of a process improvement plan.
- To lead, co-ordinate and drive all improvement activity within their respective process.
- To have a broad and detailed understanding of process management tools and techniques.
- To determine why and how the process needs to change.
- Be the first point of contact for sponsorship of breakthrough improvement projects for the respective process.

Process Team Member

- Is directly involved in the running of the process.

- Should have received appropriate process improvement training.
- Should have time for improvement activities (i.e. being involved in an improvement team is a recognized part of his/her job).

STRATEGIC PROCESS THINKING

This section of the chapter illustrates how a process-orientated organiza-tion may look in the near future and outlines a strategic process thinking approach to business management, see figure 4.4

The successful company in the not-too-distant future will be a total qual-ity organization with a fully developed process-originated viewpoint. Its processes will be defined and formally flowcharted and documented. Ownership of the processes will have been established for the key strategic business processes and ownership will be at a high level within the organi-zation. These owners will ensure that the processes are systematically man-aged by permanent, cross-functional process management teams.

A process-orientated way of working will impact the culture of the organization. People will be able to see why they do things and see the value they add to the company. Everyone will use the processes correctly, will give feedback on performance and suggest improvements. This leads to increased motivation as staff are more empowered.

Appropriate measures will be used to monitor the processes and these metrics facilitate suitable learning. These measures will be established with the requirements of the customers of those processes in mind (i.e. 'output' measurement rather than the more traditional work measurements).

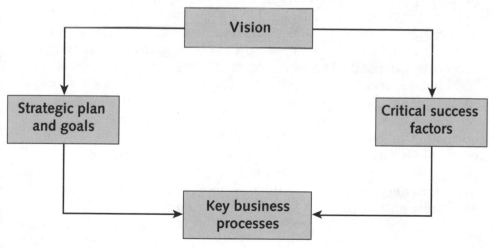

Figure 4.4   Strategic process thinking.

Zero defect goals will have been established and processes will be analysed against these with the aim of being self-sustaining and facilitating
continual improvement. Continuous improvement should ensure that the
processes are able to cope with external change and every increasing demanding customer requirements with the objective to developing robust
processes. A process is robust if its performance is insensitive to uncontrollable variations in process inputs, transformations and external factors, see
Taguchi (1986). Reduced variation in performance should facilitate gains
in process and business improvement as described in Dale (1999).

The teams undertake process improvement/process simplification. An
improvement and review mechanism is in place with targets for improvement and feedback from customers, suppliers and employees are used as
the basis for such improvement. Managers ask questions about processes
rather than outputs and manage the white spaces (i.e. the gaps between the
functions for which nobody has traditionally taken responsibility). The
processes are also benchmarked against best practice (see Love et al. (1998)
for examples of successes, problems and learning points). Occasionally,
when radical re-alignment is needed to ensure there is adequate customer
focus, business process re-engineering takes place along the lines suggested
by Hammer and Champey (1993).

The organizational systems should support the process focus by encouraging innovation and creativity amongst staff. These systems are aligned
to reflect defined cross-functional processes rather than functional hierar-
chies. The management system reflects the flat horizontal process-driven
value-chain structure rather than the traditional top-down vertical hierarchy. Employees have the necessary knowledge and empowerment to control and improve their own processes and this empowerment has enhanced
levels of staff motivation. All staff have been trained in appropriate tools
and techniques within a problem solving methodology. Process work is
centrally co-ordinated, changing the previous company approach whereby
often many independent bodies were engaged separately on process work.

A single process management tool will be utilized across the business
and also by any external consultants. The tool should be simple to use by
staff for process mapping. Process changes are easily recorded and the
information is through the tool effectively disseminated to all staff. The
tool should have clear linkages to the company's systems. This will enable
any organization to bring together in an effective manner business operation, information technology, human resources and finance information.
This allows staff to undertake data analysis and process modelling.

As a result of becoming process-focused the company becomes focused
on cross-functional processes that add the value that is sought by external
customers, rather than internally on the organization. There will be better

communication across the organization. The company has benefited from process development to gain product and service quality improvements which have taken its performance beyond that of its competitors and led to sustainable competitive advantage. The company is now proactive rather than reactive to process problems and its processes are seen as 'role models' by other organizations.

There are a variety of organizations moving towards the BPM way of thinking, as typically described by Prior-Smith and Perrin (1996) and Armistead et al. (1997) in the case of Hewlett Packard and described by Povey (1998) at IBM.

Quality costing

Ideas of what constitute quality costs have been changing rapidly in recent years. Whereas only a few years ago the costs of quality were perceived as the cost of running the quality department and a test laboratory, plus scrap and warranty charges, it is now widely accepted that they are the costs incurred in designing, implementing, operating and maintaining a quality management system, the costs involved in introducing and sustaining a process of continuous improvement, plus the costs incurred owing to failures of systems, products and/or services. Quality costs arise from a range of activities, (e.g. sales and marketing, design, research and development, purchasing, storage, handling, production planning and control, production/operations, delivery, installation and service). Suppliers, sub-contractors, stockists, distributors, agents, dealers, and especially customers can all influence the incidence and level of these costs.

This section of the chapter defines quality costs and explains why they are important to management. It also outlines how to determine, report and use quality-related costs.

DEFINITION AND CATEGORIZATION

The importance of definitions to the collection, analysis and use of quality costs is critical. Without clear definitions there can be no common understanding or meaningful communication on the topic. The definition of what constitutes quality costs is by no means straightforward and there are many grey areas where good production/operation procedures and practices overlap with quality-related activities. The comparability of data sets is dependent on the definitions of the categories and elements used in compiling them. If definitions are not established and accepted, the only alternative would be to qualify every item of data so that it might be understood, even though it may not be comparable with other data. The value of much of the published data on quality-related costs is questionable because of the absence of precise definition and lack of qualification.

Many definitions of quality-related costs are in fairly specious terms. Admittedly, there are difficulties in preparing unambiguous acceptable definitions and in finding generic terms to describe tasks having the same broad objectives in different cases. It should also be appreciated that problems of rigorous definition arise only because of the desire to carry out costing exercises. Consideration of quality in other contexts (e.g. training, supplier development, design and engineering changes, and statistical process control) does not require such sharp distinction to be made between what is and is not quality-related.

Accounting systems do not readily yield the information needed, as it is presently defined, and rigorous definitions of quality activity elements are necessary only for costing purposes. Thus there is an apparently absurd situation of defining elements in a way which makes them difficult to cost. Given that accounting systems are unlikely to change radically to accommodate quality costing difficulties there should be greater consideration of the accounting aspects when defining quality cost elements.

Overambition or overzealousness may prompt people, including management consultancies, to try to maximize the impact of quality costs on senior management. Consequently, they tend to stretch their definitions to include those costs which have only the most tenuous relationship with quality. This attempt to amplify quality costs can backfire. Once costs have been accepted as being quality-related there may be some difficulty in exerting an influence over the reduction of costs which are independent of quality management considerations. It is not always easy to disown costs once someone has claimed them, especially if ownership is in a 'grey area' and no one wants them.

Definitions of the categories and their constituent elements are to be found in most standard quality management texts. Detailed guidance is given in specialized publications on the topic, BS. 6143: Part 2 (1990), Campanella (1999) and Dale and Plunkett (1999).

The widespread use and deep entrenchment of the prevention-appraisal-failure categorization of quality costs (Feigenbaum 1956) invites analysis of the reasons for it. After all, arrangement of data into these categories is usually done for reporting purposes, after the collection exercise. It adds nothing to the data's potential for provoking action, except perhaps by facilitating comparison with earlier data from the same source, and even this may not be valid because of the relation of current warranty costs, where these are included, to other current costs.

However, there are some general and specific advantages to be gained from this type of categorization. Among the general advantages are that it may prompt a rational approach to collecting costs, and it can add orderliness and uniformity to the ensuing reports. Among the specific advantages are:

- its universal acceptance
- its conferral of relative desirability of different kinds of expenditure, and
- most importantly, it provides keyword criteria to help to decide whether costs are, in fact, quality-related or basic work (e.g. essential activities in producing and supplying a company's products and/or services) and in this way it helps educate staff on the concept of quality costing and to assist with the identification of costs

As organizations have developed their understanding of TQM and BPM the need to identify and measure quality costs across a wider spectrum of company activities has arisen. The traditional prevention-appraisal-failure approach is, in some respects, unsuited to the new requirement. Among its limitations are:

- The quality activity elements as defined do not match well with the cost information most commonly available from accounting systems.
- There are many quality-related activities in grey areas where it is unclear to which category they belong.
- In practice the categorization is often a post-collection exercise done in deference to the received wisdom on the topic.
- The categorization seems to be of interest only to quality department personnel.
- It is not an appropriate categorization for the most common uses of quality-related cost information.

In these circumstances a broader categorization which measures only the cost of conformance and the cost of non-conformances, as in Crosby's (1979) philosophy, is gaining recognition. The principal arguments in its favour are that it can be applied company-wide and that it focuses attention on the costs of doing things right as well as the costs of getting them wrong. This is considered to be a more positive all-round approach which will yield improvements in efficiency as well as improvement in product and service quality. In theory all costs to the company should be accounted for under such a system. In practice, departments identify key-result areas and processes against which to measure their performance and costs.

Details of one such process cost model are incorporated into BS 6143: Part 1 (1992).

Other alternative process cost models include:

- controllable and uncontrollable
- discretionary and consequential
- theoretical and actual
- value adding and non-value adding
- supplier, in-house and customer
- attaining, possessing and sustaining

Clearly the prospects for success of a costing system will depend on how well the system matches and integrates with other systems in the company and the way in which the company operates. Categorization of costs so that they relate to other business costs and are easy for people to identify with, must have distinct operating advantages. However, whatever categorization is preferred there is no escaping the need to decide what is quality-related and what is not. In attempting to do so there are no better passwords than prevention, appraisal and failure, despite their limitations as cost categories.

When defining and categorizing costs it is important to try to define the quality activity elements to align with the business activities of the company and fit in with existing costing structures. Warranty cost is an example of just such an element. Clearly it is quality-related. It is part of the business agreement between a company and its customers and the company must make financial provisions to meet its possible liabilities under the agreement.

COLLECTION

Purpose

Among the main purposes of collecting quality-related costs are:

- to display the importance of quality-related activities to the company management in meaningful terms (i.e. costs)
- to show the impact of quality-related activities on key business criteria (e.g. prime cost, and profit and loss accounts)
- to assist in identifying projects and opportunities for improvement
- to enable comparisons of performance with other divisions or companies to be made

- to establish bases for budgets with a view to exercising budgetary control over the whole quality management operation
- to provide cost information for motivational purposes at all levels in the company

There is little point in collecting quality-related costs just to see what they may reveal. Getting the purposes of the exercise clear at the outset can go a long way towards avoiding pitfalls and unnecessary work.

Strategies

Clearly the strategy to be adopted will be influenced by the purpose of the exercise. If, for example, the main purpose of the exercise is to identify high cost problems for improvement action, coarse scale costs in known problem areas will suffice also. If the members of the senior management team already accept that the organization's cost of quality is within the normally quoted range and is prepared to commit resources to improvement there is no point in refining the data. If, on the other hand, the purpose is to set a percentage cost reduction target on the company's total quality-related costs, it will be necessary to identify and measure all the contributing cost elements in order to be sure that costs are reduced and not simply transferred elsewhere. If the intention is only to get a snapshot from time to time as a reminder of their magnitude, the strategy will be to identify and measure large ongoing costs. Another aspect which needs to be considered is whether to collect and allocate costs on a departmental or business unit basis or across the whole company. In some cases, analysis at company level is inadequate as the problems would be set out in terms too global to generate ownership at departmental or process level. On the other hand, analysis at too detailed a level would lead to a trivialization of problems. These types of issues will also have a bearing on the definition and identification of cost elements. The incidence of such diverse objectives with their differing requirements serves to reinforce the case for a rational approach in which the purpose of the exercise is clearly established at the outset. However, whatever the purpose, key elements in any strategy are to involve the accounts department right from the outset and to start with a pilot exercise on an important operation, process or department.

Scope

As mentioned earlier, deciding the scope of the exercise in the sense of agreeing what should be included under the quality-cost umbrella may be far from straightforward. There are many 'grey areas'. For example, there are those factors which serve to ensure the basic utility of the product, guard against errors, and protect and preserve quality. Whether such factors give rise to costs which may be regarded as being quality-related is a matter for judgement in individual cases. Often there are activities, usually of a testing or running-in type, where it is unclear whether it is a peripheral quality activity or an integral and essential part of the operations activities.

Problems of categorization may arise for costs generated by functions other than quality and production/operations. Examples are the contributions of the purchasing function and supplier development team to supplier quality assessment, assurance and development, and the activities of engineering design departments involved with concessions and design modifications prompted by quality considerations. Quantifying, classifying and costing such inputs is difficult but they can amount to significant expenditures.

These are the kinds of problems which will need to be addressed when deciding the scope of the exercise. Because each case is different it is not possible to offer general solutions other than to suggest that if there is serious doubt, the cost should not be defined as being quality-related where it is unlikely to be amenable to change by quality management influences. Other suggested criteria are that an item or activity is quality-related when: (i) if less is spent on it, failure costs will possibly increase and; (ii) if more is spent on it failure costs will possibly decrease. It is always better to underestimate rather than overestimate the costs of quality and if in doubt an activity should not be treated as a quality cost element.

Cost collection

When establishing a cost collection procedure for the first time, three important points to be noted are:

1. There is no substitute for a detailed thorough examination of the operating processes in the beginning. Modifications to the procedure may be made later, if necessary, with hindsight and as experience of applying the procedure grows.
2. People will readily adopt ready-made procedures for purposes for which they were not intended if they appear to fit their situation. Hence it is very important that the 'first-off' should be soundly based.
3. Procedures should be 'user friendly' (i.e. the information needed should be readily obtainable from a relatively small number of

sources). Nothing inhibits information gathering so much as have to gather it from a large number of sources. It is strongly recommended that the system used to collect quality costs should be made as automatic as possible with minimum intervention of the cost owners.

The methodology adopted by an organization for the collection of costs must be practical and relevant in that it must contribute to the performance of the basic activities of the organization. Approaches to quality cost collection include:

- using the list of cost elements in BS 6143: Part 2 (1990) and Campanella (1999) as a guide
- identifying potential elements of cost from the literature
- developing a list of elements from company-specific experience
- using semi-structured methods: (i) by using education seminars, presentations, questionnaire and brainstorming techniques it is possible to identify elements of cost specific to a department or business unit and; (ii) the process cost model outlined in BS. 6143: Part 1 (1992) can be used to identify POC and PONC for a department or function

The elements identified can be based on people's activities and/or material waste.

It is most important that quality cost collection guidelines are developed. For example: apportioning staff time to a particular quality cost category; how to allocate an activity into different cost categories; what to include in a particular element and; losses caused by sub-standard products/services, etc.

Quality cost information needs to be produced from a company's existing systems. It is easier to develop a quality costing system in a 'greenfield' situation as opposed to attempting to break into an established system. A common fallacy is that larger companies have accounting systems from which it is relatively easy to extract quality-related costs. Often such companies have large immutable accounting systems and practices imposed by a head office and have little flexibility to provide quality costs. On the other hand, smaller companies are less likely to have a full-time professionally qualified person responsible for management accounting. Some of the difficulties in obtaining quality costs data are related to organizational structures and with the accounting system. For example, it has been found on more than one occasion that in a functional structure there is no real incentive to report and reduce costs of quality, and in relation to the accounting system, activity based costing has been found to be useful in identifying cost of quality in non-manufacturing areas.

A noticeable feature of accounting systems is the greater accountability the nearer one gets to the operations areas. This has implications for the cost collection exercise because a number of quality costs are incurred close to the operations area. Hence the accountability bias is in the quality cost collector's favour. A factor working in the opposite direction is the involvement of personnel from a wide spectrum of functions. It is important that the quality costing exercise does not concentrate purely on the production/operations. A considerable amount of non-value added activity (waste) and rework is incurred in the non-producing or service functions.

When seeking to measure costs under quality-related headings it is sometimes easy to overlook the factor that the task is primarily a cost collection exercise and that these exercises have other, different, criteria to be considered which are sensibly independent of the cost topic. It is suggested by Plunkett and Dale (1985) that an appropriate set of criteria for any cost collection exercise is:

- purpose
- relevance
- size of costs
- ease of collection
- accuracy of data
- potential for change
- completeness

A set of back-up criteria like these can often provide a useful way out of the dilemma about whether or not particular activities and costs should be included in a costing exercise.

In the cost collection stage it should be clearly understood that quality costs can increase if the exercise is undertaken as part of an ongoing approach to the development of TQM way of managing a business. In this culture managers and staff will not hide the elements of failure costs and will declare these items. Consequently, the previously accepted levels will go up rather than down.

TYPE OF COSTS

There are a number of cost aspects – hidden in-house quality costs, scrap and rework, appraisal costs and warranty costs – which occur in manufacturing industry which warrant discussion. Commercial organizations and those providing a service will have their equivalents of these types of costs.

Hidden in-house quality costs

Hidden quality costs occur in two forms: (i) those owing to in-built ineffi-ciencies in processes and systems, and; (ii) activities which are clearly qual-ity-related but do not carry a quality tag.

Many in-built inefficiencies such as excess materials allowances, excess starts, poor material utilization and deliberate overmakes because of yield difficulties, though sometimes not regarded as costs, may in fact have their origins in production inefficiency. The same may also be true of the provi-sion of standby machines and personnel, additional supervision, and some safety stocks. Similarly excess and selective fitting owing to variability of machined parts is often an accepted practice.

Snagging facilities to avoid stopping production in line manufacturing are a form of in-built inefficiency. Many people would reason that because systems are imperfect it is necessary to provide contingency facilities, such as snagging areas, and that their operating costs are just another built-in burden. But there is no reason why the principle of accountability should not apply and the function responsible for the failure made accountable for the cost.

Inattention to maintenance of process performance may result in built-in costs by acceptance of lower levels of process capability and more non-conformances than are necessary. Maintenance budgets are frequently de-cided on an arbitrary or general experience basis without taking due regard of the particular process needs. Maintenance should be preventive in the sense of prevention of non-conformances rather than preventing break-down. Failure to do this is tantamount to building in unnecessarily high levels of non-conformance with consequential in-built costs. The use of techniques such as SPC and TPM will draw attention to changes in capabil-ity and cause maintenance work to become more process- than machine-oriented.

Major activities in the second category are concessions, modifications and engineering changes. It is suspected that in many companies conces-sions are an expedient way of maintaining production schedules and that little account is taken of the disadvantages incurred in deciding to over-look non-conformances. Not least among these are proliferation of paper-work and lax attitudes towards product quality and its improvement among managers, supervisors and operatives. In fact, frequent concessions on non-conforming goods are a positive disincentive to operators and first-line supervisors to get it right first time.

In many companies goods passed on concession do not feature in quality reporting systems because they have escaped the company's defect reporting system. In some companies goods are supposed only to be passed on concession if they can not be rectified. It is often easier to find reasons why goods cannot be rectified than it is to rework them. Hence concession systems may become an engineering/technical expediency, or, equally, they may be seen as a production expediency to avoid impediments to output or delays in delivery.

Other examples of hidden costs are: provision of 'clean areas' and 'protection' for components and assemblies; segregation; marking, and handling of scrap; movement of goods for inspection purposes; the activities of purchasing and accounting personnel in dealing with rejected supplies; the effects of order-splitting (for quality reasons) on planning and manufacture and; the costs of machine downtime for quality reasons.

Scrap and rework

These costs are collected and reported in most companies. Frequently they are regarded as important costs which feature in companies' business decisions. Yet the economics of scrapping or rectification are by no means clear in many companies.

The first difficulty is the valuation to be placed on scrapped goods. Some popular views encountered are that the value should be the factory selling price, the market price, the raw materials price or the materials cost plus the cost of processing to the point of scrapping. These different bases will obviously give rise to very different valuations. The second difficulty is that the decision about whether to scrap or rework is often taken by personnel who do not have access to the financial information necessary to make an economic choice. And in any case the economics will vary depending on workload, urgency of delivery, etc.

Appraisal costs

Though appraisal costs cover a wider range of activities, the majority of the expenditure is on in-house inspection and test activities. Opinions differ about whether testing is an appraisal cost. Testing is effectively proving the fitness-for-purpose of the product in one or more respects. There may well be cases where such testing ought not to be necessary, but is, and hence incurs a quality cost. However, in many cases the state of the technology may be such that testing is unavoidable. A manufacturer may be unable to give guarantees without testing the product, he may be unable to get insurance cover without testing, and it may be a contractual requirement of the customer. In the end, the decision whether to test or not may be taken out of his hands, whatever he thinks he can achieve without testing. Whether testing is a quality-related or a purely production activity is a matter to be decided in individual cases.

The economics of appraisal are not known in most companies. High costs of failure are apparently used to justify inspection and its frequency, without any attempts being made to determine the true economic balance. It is somewhat surprising that the economics of inspection are not well established and widely known.

Warranty costs

Warranty costs are usually met from a provision set aside for the purpose. Care needs to be taken when determining costs from changes in provisions because the provision may be used to meet some other charge or may be topped-up from time to time with arbitrary amounts of money. Hence it is necessary to know about all the transactions affecting the provision.

REPORTING

An important consideration in the presentation of quality-related costs is the needs of the recipients. It may be worth presenting information in several different formats. For example: weekly reports of costs of scrap and rework may be of greatest value to first line supervisors; monthly reports of total costs highlighting current problems and progress with quality improvement projects would be suitable for middle management; while total costs and costs on which to act are needed by senior managers. While selective reporting of this kind has its merits it should always be done against a background of the total quality-related cost. Ideally quality cost reports should show opportunities for cost savings leading to increased profits or price reductions.

For maximum impact quality costs should be included in a company's cost-reporting system. Unfortunately, the lack of sophistication of quality cost collection and measurement is such that it does not allow quality cost reporting to be carried out in the same detail and to the same standard as, for example, the production/operations and marketing functions. Reporting of quality costs is, in the main, a sub-section of the general reporting of quality department activities and, as such, loses its impact. Often quality reports do not separate out costs as an aspect of quality worthy of presentation and comment in its own right. This usually results in cost informa-

LIVERPOOL
JOHN MOORES UNIVERSITY
AVRIL ROBARTS LRC
TITHEBARN STREET
LIVERPOOL L2 2ER
TEL. 0151 231

tion not being used to its full potential. Separating costs from other aspects of quality and discussing them in the context of other costs would improve the clarity of reports and help to provide better continuity from one report to the next.

Good standards of reporting are essential if the costs are to make an impact and provoke action. Managers are like everyone else in wanting easy decisions to make. Having costs, which are the basis of business decisions, tangled up with technical information makes the data less clear than they could be and may provide a reason to defer action. The manager's problem should not be to disentangle and analyse data in order to decide what to do; it should be to decide whether to act, choose which course of action to pursue and ensure provision of the necessary resources. Problems, possible solutions and their resource requirements should be presented in the context of accountability centres which have the necessary authority to execute the decisions of the senior management team.

The long intervals of time which may occur between manufacture and receipt of warranty claims can have some special implications for cost reporting. Warranty costs in any period may bear no relation to other quality costs incurred in the same period and should not be reported in the same context. To include warranty costs can distort considerably the quality performance of the company or department as depicted by the levels and ratios of quality-related costs. The delays may also mean that the causes underlying the failures leading to the claims may no longer be a problem.

One of the maxims of cost collecting seems to be that, in general, costs need to be large to hold attention. This creates something of a dilemma for the cost collector because large costs are often insensitive to changes. But the collector cannot omit large costs and concentrate only on smaller costs which may readily be seen to change. Hence cost groupings need to be chosen carefully so that cost reductions achieved are displayed in such a way that both the relative achievement and the absolute position are clearly shown. Another dilemma arises from the fact that one-off estimates do not change and that there is no point in collecting costs which do not change.

The format for the collection of costs should make provision right at the outset for all those elements and cost sources which are thought to be worth collecting. The creation of a quality-related cost file, integrated with existing costing systems but perhaps with some additional expense codes, should not present many problems. As stressed earlier, it is important to make provision in the file for collecting data which are not readily quantifiable even though it may take a long time to obtain satisfactory returns on a routine basis.

When reporting costs at regular intervals it is important to ensure that sets of data remain comparable one with another. If additional cost elements are introduced as an organization becomes more experienced in quality costing, these must be reported separately until an appropriate opportunity arises to include them among related costs. It is also worth coding each cost element to indicate its source and status.

Presentation of costs under prevention, appraisal, and internal and external failure, is the most popular approach, albeit with different cost elements appropriate to different industries, whether manufacturing, commercial or service-related. This format is favoured by quality managers perhaps because, on the face of it, it forms a quality balance sheet for the quality management function with prevention equivalent to investment, appraisal to operating cost, and failure to losses. This categorization of costs is of interest and some value to quality managers, but less so to other functional managers on the grounds that they do not relate directly to the activities of the business. The influence of senior management is vital in the reporting of quality costs. If there is no pressure to reduce costs against mutually agreed targets then the reporting will become routine and people, quite naturally, will devote their efforts to what they believe are the most important events. It is important that senior management develop a quality cost reduction strategy.

USES

Many of the uses of quality costs can be grouped into four broad categories:

1. quality costs may be used to promote product and service quality as a business parameter
2. they give rise to performance measures
3. they provide the means for planning and controlling quality costs
4. they act as motivators.

The *first* use – promoting quality as a business parameter – is usually interpreted as gaining the attention of higher management by using higher management's own language – i.e. money. But costs can also be used to show that it is not only the quality department that is involved in quality; everyone's work can impinge on quality and that it is indeed an important business parameter, especially if the influences of suppliers and customers are made clear. Clearly, knowledge of quality-related costs will enable decisions about quality to be made in an objective manner.

The *second* use – giving rise to performance measures – includes a wide variety of activities. Among them are:

- Trend analyses to show changes in costs or cost ratios with time. Diagnosis of the cause of change can often prompt pilot exercises in the use of specific tools and techniques.
- Pareto analyses to identify improvement projects. This is the quickest route to the exploitation of quality cost data.
- Identification of investment opportunities. Progressive companies are always looking for profitable ways to invest in improvement projects and initiatives, but their task is made very difficult by the lack of data and understanding of the economics of investment in quality. While it may be axiomatic that prevention is better than cure, it is often difficult to justify investment in prevention activities. To some extent such investments are regarded as acts of faith. Little is known and nothing has been published on the appropriate levels and timing of investments, payoffs or payback periods. However, there are many opportunities for investment in prevention, with consequential real cost savings. Employing qualified experienced staff, encouraging continuing education and providing training are examples of investment in personnel.

  Of more direct interest to engineers and technical personnel are the possibilities of effective savings through investment in tooling, equipment and machinery and mistake proofing devices. Poor standard of tooling are frequently responsible for non-conforming product and the extra costs of providing a higher standard of tooling is often a worthwhile investment. Quality considerations also enter into the selection of machinery and equipment inasmuch that a premium is paid for machine tools with the potential to achieve a capable process, thus avoiding failure costs, and maybe some appraisal costs.
- Performance indicators and quality efficiency indexes. Business efficiencies are commonly analysed and expressed using a variety of criteria (mostly financial). Maintenance and improvement of product and service quality are not among the criteria used. Quality managers' efforts to persuade fellow managers and directors of the value of continuous improvement to a company are often frustrated by a lack of well-known and accepted indices or standards. Some companies have developed measures for the purpose of internally monitoring their processes of continuous improvement but no general guidelines or methods of calculation exist which would readily allow a company to assess its standards against a norm or other companies' performances.

  The most popular comparative measure against which quality costs are measured is gross sales, followed by manufacturing or operating cost and value added. Other useful bases are hours of direct production labour, units of product, and processing cost. It is widely held that single ratios do not tell the whole story and may always need to be considered alongside other ratios.

The *third* use of quality costs – as a means of planning and controlling quality costs – is widely mooted in the literature. Costs are the bases for budgeting and eventual cost control. Contributions from the quality fraternity tend to see establishment of quality cost budgets for the purpose of controlling costs as the ultimate goal which may be achieved after accumulating a loss of data over a long time in pursuit of quality improvements of specific cost reductions.

Fourthly, quality costs can be used for motivational purposes at all levels in a company. Costs have been used traditionally to motivate senior managers to become interested and take part in the promotion of quality. As companies move towards TQM the use of costs as a motivator becomes more widespread. Thus, for example, costs of scrapped goods are displayed to line supervision, operatives and clerical staff because they can see the relevance of them to their work. It is found that these groups of people respond positively in terms of increased quality awareness, improved handling of the product, housekeeping disciplines, etc. Although the costs may be relatively small in company terms they are usually large in relation to operatives' salaries. Thus a strong impact is made, in particular, when poor trading conditions result in restrictions being placed on salary increases and even freezes or reductions imposed, without disclosing sensitive cost information.

SUMMARY

The capability of an organization to use and develop processes is important for future and existing customers. It may be the case that they have to develop existing processes inherited from the customer and cannot apply the appropriate approaches. However, in all cases they need to demonstrate their ability to do this.

If an organization is to move towards being at the leading edge of process management it needs:

- A clear statement of the direction it is setting for process management.
- A pragmatic approach to organizing the necessary supporting resources. All of the resources currently working in this area should be brought together and given a common framework from which to operate.

- The adoption of process benchmarking is a necessity as described by Love et al. (1998).
- An appropriate means of educating all personnel in process management methods and techniques needs to be in place.
- Use a standard format and methodology for process management and improvement (e.g. 'Casewise' software suite).

Process management and improvement constitute a significant section of the EFQM Model as described in chapter 8. Adhering to the above will enable an organization to deploy Business Excellence throughout the hierarchy, promote the development and improvement of processes and demonstrate to the external market, its commitment to TQM. This will aid the organization in ensuring that it is differentiated as a preferred service provider to its current and future customers, and will ensure the long-term viability for it in the marketplace.

The value of cost data should not be underestimated in promoting process management and improvement. Costs are a most effective way of drawing attention to and illuminating situations in ways that other data cannot. It has been found that even the most rudimentary attempts at quality costing have been beneficial in identifying areas of waste and trends in continuous improvement performance. It should also not be forgotten that quality costs are already being incurred by an organization, the whole purpose of the quality costing exercise is to identify these 'hidden costs' from various budgets and overheads. The objective is to allocate these indirect costs to a specific cost activity.

Unfortunately, the whole process of definition, collection, reporting, and use of quality-related costs is not yet well enough developed to be used in ways that many other costs are. A major influence in this is undoubtedly the solid entrenchment of the prevention-appraisal-failure categorization of quality-related costs. The potential uses of cost data derived from elements defined via this categorization are restricted and do not fit well with companies' day-to-day operating modes and experience. Nor do they lend themselves to sophisticated business uses. However, even with restricted potential, there is still much to be gained, as shown in this chapter. Sizes and proportions of costs can be used successfully as criteria for deciding whether to act, what resources should be committed, priorities to be allocated, etc.

As things stand now, the most widely accepted and used categorizations and definitions of quality cost elements cause the definition-collection-reporting-use process sequence to be definition-driven with companies making the best use they can of the outcome. But companies should be looking for more effective ways of using quality cost data. Perhaps taking a different approach to the categorization and definition of costs will assist with this.

However, what is more important is to make the process sequence dynamic. Use is the most important part of the sequence, but at present there is little or no feedback from uses to definitions. There is a need for use-driven definitions which will in turn affect the collection and reporting stages. The system can then become dynamic, changing as business requirements change. It is a task which needs to be tackled jointly by accountants and the manager responsible for quality in the company. The question to be answered is 'How can cost information be used to improve the company's quality status?' keeping in mind that quality status is determined by customers, supplier performance and in-house quality management.

REFERENCES

Armistead C., Machin S. and Pritchard J. P. 1997: *Approaches to Business Process Management*, Fourth International Conference of the European Operations Management Association, Barcelona.

BS 6143: Part 1 1992 *Guide to the Economics of Quality-Process Cost Model*, British Standards Institution, London.

BS 6143: Part 2 1990: *Guide to the Economics of Quality-Prevention Appraisal and Failure Model*, British Standards Institution, London.

Caldwell B. 1994: 'Missteps, Misuses', *Information Week*, 20 June, 50–60.

Campanella J. (ed.) 1999: *Principles of Quality Costs: Principles, Implementation and Use*, (Third Edition), ASQ Quality Press, Milwaukee.

Crosby P. B. 1979: *Quality is Free*, McGraw Hill, New York.

Dale B. G. 1994: *Managing Quality* (Second Edition), Prentice Hall, Hertfordshire

Dale B. G. and Plunkett J. J. 1999: *Quality Costing*, (Third Edition), Gower Press, Hants.

Deakin E. and Makgill H. H. 1997: 'What Killed BPR? Some Evidence from the Literature', *Business Process Management Journal* 3 (1), 81–107.

De Toro I. and McCabe T. 1997: 'How to Stay Flexible and Elude Facts', *Quality Progress*, 30 (3), 55–60.

Ezinga D. J., Horak T., Chung Yee L. and Bruner C. 1995: 'Business Process Management; Survey and Methodology', *IEEE Transactions on Engineering Management*, 24 (2), 119–28.

Feigenbaum A. V. 1956: 'Total Quality Control', *Harvard Business Review*, 34 (6), 93–101.

Hammer M. and Champey J. 1993: *Re-Engineering the Corporation*, Nicholas Bradley, London.

Love R., Bunney H. S., Smith M. and Dale B. G. 1998: 'Benchmarking in

Water Supply Services: the lessons learnt', *Benchmarking for Quality Management and Technology*, 5 (1), 59–70.

Macdonald J. 1995: 'Together TQM and BPR are Winners', *The TQM Magazine*, 7 (3), 21–5.

Plunkett J. J. and Dale B. G. 1985: 'Some Practicalities and Pitfalls of Quality-Related Cost Collection', *Proceedings of the Institute of Mechanical Engineers* 199, (B1), 29–33.

Povey B. 1998: 'The Development of a Best Practice Business Process Improvement Methodology', *Benchmarking for Quality Management and Technology*, 5 (1), 27–44.

Prior-Smith K. and Perrin M. 1996: 'Ideas on Motivating People, Addressing complaints and training (IMPAC): an application of Benchmarking Learning Best Practice', *Business Process Re-engineering and Management Journal*, 2 (1), 7–25.

Taguchi G. 1986: *Introduction to Quality Engineering*, Asian Productivity Organization, New York.

Zairi M. 1997: 'Business Process Management: a Boundaryless Approach to Modern Competitiveness', *Business Process Management Journal*, 3 (1), 64–80.

ACKNOWLEDGEMENTS

Barrie Dale is indebted to the late Jim Plunkett for the use of some of his research findings on quality costing to be used in this chapter.

5

Quality management systems

INTRODUCTION

This chapter opens by examining the concept of quality assurance and the responsibilities of people within an organization for carrying out the activity. A quality system is defined and the background of quality system standards traced. The key features of the ISO 9000 series (1991, 1993, 1994) are examined, implementation guidelines and issues outlined, the quality system assessment and registration reviewed and the benefits and limitations highlighted. Much has already been written about quality systems and standards (Dale and Oakland 1994, Hall 1992, Jackson and Ashton 1993, Lamprecht 1992 and 1993 and Rothery 1993) and there are the standards themselves. Therefore, this chapter is constrained to an overview of the key features and issues.

WHAT IS QUALITY ASSURANCE?

Quality assurance is defined in BS EN ISO 8402 (1995) as:

> All the planned and systematic activities implemented within the quality system, and demonstrated as needed, to provide adequate confidence that an entity will fulfil requirements for quality.

Quality assurance is often regarded to be discrete policing by the Quality Assurance Department. This is not so. The ideal role of the department is to oversee the whole process of quality assurance within an organization, provide guidance, advice on the assignment of roles and responsibilities to be played by each function and person and address weaknesses in the system. Quality assurance needs to be an integral part of all an organization's processes and functions, from the conception of an idea and throughout the life cycle of the product or service – determining customer needs and requirements, planning and designing, production, delivery and after-sales service. It is an integrated management system.

The objective should be to get every person in the organization to take personal responsibility for the quality of the processes for which they are accountable. This includes treating following processes as customers and endeavouring to transfer conforming products, services, materials and documents to them, monitoring quality performance, analysing non-conformance data, taking both short and long-term action to prevent the repetition of mistakes, and feedforward and feedback of data. The emphasis should be on the pursuance of corrective and preventive action procedures and non-conformance investigation in a thorough manner with closed loop effectiveness. It is also necessary for everyone to perform their tasks as defined by the quality system.

The main objective of quality assurance is to build quality into the product and/or service during the upstream design and planning processes. Quality function deployment, FMEA, design of experiments, design reviews, design for manufacturability and quality audits are of considerable assistance in the pursuance of this goal. Quality assurance which is planned and managed along these lines will strengthen an organization's TQM efforts.

WHAT IS A QUALITY SYSTEM?

A quality system is defined in BS EN ISO 8402 (1995) as:

> Organisational structure, procedures, processes and resources needed to implement quality management.

The purpose of a quality system is to establish a framework of reference points to ensure that every time a process is performed the same information, methods, skills and controls are used and applied in a consistent manner.

The three levels of documentation, which is hierarchial in nature, which are required of a quality system are:

Level 1   Company quality manual – this is the fundamental document and provides a concise summary of the quality policy and quality system along with the company objectives and its organization. ISO 10013 (1995) provides useful guidelines on the development and preparation of quality manuals.

Level 2   Procedures manual – describes how the system functions, structure and responsibilities in each department.

Level 3   Work instructions, specifications, methods of performance and detailed methods for performing work activities.

In addition there should be a database (level 4) containing all other reference documents (e.g. forms, standards, drawings, reference information, etc.).

The quality system should define and cover all facets of an organization's operation from identifying and meeting the needs and requirements of customers, design, planning, purchasing, manufacturing, packaging, storage, delivery, installation and service, together with all relevant activities carried out within these functions. It deals with organization, responsibilities, procedures and processes. Put simply, a quality system is good management practice.

A quality system, if it is to be comprehensive and effective and cover all these activities and facets, must be developed in relation to a reference base against which its adequacy can be judged and improvements made. This reference base is a 'quality system standard'.

A documented quality system which embraces quality management objectives, policies, organizationand procedures and which can demonstrate, by assessment, compliance with the ISO 9000 series of quality system standards or that of a major purchaser, provides an effective managerial framework on which to build a company-wide approach to continuous improvement.

THE DEVELOPMENT OF QUALITY SYSTEM STANDARDS

Irrespective of the approach taken to TQM and the quality management maturity of the organization, a business will need to demonstrate to customers that its processes are both capable and under control and there is effective control over procedures and systems. This pressure for proof that systems and procedures are in place, and working in an effective manner, led to the development of quality system standards.

The early standards were provided by major purchasers to their suppliers. These standards were customer and sector specific and designed to be used in contractual situations in the industries for which they were designed and operated; the standards had a strong bias towards inspection activities. Each purchaser developed its own methods of assessment, which involved visiting the supplier to examine the degree to which the supplier's operating procedures and systems followed the requirements of the standard. This method of assessment is called second party certification.

Most of the current quality system standards evolved from military standards (e.g. Mil-Q-9858, American Military Standard and the North Atlantic Treaty Organisation (NATO), Allied Quality Assurance Publications (AQAPs)). There has also been a considerable contribution to formalized quality assurance procedures by NASA, the controlling body for the American space programme. A United Kingdom standard for quality systems was first published in 1973 by the Procurement Executive of the British Ministry of Defence (MoD) as Defence Standards – the DEF-STAN O5–21 series (05–21 to 05–29). These were virtual copies of the American-derived NATO AQAPs (AQAP-1 to AQAP-9), used by NATO in defence procurement. The AQAP standards addressed the problem of achieving consistency and total interchangeability in the supply of standardized weapons and ammunition coming from many different suppliers and intended for the different national military units which make up NATO. The MoD used the DEF-STAN O5–21 series to approve potential suppliers and audit current suppliers in contractual situations. It was a requirement that a supplier developed their quality system to meet the clauses set-out in these standards for them to be included on the list of MoD assessed contractors. These standards became the basis for contracts with the MoD from April 1973 onwards. One principle is that the prime contractors must conduct audits of their own suppliers in line with the requirements of these standards. The O5–21 series were withdrawn in 1985 and MoD assessments were carried out using the AQAP standards. From September 1991, the MoD has, in the main, relied on third party assessment against the ISO 9000 series of standards. The MoD only assesses suppliers/contractors who are outside the current scope of the accredited certification bodies. This type of situation relates to specific military applications such as aircraft construction, ammunition and explosives, packaging and software. A new set of defence standards (the 05–90 series, 05–91 to 05–95), which includes the ISO 9000 series plus special military purchase requirements, is used to audit suppliers in contractual situations.

In 1972 the British Standards Institution (BSI) published BS 4891 (1972) *A Guide to Quality Assurance* which set out recommendations on organizations for, and the management of, quality and was intended as a guide to companies developing their quality management system. This standard was withdrawn in 1994. It was followed in 1974 by the issue of BS 5179 which was a three part standard *A Guide to the Operation and Evaluation of Quality Assurance Systems*. This standard was withdrawn in 1981 after being superseded in 1979 by the first issue of BS 5750.

During the mid-1970s there was a proliferation of quality system standards produced by a variety of second and third-party organizations. The Warner (1977) report on *Standards and Specifications in the Engineering Industries* stressed the need for a national standard for quality management systems, to reduce the number of assessments with which suppliers were being subjected to by their customers. It pointed to the shortcomings and fragmented nature of the British system of quality system standards. It was recommended that British Standards be produced to provide the single base document for quality systems. Subsequently in 1979, the British Standards Institution issued the BS 5750 series of quality management system standards.

It was the British Standards Institution who formally proposed the formation of a new technical committee to develop international standards for assurance, techniques and practices (ISO/TC 176). Some 20 countries participated in the development of the ISO 9000 series. In 1987, the series of international standards on quality management systems was first published by the International Organization for Standardization (ISO). This 1987 version of the standards, whilst reflecting various national approaches and international requirements, was based largely on the 1979 version of the BS 5750 series and the eight or so years of UK user experience, mainly in the manufacturing industry. The text of these international standards was approved as suitable for publication as a British Standard without deviation – BS 5750: Parts 0 to 3 (1987) and extended in 1991 to services and software as Parts 8 and 13 (1991). The ISO 9000 series was revised and reissued in the Summer of 1994 and approved as a British Standard, the BS EN ISO 9000 series. This revision was meant to be interim involving minor changes pending a full revision (ISO standards are meant to be revised every 5 years). The Phase 1 revisions were undertaken with the aims that no new requirements were introduced and that the standards should be clarified to aid implementation and assessment. The revision is part of a broader programme, resulting from a long-term strategy adopted by ISO/TC 176 and termed 'Vision 2000', see PD 6538 (1993). In the 2000 revision there will be just four primary standards:

- ISO 9000: Quality management systems – Concepts and Vocabulary
- ISO 9001: Quality management systems – Requirements
- ISO 9004: Quality management systems – Guidelines
- ISO 10011: Guidlines for auditing quality systems

The ISO 9000 series was adopted by CEN (the European Committee for Standardization) and CENELEC (the European Committee for Electrotechnical Standardization) as the EN 29000 series, thus harmonizing the approach to quality systems amongst the European Community. The ISO 9000 series has perhaps had the most significant and far reaching impact on international standardization of any other set of standards. An excellent account of the historical background of the ISO 9000 series is provided by Spickernell (1991).

Government initiatives

In July 1982, a White Paper was published on Standards, Quality and International Competitiveness which suggested that to maintain standards, certification bodies should be accredited by a central agency in order to uphold the standards of the certification bodies. The National Accreditation Council for Certification Bodies (NACCB) was the national statutory body established in June 1985 with the task of assessing the independence, integrity and technical competence of leading certification bodies applying for government accreditation in four areas – approval of quality systems, product conformity, product approval, and approval of personnel engaged in quality verification. At the same time the National Measurement Accreditation Service (NAMAS) was set-up to deal with laboratories. NAMAS was formed by the amalgamation of the British Calibration Service (BCS) and the National Testing Laboratory Accreditation Service (NATLAS), also in 1985. In August 1995 and in response to market demand NACCB and NAMAS merged to create a single accreditation authority – the UK Accreditation Service (UKAS). The objective is to bring economies of scale and improved efficiency to UK accreditation. Accreditation, which is awarded in the UK by the Secretary of State for Trade and Industry, allows a certification body to demonstrate its competence and independence. To be eligible for accreditation, third party certification bodies are required to meet criteria outlined in three standards:

- BS 7511 (1989) for certification bodies issuing certificates of product conformity
- BS 7512 (1989) for certification bodies certificating that suppliers' quality systems comply with appropriate standards, normally BS EN ISO 9001, 9002 and 9003
- BS 7513 (1989) for certification bodies certificating the competence of personnel

This set of standards helps to promote confidence in the way in which product and quality system certification activities are performed and in the accreditation systems and bodies themselves. From the accreditation granted it will be clear whether the body is accredited for quality system assessment only, and in which fields, or whether it has the additional qualification of being accredited to certificate conformity of product.

Those companies who have been assessed by an accredited certification body can use the symbol of a gold crown (signifying government) and gold tick (signifying approval) if the scope of certification applied for falls within the scope of accreditation of the accredited certification body.

The Department of Trade and Industry through its National Quality Campaign (initiated as a result of the White Paper 1982) and 'Managing into the 1990s' programme, actively encourages British Industry to consider more seriously its approach to quality management and one of the methods advocated is registration to the BS EN ISO 9000 quality management system series. The DTI issues a central register of Quality Assured Companies. This register lists the firms whose quality management system has been approved by major users or independent third-party assessment bodies – this means the investigation is done by an independent organization, unrelated to buyer or seller. It also describes the assessment standard used – the BS EN ISO 9000 series or its equivalent and details of the certification body.

Acceptance of the ISO 9000 series of standards

Major industrial purchasers, in particular within the motor industry, have their own system standards and procedures for assessing their suppliers systems. These standards, because they tend to be specific, are often more demanding in certain areas than the ISO 9000 series.

The use of the ISO 9000 series has not been accepted and used universally across the UK motor industry, but this situation is moving ever close. The Society of Motor Manufacturers and Traders (SMMT) in their booklet *Quality Systems and the Motor Industry* (1990) issued a quality policy statement which 'recommends that member and non-member companies recognise and take account of approvals to BS 5750/ISO 9000/EN 29000 Quality Systems Standard as a minimum when contracting work out and buying in supplies. It is strongly recommended that all UK automotive industry companies obtain approvals as applicable to this standard through accredited third party certification'. For example, Nissan Motor Manufacturing (UK) Ltd have structured their quality management system requirement for suppliers (QA 001, Section 4.0, Nissan Motor Manufacturing (UK) Ltd 1991) in line with the 20 clauses of ISO 9001 with five additional requirements of: quality cost, housekeeping, site and equipment maintenance, visual management and warranty. The Chrysler Corporation, Ford Motor Company and General Motors Corporation have produced a common quality system assessment standard – QS 9000. This standard, first released in August 1994 with a worldwide version in February 1995, harmonizes their own three separate quality system standard requirements and will reduce the current level of duplication in terms of information requested from suppliers, leading to economic advantage. The first section of QS 9000 aligns itself with the 20 elements of ISO 9001. The second section (sector-specific) contains additional but common and harmonized requirements of Chrysler, Ford and General Motors covering the production part approval process, continuous improvement, identification of key product and process parameters, process capability performance and measurement system studies on product and process parameters, and development of control plans. The third section addresses customer specific additional requirements.

Registration to ISO 9001, ISO 9002 or ISO 9003 is a useful foundation leading to the development of a quality system to meet the independent system requirements of customers. A number of major purchasers use this registration as the 'first-pass' over a supplier's quality system. They will take the ISO 9000 series as the base, and only assess those aspects of the system which they believe are important (e.g. for those clauses which are not covered in the ISO 9000 series customers often require the supplier to have additional features to the series supplanted within the system, or those clauses without sufficient detail, to the satisfaction of the customer). On the other hand, many major customers are not prepared to accept a supplier's ISO 9001, ISO 9002 or ISO 9003 registration and wish to carry out a full assessment of their quality system. For example:

- Dale and Plunkett (1984) reporting on a study carried out in 12 fabricators found that most were subjected to about six audits a year.
- Singer et al. (1988) in a study of the impact of quality assurance on 13 suppliers to the nuclear industry found that most companies are audited four or more times each year.
- Galt and Dale (1991), in a study of the supplier development programmes of a cross-section of ten UK-based organizations, found that five of the firms studied relied totally on their own evaluation of suppliers, three considered it to be a good starting point and only two accepted third-party recognition as being adequate for their supplier evaluation purposes. They go on to say 'It was clear that most of the firms considered their own quality standards to be above those required for the ISO 9000 series registration.'
- Boaden et al. (1991) reporting on a study of TQM in the UK construction industry make the point 'One of the main arguments put forward for the ISO 9000 series of standards is that it will help to reduce second party assessments, the responses indicate that this has not happened in the construction industry; clearly a disappointment.'

It is clear from these four studies and, at the time they were carried out, that a number of organizations were not prepared to accept the approvals and certification of recognized bodies which have been awarded to suppliers with whom they are dealing; a company may be approved to ISO 9001, ISO 9002 or ISO 9003 but some of its customers still intend to audit them on a regular basis. However, this situation is now changing as companies operating on a global basis have become registered to the ISO 9000 series and, in turn, are encouraging the same of their suppliers and also as confidence grows in third party schemes. The latest (seventh cycle) ISO Survey of ISO 9000 and ISO 14000 certificates (ISO 1998) reveals that up to the end of December 1997 at least 226,349 certificates have been awarded in 129 countries worldwide.

THE ISO 9000 SERIES OF STANDARDS: AN OVERVIEW

Introduction

In simple terms, the objective of the ISO 9000 series is to give purchasers an assurance that the quality of the products and/or services provided by a supplier meets their requirements. The series of standards defines and sets-out a definitive list of features and characteristics which it is considered should be present in an organization's management control system through documented policies, manual and procedures, which help to ensure that quality is built into a process and it is achieved. Amongst other things it ensures that an organization has a quality policy, procedures are standardized, defects are monitored, corrective and preventive action systems are in place and management reviews the system. The aim is systematic quality assurance and control. It is the broad principles of control, in general terms, which are defined in the standards, and not the specific methods by which control can be achieved. This allows the standard to be interpreted and applied in a wide range of situations and environments, and allows each organization to develop its own system and then test them out against the standard. However, this leads to criticisms of vagueness.

The original BS 5750 series was developed primarily by the engineering sector of industry, and consequently many of the terms and definitions are engineering based. Therefore they require interpretation for the specific needs of individual organizations, and this has led to problems in some sectors of manufacturing industry and in the majority of non-manufacturing organizations. For example, Owen (1988) writing from the chemical industry is critical of the standard for being too orientated to the engineering industry and Oliver (1991) expresses the view that it 'Uses language that the construction industry does not use and, by and large, does not understand.'

Despite these types of difficulties, it has been applied in a wide variety of manufacturing situations and registration is being received in an increasing number of non-manufacturing environments – banking, consumer, education, financial services, gardening, hotel and catering, legal, local authorities, marketing services, recruitment, transport and travel agencies.

The series of standards can be used in three ways:

1. Provision of guidance to organizations to assist them in developing their quality systems.
2. As a purchasing standard (when specified in contracts).
3. As an assessment standard to be used by both second party and third party organizations.

Functions of the standards and their various parts

The ISO 9000 series consists of five individual standards (i.e. ISO 9000, ISO 9001, ISO 9002, ISO 9003 and ISO 9004) divided into four parts (i.e. guidelines; model for quality assurance in design, development, production, installation and servicing; model for quality assurance in production, installation and servicing; and model for quality assurance in final inspection and test).

The standards have two main functions. The first function is an introduction to the series and this identifies the aspects to be covered by an organization's quality system. The guidelines contained in ISO 9000 and ISO 9004 give guidance in quality management and their application. The second function defines in detail the features and characteristics of a quality management system that are considered essential for the purpose of quality assurance in contractual situations, for three main different types of organization, depending upon the services they offer. Organizations usually register for one of the following categories:

- design, development, production, installation and servicing – ISO 9001
- production and installation, and servicing – ISO 9002
- final inspection and test – ISO 9003

The Guidelines: ISO 9000-1 to 4 and ISO 9004-1 to 4

ISO 9000 *Guidelines for selection and use* and ISO 9004 *Guidelines for specific applications* (which are considered as one part of this series of standards) consist of a number of parts and are intended only as guidelines. They cannot be used as reference standards with which to assess the adequacy of a quality management system. These two parts are more reader friendly than ISO 9001, ISO 9002 and ISO 9003. Organisations embarking on the development of a quality system to meet the requirements of ISO 9001, ISO 9002 or ISO 9003, should find ISO 9000-1 to 4 and ISO 9004-1 to 4 of considerable help in the initial stages where an overview is needed.

ISO 9000-1   is a guide to the use of other standards in the series, and a thorough understanding of its content is essential if the series of standards are to be interpreted and used correctly.

ISO 9000-2   is a guide for the application of ISO 9001, ISO 9002 and ISO 9003. This is a guidance document and is useful to organizations in understanding the requirements of these three standards. It is structured in line with ISO 9001 and needs to be read in conjunction with that part of the ISO 9000 series with which compliance is sought.

ISO 9000-3   sets out guidelines to facilitate the application of ISO 9001 to organizations developing, supplying and maintaining software.

ISO 9000-4   is a guide to dependability (i.e. reliability, maintainability and availability) programme management and covers the essential features of such a programme.

ISO 9004-1   is a guide to good quality management practice and in this it provides more detail than ISO 9001, ISO 9002 and ISO 9003. It also contains reference to a number of quality aspects (e.g. quality risks, costs, product liability and marketing) which are not covered in the same level of detail in ISO 9001, ISO 9002 and ISO 9003. Considerable emphasis is placed throughout on the satisfaction of customer needs and requirements.

ISO 9004-2   gives guidance and a comprehensive overview for establishing and implementing a quality system specifically for services.

ISO 9004-3   provides guidance on quality system elements for processed materials.

ISO 9004-4   gives guidelines for quality improvement, covering concepts, principles, methodology, and tools and techniques.

Detailed definition of features – ISO 9001, ISO 9002, ISO 9003

ISO 9001 *Model for quality assurance in design, development, production, installation and servicing* covers circumstances in which an organization is responsible for conceptual design and development work, and/or where it may be required to cover post delivery activities such as commissioning and servicing. It contains 20 elements and is the most comprehensive in scope.

ISO 9002 *Model for quality assurance in production, installation and servicing* covers circumstances where an organization is responsible for assuring the product and/or service quality during the course of production or installation only. This part consists of 19 elements, excluding design control.

ISO 9003 *Model for quality assurance in final inspection and test* is used when conformance to specified requirements can be assured solely at final inspection and test. This contains 16 of the elements of ISO 9001, excluding, design controls purchasing, process control and servicing.

Principal clauses in ISO 9001

The 20 principal clauses in ISO 9001 together with key factors of the quality system are given below. The ISO 9002 standard includes all the clauses of ISO 9001 apart from design control whilst the ISO 9003 standard does not include the clauses of design control, purchasing, process control and servicing.

1. Management responsibility

- Corporate quality policy development, definition statement, organizational goals, aims and objectives, deployment, implementation, communication, understanding and review.
- Organisation, structure, resources, trained personnel, responsibility and authority.
- Management representative.
- Management review and reporting of the system to ensure its effectiveness, including policy and objectives.

2. Quality system

- Documentation and implementation of procedures and instructions.
- Quality manual – the first part of the manual should describe how the company operates and the second part should list the requirements of various standards against which registration of approval may be sought and references the procedures to satisfy these requirements.
- Quality planning, quality plans, work instructions, inspection instructions, etc.

3. Contract review

- Definition and documentation of customer (internal and external) needs and requirements, including records.
- Contract and tender compatibility.
- Quality planning.
- Capability of compliance with requirements.
- Amendment to contract.

4. Design control

- Design and development planning, including statutory and regulatory requirements.
- Identify and allocate resources.
- Organizational and technical interfaces.
- Definition and control of design inputs, outputs and interfaces.
- Design verification to confirm outputs meet input requirements.
- Design validation.
- Review, approve, record and control design changes.

5. Document and data control

- 'Document' (in the form of any type of media) needs to be defined.
- Formal review and approval of documents by authorized personnel.
- Correct issues of necessary documents available at appropriate locations.
- Obsolete documents removed or assured against intended use provided suitable documentation is maintained.
- Changes to documents are authorized and recorded.

6. Purchasing

- Suppliers/sub-contractors' evaluation, and monitoring of performance and capability.
- Records of acceptable suppliers.
- Formal written definition of requirements and specification.
- Verification of sub-contracted product by the customer, if required in the contract.

7. Control of customer – supplied product

- Verification, storage and maintenance of 'free issue' or customer supplied material for use on their order.

8. Product identification and traceability

- Unique and positive identification of material, parts and work-in-progress from receipt and through all stages of production, delivery and installation.
- Demonstrated traceability and its recording as and to the extent specified.

9. Process control

- Identify and plan the processes.
- Process control procedures, where their absence would adversely affect quality.
- Monitoring of key characteristics and features during production.
- Process definition and qualification.
- Processes carried out under controlled conditions.
- Criteria for workmanship, including illustrations, written standards and samples.
- Provision and control of equipment.
- Maintenance of equipment to ensure process capability.

10. Inspection and testing

- Established procedures.
- Goods receiving inspection and testing, or other means of verification.
- In-process inspection and testing.
- Final inspection and testing.
- Inspection and test records, including responsibilities.

11. Control of inspection, measuring and test equipment

- Control, calibration and maintenance of equipment needed to demonstrate compliance with requirements.
- Consideration of other measurements needed.
- Calibration procedures and processes defining equipment, location, methods of checking, acceptance criteria, etc.
- Documentation and calibration records.
- Traceability to reference standards, where applicable.
- Handling and storage.

12. Inspection and test status

- Identification of inspection and test status (i.e. untested, tested, checked, reject, meets the requirements) throughout all processes.
- Confirmation that tests and inspections have been carried out.
- Authority for release of conforming product.

13. Control of non-conforming product

- Identification and control to prevent unauthorized use.
- Segregation of non-conforming materials, parts and products, where practicable.
- Review and decide on appropriate remedial action (e.g. destroyed, repaired, reworked or regraded).
- Reinspection.

14. Corrective and preventive action

- Procedures, routines and reporting of customer complaints and product non-conformities.
- Detection, investigation and analysis of causes.
- Elimination of causes and abnormalities.
- Corrective action control.
- Preventive action to analyse and eliminate potential problems.
- Assignment of responsibilities.
- Changes to procedures, working instructions.

15. Handling, storage, packaging, preservation and delivery

- Methods and equipment which prevent product damage, preservation, segregation, and deterioration.
- Maintenance of product integrity.
- Use of designated storage areas to prevent damage and/or deterioration.
- Receipt and delivery of items into and out of storage.
- Procedures to ensure that the product is packed to prevent damage throughout the entire production to delivery cycle.

16. Control of quality records

- Adequate records relating to inspections, tests, process control, etc. to demonstrate achievement of product quality and effective operation of the quality system.

- Traceability and full history.
- Retention time for records.
- Storage, retrievable, legibility and identification.
- Method of disposition when no longer required.

17. Internal quality audits

- Audit plan, verification, responsibility, and auditor independence.
- Procedures to ensure that the audit method is clear.
- Compliance with the documented system.
- Reporting of discrepancies and results to personnel responsible for the area audited.
- Assessment of the effectiveness of actions taken.
- Review and implementation of corrective action by management to bring activities and the quality system into agreement with the planned arrangements.

18. Training

- Assessment and identification of needs.
- Provision of the required training.
- Written job responsibilities and specification.
- Determine degree and method of competency.
- Planned and structured training programme.
- Training records.

19. Servicing

- Contractual specification.
- Procedures for performing and verifying that needs and requirements are met.

20. Statistical techniques

- The use of samples to determine product and service quality.
- Identify the need for statistical technique.
- Process capability determination, acceptability and certification.
- Product characteristic verification.

The set of requirements outlined in ISO 9001 can be supplemented for specific industries or products by 'quality assurance specifications', 'quality assurance guidance notes' and 'codes of practice' which provide more detail.

It is worth mentioning that BS EN ISO 14001 (1996) *Environ-* *agement Systems: Specification with Guidance for Use* shares man management principles with the BS EN ISO 9000 series and a organizations are considering how they may develop their qu agement system as a basis for environmental management.

IMPLEMENTATION GUIDELINES FOR THE ISO 9000 SERIES

At this point in the chapter it is useful to look at the guidelines, with some additions and amendments by the authors, advanced by Long et al. (1991) based on their research into the application and use of the ISO 9000 quality system series in small and medium sized enterprises. The guidelines are also applicable to larger organizations.

- An organization should be clear on the reasons for seeking ISO 9001, ISO 9002 or ISO 9003 registration. Implementation for the wrong reasons will prevent the organization from receiving the full benefits. In addition, it may be found that implementing and maintaining the requirements of the chosen standard is a burden in terms of costs and extra paperwork with no compensating benefits. ISO 9001, ISO 9002 or ISO 9003 registration must therefore not be sought just to satisfy the contractual requirements of major customers or for marketing purposes. Indeed when most competitors have ISO 9000 series registration there is little marketing advantage, and in many markets it is now an order to qualify criterion.
- The development of a quality system to meet the requirements of ISO 9001, ISO 9002 or ISO 9003 should be managed as a project, with the identification of key steps, milestones and timescales. This will prevent progress being sporadic and variable.
- Prior to a programme if ISO 9000 series implementation it is important that an internal quality audit is conducted of the existing quality system against the appropriate part of the standard by a qualified auditor. This will determine the initial status of the company's quality management system, enable management to assess the amount of work required to meet the requirements of ISO 9000 series and also to plan for systematic implementation of the standard. Without this knowledge the project planning process mentioned above would be impossible. It is important that a realistic timescale is established, because if it is set too tight there will be a tendency to do things artificially and this will result in considerable time spent later in de-

bugging the system. Involvement of the appointed management representative during the quality audit is essential.

- For those organizations developing a quality management system for the first time a steering committee should be established comprised of all the heads of departments and chaired by the CEO. This type of representation is essential to gain cross-functional support for the project and to help ensure the smooth development and implementation of the system. Participation and commitment from all the heads of departments is essential in order to gain employee support for the project, and this will help to ensure the smooth implementation and subsequent maintenance of the standard. In extremely small companies where there is little or no second-tier management the whole-hearted commitment and involvement of the CEO is critical and essential.

- The ISO 9000 series should be considered as the minimum requirement. Without a documented quality management system there is neither basis nor connected reliable data to monitor the process of quality improvement. Organisations should, however, aim to have a quality system which surpasses the standard's requirements, with new quality initiatives built into the system. A quality system which meets the requirements of ISO 9001, ISO 9002 or ISO 9003 should in no sense be regarded by senior management as the pinnacle of their quality management achievements. All it says to the outside world is that the organization has controls, procedures and disciplines in place. The organization should treat ISO 9000 series registration as a precursor to developing their approach to TQM.

- There is a need to create a conducive environment for the development of a quality system which meets the requirements of the ISO 9000 series. This can be achieved by the formulation of organizational quality policy and quality objectives. The responsibility of executives in the establishment, maintenance, and development of the ISO 9000 series cannot be understated. The total commitment and leadership of senior management to the process of quality system registration to ISO 9001, ISO 9002 or ISO 9003 is vital, and it is only they who can deliver the resources and co-operation of appropriate personnel and provide the necessary direction. The CEO whilst accepting ultimate responsibility, has, as one would expect, to delegate a variety of tasks. Senior management must not only understand the principles of the ISO 9000 series but should ensure that the quality policy is implemented and understood by all employees and everyone in the organization has improvement objectives for their jobs. Senior management also needs to react positively to the actions resulting from quality audits.

- Training at all levels within the company is required on the importance of product and service quality, in general, and the reasons for the quality system and its benefits, in particular. This will help to facilitate the right type of behaviour, attitude and values of employees towards the ISO 9000 series and will encourage total participation. A systematic approach to quality, education and training will reduce resistance to change and other obstacles. An element of this awareness can occur if the initial audit is well explained and sympathetically carried out, explaining the reasons for recommendations.
- Once all the above steps have been taken the organization is in a position to commence developing its system to meet the requirements of the ISO 9000 system series. Accurate procedures including operating and working instructions are required. These procedures must be practical, workable and easily implemented. Wherever possible, they should document what employees are currently doing, they are most likely then to continue in the same way and fulfil assessment requirements naturally. Only where the standard would suggest that some modification is required should they be introduced. In writing the procedures it is worthwhile to keep in mind how to demonstrate to the auditor that the ISO 9000 series requirements have been fulfilled. The personnel who are given responsibilities for writing the procedures must be familiar with the requirements of the ISO 9000 series and be fully conversant with the procedures they are drafting. The use of consultants and management specialists to write procedures is not desirable as they are less likely to understand fully all the activities of the company. It is often found that when procedures are written in 'ivory towers' and then pushed into the working environment as required mandates, this leads to two main problems. Initially, there is the confrontation of changing the way the people work without any perceived gain and benefit. Secondly, when a formal assessment of the system is due there is an intense period of activity when people start to check the system and work to the procedures to ensure that they pass the audit. In addition 'ownership' of the processes by those operating them is lessened. The procedures as they are being developed and/or documented need to be checked to see that they meet the requirements of the ISO 9000 series and how they impact on other procedures, systems and activities.
- As a final point it should be emphasised that the quality management system must become an integral part of the management process. When managed in this way it will ensure that business improvements are incorporated into the system.

QUALITY SYSTEM ASSESSMENT AND REGISTRATION

When the organization has written the necessary procedures and instructions, and developed its quality system to meet the requirements of that part of the ISO 9000 series for which registration is sought, the following key activities need to be accomplished:

- Train and educate staff in the workings and operation of the system and test-out the procedures which have been developed. Education and training is a key determinant of people following procedures, completing the appropriate documentation, taking corrective action seriously, providing timely and accurate information and being aware of their responsibilities. In some companies, plans for training are supplemented by people's involvement for which departmental achievements are rewarded. For example, snapshots of audit requirements undertaken by an ISO 9000 series implementation team and recognition of performance given by rewards such as mugs, writing blocks, pens, etc.
- Arrange for a pre-assessment of the system to be carried out by a suitable qualified person.
- Decide the most appropriate time to go for assessment.
- ISO 9000 series registration is conferred by certification bodies who have, in turn, been accredited in the UK by the UKAS. The list of accredited certification bodies should be consulted and a 'supplier audit' of them carried out. It is important to establish the scope of the certification body's approval, their fee structure, relevant experience and knowledge in the organization's field of work, reputation, current workload, etc. Goodman (1997) lists 12 tips for choosing a certification body and this serves as a useful check list.
- Apply to the chosen accredited certification body who will then supply an information pack. Upon completion of the necessary forms, the certification body will provide a quotation and details of fees. After agreeing a contract, the appropriate documentation (including the quality manual) is then sent to the certification body to check compliance against the standard. In general, a certification body will usually want to see proof that the quality system has been in effective operation for a period of 6 months. However, this depends on the size of the company and the maturity of its quality management system.
- If the documentation reaches the standard, some certification bodies proceed to the on-site assessment for a preliminary review (pre-audit

assessment). At this stage, the company is able to make appropriate modifications and establish corrective actions to take account of the assessors' initial findings and comments.

- The formal assessment involves an in-depth appraisal of the organization's quality management system for compliance with the appropriate part of the standard. This is carried out by a small team of independent assessors appointed by the certification body and under the supervision of a registered lead assessor, the assessors should be knowledgeable in the organization's field of activity. If the assessors discover a deviation from the requirements or identify a non-compliance with the documented procedures, a discrepancy report is raised. At the end of the assessment, the non-conformances are reviewed and the assessors make a report on their recommendations, this includes a verbal report to management by the lead assessor. The recommendation can be unqualified registration, qualified registration and non- registration. Any non-compliance with the appropriate part of the standard must be rectified, within a prescribed time, before approval is given.

- Once registered the certification bodies have a system of routine surveillance. The frequency of these surveillance visits varies with the certification body but is generally twice a year. The certification body have the right to make these visits unannounced. The registration usually covers a fixed period of three years, subject to the regular surveillance visits. After three years a quality system reassessment is made. However, the main approach these days is continuous assessment visits of which there are a minimum of two per year. Continuing assessment is planned so that the cumulative effect over a two year cycle results in a complete audit of the quality system. This not only reduces the cost of registration but also minimizes the inconvenience caused to the organization. The continued compliance with the requirements of the standard is confirmed in writing following the site visit.

Long et al. (1991) from their research into the implementation of the ISO 9000 series have identified four factors that determine the time taken by organizations to implement the standard.

1. The status of the quality system prior to seeking ISO 9001, ISO 9002 and ISO 9003 registration. This status is determined by the presence or otherwise of activities which are in accordance with one of these three standards and their existence in a documented form. When few activities are in place and/or activities are not documented then

more time is required first to document and then to develop the system to meet the appropriate requirements.

2. The complexity of the company in terms of work locations, products manufactured, services offered, type of production and the type and number of production processes and operating instructions. With increasing complexity more procedures and work instructions are required to be documented.

3. The priority given by management to implementing the requirements of the standard and the time they are prepared to set aside for the activity from their normal day-to-day work responsibility affects the progress of implementation. This is especially the case when there are no full-time personnel responsible for quality assurance.

4. The existence of a conducive environment is required for the implementation and development of the standard. Resistance to change, lack of understanding about product and service quality and poor attitudes among employees toward quality improvement are major obstacles in implementing the requirements of the chosen standard.

BENEFITS AND LIMITATIONS OF THE ISO 9000 SERIES

The data are based on the type of discussions mentioned above. These are supplemented with comments made by directors, managers and technical and quality specialists on the Ford Motor Company three day SPC training courses for suppliers held at UMIST, various discussions with executives, consultants during the course of the UMIST TQM research both on a national and international front and comments made by executives on early drafts of this chapter.

* A quality system is a fundamental pillar in an organization's approach to TQM and it helps to ensure that any improvements made are held in place, see figure 5.1. However, ISO 9000 quality system series registration is not a prerequisite for TQM. Some organizations, in particular, those from the non-manufacturing sector have analysed and improved their systems and working practices and then have gone straight to TQM.

The guidance provided in the 20 clauses of ISO 9001, and the independent assessment surveillance, is an undisputable aid in developing and maintaining the procedures, controls and discipline required in a quality management system. The system should help to ensure that more people within the organization are touched by quality and in this way quality awareness is raised. The ISO 9000 series does, however, tend to encourage the separation of a business into areas that complete the recording of requirements and those areas which do not. For example, functions such as finance, management information systems and human resources are little affected, except for training requirements. It is TQM which stimulates the business by creating the understanding that all its component parts have customers, that waste must be systematically eliminated and improvement is a continuous process. To help eradicate these weaknesses relating to the separation of functions BSI Quality Assurance introduced in 1991 Company-Wide Registration to extend quality system accreditation to the whole of the company (core businesses as well as supporting functions), see Perry (1991) for details.

The UMIST TQM research experience indicates that, in most companies, it is not easy to get every function and person involved in taking responsibility for their own quality assurance and to make continuous improvements in the processes for which they are responsible, see Lascelles and Dale (1993). The ISO 9000 series of standards, albeit limited in respect of the point made above, can assist in making this happen.

* It is a contractual requirement of many customers that their suppliers are registered to the ISO 9000 series of standards. Registration is also required to get on bid lists. Once a company has become registered, it is more than likely that it will ask its suppliers, distributors and providers of service to do the same, setting into motion a chain reaction or what might be classed as a form of pyramid selling. Therefore, in many sectors of industry and government procurement agencies, it is necessary from a marketing

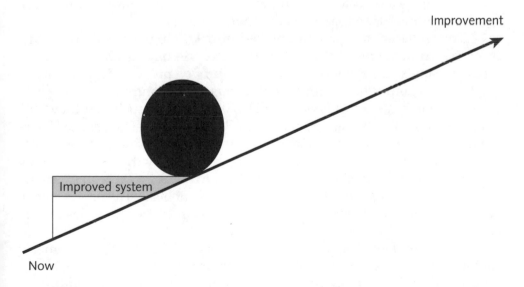

Figure 5.1 Performance improvement.

viewpoint to be registered, and without it a company will simply not get orders. In much of the world it is now a prerequisite condition to doing business. An increasing number of long standing suppliers to companies have been told by them that they must get ISO 9000 quality system series registration to continue to be a supplier. This is in spite of the supplier being the supplier of choice for a considerable period of time. Once ISO 9001, ISO 9002 or ISO 9003 registration has been achieved an organization cannot afford to lose it.

Suppliers have a habit of doing what their customers want and many organizations have achieved ISO 9001, ISO 9002 or ISO 9003 registration to provide documented proof that they have an adequate quality system in place just to satisfy the demands of their major customers. This may not produce the required improvement ethos naturally and any gains made will be short-lived if registration is perceived as a contractual condition rather than a foundation for ongoing improvement. Some suppliers also use it to demonstrate to customers (actual and potential) that they are committed to quality and have achieved what they often call 'the right level of quality'.

*   A system based on the ISO 9000 series provides only the foundation blocks and registration to the relevant part of the ISO 9000 series should be viewed as the minimum requirement and the objective should be to develop and improve the system in relation to the needs of the organization. An organization does not achieve superior performing company status merely by ISO 9001, ISO 9002 or ISO 9003 registration. The winners will be those who have a dedicated commitment to company-wide improvement through continuous self-assessment of what they do.

*   The preparation of systems, procedures, working instructions, etc., to meet the requirements of the ISO 9000 series, will have a beneficial affect on a company's performance in terms of improved process yields, reduced levels of non-conformance, improved management control, etc. However, the underlying mechanisms of the ISO 9000 series are such that they will tend towards a steady state performance. The ISO 9000 series of standards are designed to produce consistency both in actions, products and services. An organization can have a consistent performance with a high level of non-conformance. In the words of one Executive, 'ISO 9000 is an excellent system for telling us where we have produced rubbish'. The achievement of consistency whilst meritious, leads to the goal and once achieved can result in complacency.

The question 'Does the quality system reflect the needs of the customer?' should forever circulate in the minds of senior managers.

Only if there is strong leadership and a written commitment to improvement in the management review of the system will an improvement cycle be triggered. Some organizations have done this by building-on and widening their quality systems management review meetings which deal with issues such as: quality audit, corrective and preventive action; production rejections, concessions and corrective actions; waste levels; supplier performance/concessions; customer complaints; and market trends and requirements and into monthly steering meetings for process improvement. In this way the quality system is integrated into the continuous improvement process. It is not uncommon to find they are operated in parallel.

   * Having an ISO 9000 series certificate of registration does not as a matter of course imply that non-conformities at all stages of the process will not occur. The standard is not prescriptive as to the means of prevention. Detection methods which rely very heavily on inspection techniques, human or mechanical, would satisfy the standard in many aspects. This may be an acknowledgement of the fact that there are many processes where, given the state-of-the-art technology, it is not possible to achieve 'zero defects'. The standard does clearly indicate that corrective and preventive actions procedures should be established, documented and maintained to prevent recurrence of non-conforming products and that the system is maintained and developed through the internal audit and management review. However, there is a lack of evidence to suggest that improvement is an explicit criterion by which ongoing registration is monitored. In general, the ISO 9000 series tends to measure the effectiveness of documentation, paperwork and procedures (the requisite assessments are often termed a paperchase); this leads to the claim that they encourage bureaucracy.

   * Experience indicates that the ISO 9000 series has a limited impact on the total improvement operation of an organization simply because it does not get at the root cause of problems. Most problems are resolved at branch level and this is a failure in a number of businesses.

   By way of a comparison, QS 9000 requires suppliers to demonstrate ongoing improvements in their quality system and processes, and these improvements are assessed by documentation, reports and visits to the supplier. However, there is no published data about inter and intra industry comparisons. There is also no evidence that companies who are registered to ISO 9001, ISO 9002 or ISO 9003 exhibit a better quality performance and have a more positive approach to continuous and company-wide quality improvement, than those who are not registered.

   * Some people are confused about the relationship between the ISO 9000 series and TQM. They are not alternatives; a quality system is an essential feature of TQM. However, some organizations see ISO 9001, ISO 9002 or ISO 9003 registration as the pinnacle of their TQM achievements and no plans are laid for building on this registration. A small number of

people even believe that improvements driven through internal audits of the ISO 9000 series will lead their organization to TQM. As previously mentioned, registration often results in a sense of complacency, in particular, after successful third party assessment of the system.

* It should be obvious from the above discussion that ISO 9001, ISO 9002 or ISO 9003 registration or for that matter any other quality system registration or certification or approvals will not prevent a supplier from producing and delivering non-conforming products and/or services to its customers. The standards are a specification for the management of quality and there is clear distinction between registration and capability, and this fundamental fact needs to be recognised. Product and/or service quality is determined by the individual organization and its people and processes and not by a quality system standard.

Proof of this difference is provided from an investigation carried out by Judy Mone of the initial samples submitted by some 300 suppliers to the Leyland Daf assembly plant (it was a contractual requirement of the then Leyland Daf organization that all its suppliers are registered to the ISO 9000 series or its equivalent). She found that over 30 per cent of initial samples did not conform to requirements, see Mone et al. (1991) for details.

* Many organizations and executives have inflated views of the ISO 9000 series; these are often picked up from the hype generated by those selling advisory services. These views can lead to high expectations of what the standard can achieve which, in the long term, may do it a disservice. The following are typical of the comments (not referenced and attributed to individuals).

> Quality recognition of the ISO 9000 series from a National accredited certification body is prized nationwide because it is known to be difficult to achieve the high standards required by their impartial testing procedures.

> It will give the car-buying public a guarantee of complete satisfaction or their money back. What it aims to achieve is the world's coveted benchmark of quality: ISO 9000. . . . it is a standard that is recognized as being truly superb and is a move that no other rival car maker can afford to ignore.

> How can it be coveted and difficult to achieve when many thousands of companies in the UK have already met this requirement?

Such and such a company are the first in their industrial sector to obtain the prestigious ISO 9001, ISO 9002 or ISO 9003 registration – tremendous achievement, very proud to have achieved to the registration, the most significant event in the company's history, breaking new ground for quality, etc., etc. (write-up and picture in the local paper).

To the informed what these motherhead statements and platitudes are saying is that the organization has taken the first step down the TQM journey.

SUMMARY

A quality system is one of the key building blocks for an organization's TQM activities. The ISO 9000 generic series of quality system standards defines and sets-out a definitive list of features and characteristics which should be present in an organization's quality management system through documented policies, manual and procedures, whatever the product manufactured or offered, or the service provided, or the technology used. In this way sound advice is provided on how an organization may develop a quality system.

Seeking registration for the wrong reasons and a system which is too inflexible and bureaucratic are some of the major pitfalls. Registration to the ISO 9000 series will improve an organization's systems, procedures and processes but on its own will not deliver continuous company-wide improvement. To make best use of the ISO 9000 series it is important that the implementation is carried out in the right spirit and for the right reasons. This is an area in which management commitment is vital. The solution to many of the reported difficulties, shortcomings and criticisms against the standard lies in the hands of an organization's senior management team. The saying 'you only get out what you put in' is so relevant to the ISO 9000 series. All too often the ISO 9000 series system is left solely in the hands of the Quality Department.

Registration to the ISO 9000 series of standards is not the only way to achieve quality assurance neither is it a prerequisite for TQM. It is, however, becoming necessary to have the appropriate registration in order to do business at both a national and international level and in this respect it is a key marketing tool. It is the fear of loss of business and substitution in the marketplace that have caused many organizations to attain ISO 9000 series registration. The ISO 9000 series provides a common benchmark for good quality management system practice which is recognized throughout the world. An organization which is registered to the appropriate part of the series should be working in an organised, structured and procedural way with defined methods of operating.

It is important that organizations do not view ISO 9000 series registration as their pinnacle of success in relation to quality assurance and quality management. It only provides the basic foundation blocks and they must have strategies and business plans in place to move on and cater for areas which are not addressed by the standard and develop to TQM. This is particularly important in smaller businesses who, in a number of cases, attain ISO 9000 series registration and have no interest and vision to developing further their quality management activities.

REFERENCES

Boaden R. J., Dale B. G., Polding E. 1991: *A State-of-the-Art Survey of Total Quality Management in the Construction Industry*, Research Report to the European Construction Institute, Loughborough.

BS 4891 1972: *A Guide to Quality Assurance*, British Standards Institution, London.

BS 5750: Part 1 1979: *Specification for Design/Development, Production, Installation and Servicing*, British Standards Institution, London.

BS EN ISO 8402 1995: *Quality Management and Quality Assurance*, British Standards Institution, London.

BS EN ISO 14001 1996: *Environmental Management Systems: Specification with Guidance for Use*, British Standards Institution, London.

Dale B. G. and Oakland J. S. 1994: *Quality Improvement Through Standards*, (Second Edition), Stanley Thornes, Cheltenham.

Dale B. G. and Plunkett J. J. 1984: 'A study of Audits, Inspection and Quality Costs in the Pressure Vessel Fabrication Sector of the Process Plant Industry'. *Proceedings of the Institution of Mechanical Engineers*, 198, (B2), 45–54.

Galt J. D. A. and Dale B. G. 1991: 'Supplier Development: A British Case Study', *International Journal of Purchasing and Materials Management*, Winter 16–22.

Goodman S. 1997: 'Tips on How to Choose Your Certification Body', *Quality World*, February, 114–15.

Hall T. J. 1992: *The Quality Manual: the Application of BS 5750, ISO 9001, EN 29001*, John Wiley, Chichester.

ISO 9000-1 1994: *Quality Management and Quality Assurance Standards – Part 1: Guidelines for selection and use*, International Organization for Standardization, Geneva.

ISO 9000-2 1997: *Quality Management and Quality Assurance Standards – Part 2: Generic Guidelines for the Application of ISO 9001, ISO 9002 and ISO 9003*, International Organization for Standardization, Geneva.

ISO 9000-3 1997: *Quality Management and Quality Assurance Standards – Part 3: Guidelines for the application of ISO 9001 to the Development, Supply and Maintenance of Software*, International Organization for Standardization, Geneva.

ISO 9000-4 1993: *Quality Management and Quality Assurance Standards – Part 4: Guide to Dependability Programme Management*, International Organization for Standardization, Geneva.

ISO 9004-1 1994: *Quality Management and Quality System Elements – Part 1: Guidelines*, International Organization for Standardization, Geneva.

ISO 9004-2 1991: *Quality Management and Quality System Elements – Part 2: Guidelines for Services*, International Organization for Standardization, Geneva.

ISO 9004-3 1993: *Quality Management and Quality System Elements – Part 3: Guidelines for Processed Materials*, International Organization for Standardization, Geneva.

ISO 9004-4 1993: *Quality Management and Quality System Elements – Part 4: Guidelines for Quality Improvement*, International Organization for Standardization, Geneva.

ISO 8402-1 1994: *Quality Management and Quality Assurance – Vocabulary*, International Organization for Standardization, Geneva.

ISO 9001 1994: *Quality Systems – Model for Quality Assurance in Design, Development, Production, Installation and Servicing*, International Organization for Standardization, Geneva.

ISO 9002 1994: *Quality Systems – Model for Quality Assurance in Production, Installation and Servicing*, International Organization for Standardization, Geneva.

ISO 9003 1994: *Quality Systems – Model for Quality Assurance in Final Inspection and Test*, International Organization for Standardization, Geneva.

ISO 10013 1995: *Guidelines for Developing Quality Manuals*, International Organization for Standardization, Geneva.

International Organization for Standardization 1998: *The ISO Survey of ISO 9000 and ISO 14000 Certificates*, (Seventh Cycle) ISO, Geneva.

Jackson P. and Ashton D. 1993: *Implementing Quality Through ISO 9000*, Kogan Page, London.

Lamprecht J. L. 1992: *ISO 9000, Preparing for Registration*, Marcel Dekker, New York.

Lamprecht J. L. 1993: *Implementing the ISO 9000 Series*, Marcel Dekker, New York.

Lascelles D. M. and Dale B. G. 1993: *Total Quality Improvement*, IFS Publications, Bedford.

Long A. A., Dale B. G. and Younger A. 1991: 'A Study of BS 5750 Aspirations in Small Companies', *Quality and Reliability Engineering International*, 7 (1), 27–33.

Mone J., Hibbert B. and Dale B. G. 1991: 'Initial Samples and Quality Improvement: a Study', *Proceedings of the Sixth National Conference on Production Research*, Hatfield Polytechnic, Bell and Bain, September 1991, 459–63.

Nissan Motor Manufacturing (UK) Ltd 1991: *Nissan Quality Standard for Suppliers*, Nissan Iberica SA and Nissan Motor Manufacturing (UK) Ltd, Washington.

Oliver B. 1991: 'Further Thoughts on ISO 9000', *Quality News*, 17 (3), 122–23.

Owen F. 1988: 'Why Quality Assurance and its Implementation in a Chemical Manufacturing Company', *Chemistry and Industry*, August, 491–4.

PD 6538 1993: *Vision 2000: A Strategy for International Standards, Implementation in the Quality Arena during the 1990s*, British Standards Institution, London.

Perry M. 1991: 'Company-Wide Registration: A Foundation for Total Quality', *BSI Quality Assurance*, British Standards Institution, Milton Keynes.

Rothery B. 1993: *ISO 9000*, Gower Press, Hants.

Singer A. J., Churchill G. F. and Dale B. G. 1988: 'Supplier Quality Assurance Systems; a Study in the Nuclear Industry'. *Proceedings of the Institution of Mechanical Engineers*, 202, (B4), 205–12.

Society of Motor Manufacturers and Traders 1990: *Quality Systems and the Motor Industry*, SMMT, London.

Spickernell D. G. 1991: *The Path to ISO 9000*, Third Business Success Seminar, November, London.

Warner F. 1977: *Standards and Specifications in the Engineering Industries*, National Economic Development Office, London.

White Paper 1982: *Standards, Quality and International Competitiveness*, Government White Paper, Cmnd 8621, Her Majesty's Stationery Office.

6

Quality management tools and techniques

INTRODUCTION

To support and develop a process of continuous improvement it is necessary for an organization to use a selection of management tools and techniques. Some of these tools and techniques are simple (sometimes deceptively so) whilst others are more complex. Tools and techniques have different roles to play in a process of continuous improvement and if applied correctly give repeatable and reliable results. Their roles include:

- data collection
- summarizing data *executive summary*
- data presentation
- discovering problems
- ✓ understanding the problem
- ✓ finding and removing the causes of the problem
- ✓ assisting with the setting of priorities
- ✓ selecting problems for improvement

- identifying relationships
- structuring ideas
- performance measurement
- capability assessment
- planning
- implementing actions
- monitoring and maintaining control

The potential user must always be aware of the main uses of the particular tool and technique they are considering applying. There is often a danger of using a tool and technique in a blinkered manner, almost expecting it to solve the problem automatically. Connected with this is the overreliance on one particular tool. A saying to describe this misconception is 'If you only have a hammer it is surprising how many things look like nails.'

This chapter provides an overview of the tools and techniques which are likely to be used in an organization's improvement process. The focus is on describing the tools and their uses and avoids detail on construction. Where appropriate, guidance for further reading is provided for those who may wish to extend their knowledge of a particular tool or technique.

BENCHMARKING

Benchmarking as it is known it today originated in Rank Xerox. It is now well documented (e.g. Camp 1989) that when the company started to evaluate its copying machines against the Japanese competition it was found that the Japanese companies were selling their machines for what it cost Rank Xerox to make them. It was also assumed that the Japanese-produced machines were of poor quality, this was proved not to be the case. This exposure of their vulnerability highlighted the need for change.

Benchmarking is defined by Rank Xerox as 'the continuous process of measuring products, services and processes against the strongest competitors or those renowned as world leaders in their field'. Put simply, benchmarking is an opportunity to learn from the experience of others. Most organizations carry out what can be termed informal benchmarking. There are perhaps two forms of this: (i) by visits to other businesses, ideas can be gleaned which can be used to facilitate improvements in one's own organization and; (ii) the collection in a variety of ways, of data, about the competitors. This is often not done in any planned way and is limited in its value.

To make the most effective use of benchmarking and use it as a learning experience as part of a continual process rather than a one-shot exercise a more formal approach is required. However, before an organization embarks on formal benchmarking it is important that it is prepared to spend time understanding how its own processes work. This will often be the key criterion of the benchmarking activity.

There are three main types of formal benchmarking.

1. Internal benchmarking: this is the easiest form of benchmarking to conduct and involves benchmarking between businesses within the same group of companies. In this way but practice and initiatives are shared across businesses.
2. Competitive benchmarking: this is a comparison against the direct competition. It is often difficult, to obtain the data for this form of benchmarking.
3. Functional/generic benchmarking: this is comparison of specific processes with 'best in class' in different industries. Functional relates to the functional similarities of organizations, whilst generic looks at the broader similarities of business. It is usually not difficult to obtain access to other organizations to perform this type of benchmarking. Organizations are often keen to swop and share information in a network or partnership.

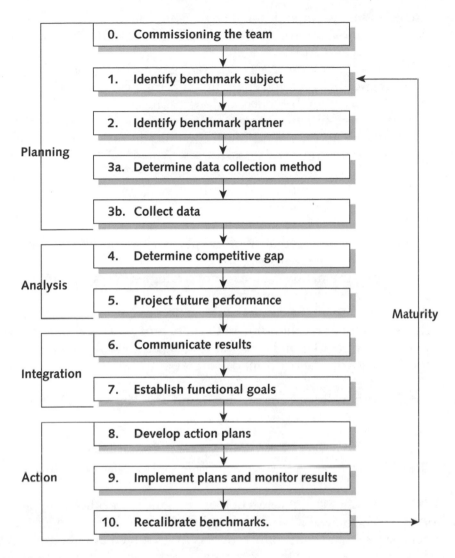

Figure 6.1 Steps in the benchmarking process.
Source: North West Water

There are a number of steps in a formal benchmarking process, see figure 6.1. They are now briefly described (more detail can be found in Camp 1989):

1. Identify what is the subject (i.e. the invoicing process) to be benchmarked, and reach agreement on the measures (i.e. number of invoices per day, per person) to be used.

2. Identify which companies will be benchmarked.
3. Agree the most appropriate means of collecting the data, who will be involved and a plan of action.
4. Determine the reasons for the current gap (positive or negative) in performance between the company and the best amongst the companies involved in the benchmarking exercise.
5. Estimate, over an agreed time frame, the change in performance of the company and the benchmark company in order to assess if the gap is going to grow or decrease.
6. Define and establish the goals to close or increase the gap in performance. This step requires effective communication of the benchmarking findings.
7. Develop action plans to achieve the goals set out in step 6. This step involves gaining acceptance of the plans by all employees likely to be affected by the changes.
8. Implement the actions, plans and strategies. This involves good project planning and management.
9. Assess and report the results of the action plans.
10. Reassessment or recalibration of the benchmark. This should be conducted on a regular and systematic basis and involves maintaining good links with the benchmark partners.

More details of benchmarking can be found in Camp (1989) and Zairi (1996).

CHECKLISTS

Checklists (sometimes called inspection or validation checklists) are used as prompts and aids to personnel. They highlight the key features of a process, equipment, system and/or product/or service to which attention needs to be given, and to ensure that the procedures for an operation, housekeeping, inspection, maintenance, etc. have been followed. Checklists are also used in audits of both product and systems. They are an invaluable aid for quality assurance and as might be imagined the variety and style and content of such lists are immense. Figure 6.2 is an example of a checklist sheet.

DEPARTMENTAL PURPOSE ANALYSIS (DPA)

Departmental Purpose Analysis is a structured quality management tool. Perhaps its main value is facilitating the internal customer/supplier

Standard Operating Procedure (SOP): Control information

Does the SOP clearly state/include the following or make cross-reference to supporting information?

	Yes	No	N/A
Job title and purpose (why)	Yes	No	
SOP reference number	Yes	No	
Scope of the job covered by the SOP	Yes	No	
Name of person responsible for construction of SOP	Yes	No	
Approval by controlling function	Yes	No	N/A
Last revision date	Yes	No	
Next revision date	Yes	No	
Acceptance by user(s), user friendly	Yes	No	
Reference to supporting information (can the user locate the information using the SOP?)	Yes	No	N/A
Training and refresher training (why?)	Yes	No	N/A
Information on one sheet	Yes	No	
Visual communication to replace words	Yes	No	

Job process information

Does the SOP clearly state/include the following or make cross-reference to supporting information?

	Yes	No	N/A
Correct (standard) sequence of operations/actions	Yes	No	N/A
Agreed critical control/check points	Yes	No	
Correct job performance by: (1) experienced operator	Yes	No	N/A
(2) inexperienced operator	Yes	No	N/A
Key job requirements (Q, D, C and P) i.e. quality, cost, delivery and performance)	Yes	No	N/A
Sampling and/or inspection procedures	Yes	No	N/A
Actions and limits of authority in dealing with abnormalities	Yes	No	N/A
Fault finding actions	Yes	No	N/A
Supplier/customer (next operation/action)	Yes	No	N/A
Technical specifications	Yes	No	N/A

Q, D, C, P (S & M) Information

Does the SOP clearly state/include the following or make cross-reference to supporting information?

	Yes	No	N/A
Possible (most common abnormalities)	Yes	No	
Methods of monitoring and recording abnormalities	Yes	No	N/A
Reference and requirements of any inspection equipment	Yes	No	N/A
Calibration/equipment checking requirements	Yes	No	N/A
Product protection and/or handling requirements (why?)	Yes	No	N/A
Process (operation, lead, queue) times	Yes	No	N/A
Delivery dates (outputs from job)	Yes	No	N/A
High cost items/features (why?)	Yes	No	N/A
Opportunities for job holder cost control	Yes	No	N/A
Potential hazards, warnings (why?)	Yes	No	
Actions in the event of a health and safety problem	Yes	No	
Skill and knowledge requirements (to do the job)	Yes	No	N/A
Location of help and assistance	Yes	No	N/A

Additional SOP Information (job-related)

Does the SOP clearly state/include the following information or make cross-reference to supporting information?

	Yes	No	N/A
Special fail safe devices and purpose (why?)	Yes	No	N/A
Certificates/permits to operate (why?)	Yes	No	N/A
Pre-kitting checks	Yes	No	N/A

Figure 6.2 Inspection and validation checklist covering construction of standard operating procedures.
Source: RHP Bearings

LIVERPOOL
JOHN MOORES UNIVERSITY
AVRIL ROBARTS LRC

relationship, determining the effectiveness of departments, and extending the quality improvement initiatives to non-manufacturing areas. The concept of DPA originated at IBM, Lewis (1984). The key features of DPA are:

- A departmental task analysis is undertaken to determine what needs to be achieved by a department in order to meet the company objectives. In this way, a department's objectives are aligned to company objectives. It helps to ensure uniformity of opinion on both departmental and company objectives.
- Identifies in a clear manner, the purpose, roles, responsibilities and total contribution of a department to adding value to an organization's activities; non-value adding work is highlighted.
- Identifies the workload of departmental staff and the current utilization of skills.
- Describes the relationship between a department and its internal customers/suppliers.
- Provides the basis for applying and establishing performance measures by which a department can ensure that it is focusing on satisfying the needs and expectations of its internal customers. From the measurements, improvement objectives and targets can be agreed with all those concerned.
- Identifies interdepartmental problems which can be the subject of a cross-functional team.

Part of a DPA is given in figure 6.3.

DESIGN OF EXPERIMENTS

Design of experiment techniques involve the identification and control of those parameters or variables (termed factors) which have a potential influence on the output of a process, choosing two or more values (termed levels) of these variables and then running the process at these levels. Each combination or experimental run is known as a trial. There are a number of methods of experimentation – trial and error (the one-at-a-time method), full factorial and fractional factorial.

The trial and error (or classical method) is to change one factor at a time while keeping all the other factors constant. The experiments are run until some optimum level is found for the single factor. Then keeping this factor at that level, variations are made to another factor to find its optimum with the other factors being kept constant and so on. This approach is quick, familiar and easy. However, it is widely criticized, not least for the fact that no information is provided about any interactions which may occur between the factors being tested and for being inefficient, resource intensive and costly. In addition, it is not easy to hold the factors constant from experiment to experiment and this in itself creates variation.

The full factorial approach is to consider all combinations of the factors. In this way investigating all possible interactions between the factors and finding the best combination of the factors. This may be feasible for a small number of factors but even with say seven factors at two levels, the minimum number of trials would be 2^7, i.e. 128. Despite the fact that both the main effects and interactions can be measured in a thorough and pure scientific manner, the time and costs associated with running such a large number of experiments is usually considered to be prohibitive and is simply unrealistic. This problem may be overcome by the use of fractional factorial designs.

Fractional factorial designs assume that higher order interactions are negligible and consequently the number of trials are a fraction of the full factorial (i.e. ½ or ¼). However, they still have the disadvantage of requiring a large number of trials. Taguchi (1986), along with others (e.g. Plackett and Burman 1946) has developed a series of orthogonal arrays to address the size of the experiment and thus aid the efficiency of conducting fractional factorial experiments. For example, the number of trials for seven factors at two levels would be reduced from 128 to 8. However, whilst economics in the design of experiment are achieved, there is an inevitable loss of information, usually that of some possible interactions between factors. Despite this drawback most practitioners appear to favour the Taguchi approach. Not only are his methods cost effective and time efficient but they also work.

Design of experiments dates back to the work for agricultural research of Sir R. A. Fisher in the 1920s and historically required a great deal of statistical knowledge and understanding, which most users found somewhat intimidating. Much effort has been devoted to simplifying the task. In the late 1970s, the work of Genichi Taguchi on experimental design made what is regarded by many as a major breakthrough in its application, (see Taguchi 1986 for details of his method).

Taguchi is a statistician and electrical engineer who was involved in rebuilding the Japanese telephone system, and has been involved in applying design of experiments in the Japanese electronic industry for over 25 years. He promotes three distinct stages of designing-in quality:

1. System design – the basic configuration of the system is developed, this involves the selection of parts and materials.
2. Parameter design – the numerical values for the system variables (prod-

(a) Main tasks – suppliers

Task	What is the input?	Who provides it?	Is it right?	How can it be modified?
Taking of orders	Phone calls, telexes, fax messages, ansafone, postal orders	Clients, salespersons unit offices	In the main yes, but some aspects such as packaging sizes, address detail, order numbers are sometimes given with the assumption we know what is missing	Personnel placing orders could be more explicit with details. Some detail could be given with the assumption we know sales office. Ansafone could be replaced by the Wang electronic mail system
Processing Orders	Computer via visual display units and internal sales office order input form	Sales office	Yes, within our abilities and constant interruptions by phone calls and visitors, which by causing distractions can lead to errors	A CSP is in the system to assist with efficiency. Sales department could specify if the checking of product programme is required as some require it and others do not
Answering enquiries and liason with shipping and transport, warehousing and customer stores	Phone calls to engineering technical, purchasing production, credit control customer stores , shipping and transport, warehousing	Clients, unit offices, salespersons	Generally yes, but clients sometimes require miracles and are annoyed and sometimes abusive if they do not get them	Sales office is manned 9 a.m.–5 p.m. Technical back-up and stores are often not available during working day. Warehouse is unmanned after 4 p.m., which makes transport ineffective as they can only answer in the main based on information from the warehouse
Daily booked order figures	Edit list	Computer department	Yes	Computer could produce the same data but would have to run in parallel for one year while it built up a year's records
Outstanding order list – chemicals	Computer listing 106	Computer department	No	Glassware and reagents should be on engineering list. Due date is required
Outstanding order – engineering	Computer listing 109	Computer department	No	Glassware and reagents should be on this list not on chemical list
New account raising	Orders	Clients, salespersons, unit offices	No	Sales office often get passed around in obtaining territory numbers; responsible sales units/offices should know their own prospects
Process	Postal orders	Clients, unit offices,	No	These are confirmatory to verbal

Task	What is the output?	Who receives it?
Processing orders	A works order set	Warehouse stores, production control, purchasing and manufacturing plants
Answering enquiries and liaison with shipping and transport, warehousing and customer stores	Fast, accurate response	Clients, unit offices, salespersons, credit control, transport and stores
Daily booked order figures	Accurate booked sales figures	Sales management and operations management
Outstanding order list – chemicals	That all booked orders are progressed to invoices	Sales office
Outstanding order list – engineering	That all booked orders are progressed to invoices	Sales office
New account raising	The facility to process client orders	Sales office
Process confirmatory orders	Processed client orders	Sales office
Ordering and progress of engineering bought out items	Purchase requisitions and progress sheet	Engineering and purchasing departments
Price list maintenance	Special price lists	Sales office and sales management
Forward order diary	Orders raided to client's requirements	Sales office
Water treatment service and supervisory contracts	Memos annotated with account numbers and account special instruction facility displaying contract	Sales office and accounts department

Figure 6.3 Departmental Purpose Analysis.
Source: Betz Dearborn

uct and process parameters – factors) are chosen so that the system performs well, no matter what disturbances or noises are encountered by the system. The experimentation pinpoints this combination of product/process parameter levels. The emphasis in parameter design is on using low-cost materials and processes in the production of the system. Parameter design is the key stage of designing in quality.

The objective is to identify optimum levels for these control factors so that the product and/or process is least sensitive to changes in the noise factors.

3. Tolerance design – if the system is not satisfactory, then tolerance design is then used to improve performance (i.e. reduce variation) by tightening the tolerances on those factors which have the largest impact on variation.

Taguchi's 'off-line' approach to quality control is well accepted in the West, in particular, with the engineering fraternity, but inevitably there are many criticisms to some of his statistical methods and rather surprisingly to the advocated philosophy. What the critics seem to forget is that Taguchi's methods have proven successful both in Japan and the West, and those organizations who have adopted his methods have succeeded in making continuous improvement; it is this which is important and not the methods used. There is little doubt that his work has led to increased interest in a variety of approaches and methodologies relating to design of experiments. It should be noted that a number of other people have made significant improvements with the other approaches to experimental design. The maxim to be applied should be 'if it works for you, use it'.

The key steps in designing and running a fractional factorial experiment are:

Step 1   Decide the project objective.

Step 2   Identify and define the main factors (e.g. temperature, pressure, speed and the percentage of constituents making up a product or mix of material) and interactions that can affect performance and these factors. The preparation of a cause and effect diagram may aid this identification. This step should be undertaken by people who are knowledgeable about the process under investigation; this would be done using engineering 'know-how', with some form of instinctive 'gut feeling'.

Step 3   List the control factors and noise factors. Control factors are those factors which may be controlled during production (e.g. temperature, speed, tension, pressure and material type). Noise factors are those factors which are difficult or impossible to control in production. They include atmospheric conditions, ageing of equipment, machine maintenance, operator skills and shift differences.

Step 4 Establish the levels at which each factor is to be tested. Identify the orthogonal array (see figure 2.1) to be used, there are a number of popular arrays with perhaps seven covering most applications. Decide which factors are to be placed in each column of the orthogonal array. It is usual to place those control factors which are more difficult to change in the first and second columns on the left hand side of the array. The rows and columns of the orthogonal array is the experimental plan.

Step 5 Organize the experiment and carry it out. This often involves con-siderable organization in tracking the products involved in the experiment.

Step 6 Analyse and interpret the results, looking for relevant interactions.

Step 7 Carry out a confirmation run at the optimum settings to validate the conclusions.

Some suggested reading, in addition to that of Taguchi (1986), includes Lochnar and Matar (1990) and Bendell et al. (1990).

FAILURE MODE AND EFFECTS ANALYSIS (FMEA)

The technique of FMEA was developed in the aerospace and defence industries. FMEA is a systematic and analytical quality planning tool for

	Gap	Straw unwind	Gaylord heater	Fluting shower	Liner wrap	Small P/heat	Roll pressure	Strength	Variation
Set 1	6	Off	On	Off	Off	Off	40	58.73	6.93
Set 2	6	Off	On	On	On	On	60	76.27	7.18
Set 3	6	On	Off	Off	Off	On	60	63.26	6.29
Set 4	6	On	Off	On	On	Off	40	67.07	7.53
Set 5	9	Off	Off	Off	On	Off	60	61.65	4.51
Set 6	9	Off	Off	On	Off	On	40	61.19	4.90
Set 7	9	On	On	Off	On	On	40	65.56	4.57
Set 8	9	On	On	On	Off	Off	60	62.73	5.41

Figure 6.4 Design of experiments: liner bond strength.
Source: Rexam Corrugated South West Ltd

identifying at the product, service and process design stages, what potentially could go wrong either with a product during its manufacture or end-use by the customer or with the provision of a service. The use of FMEA is a powerful aid to advanced quality planning of new products and services. Its effective use should lead to a reduction in:

- defects during the production of initial samples and in volume production
- customer complaints
- failures in the field
- performance-related deficiencies
- warranty claims
- improved customer satisfaction and confidence as products and services are produced from robust and reliable production and delivery methods

There are two categories of FMEA: design and process. Design FMEA assesses what could, if not corrected, go wrong with the product in service and during manufacture as a consequence of a weakness in the design. Design FMEA also assists in the identification or confirmation of critical characteristics. Process FMEA is mainly concerned with the reasons for potential failure during manufacture and in service as a result of non-compliance with the original design intent, or failure to achieve the design specification.

The procedure involved in the development of FMEA is progressive iteration. In brief it involves the following steps:

- it starts by focusing on the function of the product, service and/or process
- it identifies potential failure modes
- it assesses the effects of each potential failure
- it examines the causes of potential failure
- it reviews current controls
- it determines a Risk Priority Number (RPN)
- it recommends the corrective action which is to be taken to help eliminate potential concerns
- it monitors the corrective actions and counter-measures which have been put into place

The requisite information and actions are recorded on a standard format, see figure 6.5.

The RPN comprises an assessment of: (i) occurrence; (ii) detection and; (iii) severity of ranking and is the sum of the three rankings.

1. The occurrence is the likelihood of a specific cause which will result in the identified failure mode and based on perceived or estimated probability ranked on a scale of 1–10.
2. The detection criterion relates, in the case of a design FMEA, to the likelihood of the design verification programme pinpointing a potential failure mode before it reaches the customer; a ranking of 1–10 is used. In the process FMEA, this relates to the existing control plan.
3. The severity of effect on a scale of 1–10 indicates the likelihood of the customer noticing any difference to the functionality of the product or service.

The resulting RPN should always be checked against past experience of similar products, services and situations. After it has been determined the potential failure modes in descending order of RPN should be the focus for improvement action to reduce/eliminate the risk of failure occurring.

From the design FMEA, the potential causes of failure should be studied and actions taken before designs and drawings are finalized. Likewise, with the process FMEA, actions must be put into place before the process is set up. Used properly, FMEA prevents potential failures occurring in the manufacturing, producing and/or delivery processes or end-product in use, and will ensure that processes, products and services are more robust and reliable. It is a powerful technique and there is little doubt that a number of the product recall campaigns, which are well publicized each year, could conceivably be avoided by the effective use of FMEA. However, it is important that FMEA is seen not just as a catalogue of potential failures, but as a tool for pursuing continuous improvement. It should also not be viewed as a paperwork exercise carried out to retain business, as this will limit the perceived usefulness of the technique.

The concept, procedures and logic involved with FMEA are not new. Every forward-thinking design, planning and production engineer and technical specialist carries out, in an informal manner, various aspects of FMEA. In fact, most people in their daily routines subconsciously will use a simple, informal FMEA. However, this mental analysis is rarely committed to paper in a format that can be evaluated by others and discussed as the basis for a corrective action plan. What FMEA does is to provide a planned, systematic method of capturing and documenting this knowledge; it also forces people to use a disciplined approach and is a vehicle for obtaining collective knowledge and experience through team activity.

Process function requirements	Potential failure mode	Potential effect(s) of failure	Severity	Potential cause(s)/mechanism(s) of failure	Occurrence	Current process controls
Kit parts to the assembly line	Incorrect parts used on build	Turbo failure	7	Wrong parts presented to the line at change-over	2	Visual check by setter to the shop. Packet introduced from the bulk issue area set up on the line. Marking of the part number on the 'A' surface on compressors to identify. Marking of the part number the turbine flange.
Kit parts to the assembly line	Contaminated parts	Turbo failure	7	Contaminated parts due to lack of cleanliness of holding containers, organic material in spacer	2	Visual check, work instruction by station describing method of assembly.
Check cross-over holes	Cross-over hole not drilled	No oil flow turbo failure	8	Broken drill, missed operation	5	Air gauge on assembly 100% prior to build; work instruction by station describing method assembly.
Affix label to centre housing	Wrongly orientated to customer requirements or on the wrong side of centre housing	Unable to read customer no. on the engine, engine, reject unit which customer will have to adjust label to correct orientation and record ppm	5	Process controlled by the operator and is capable of producing defects	4	100% visual check by operators; work instructions by station describing method assembly.
Affix label to centre housing of compressor housing	Incorrect data on label	Customer dissatisfaction, could use the wrong turbo	7	Wrong input	2	Software provides for a check so that the data have to be inputted twice to verify; work instructions by station describing method assembly.
Affix label to centre housing of compressor housing	Label not properly affixed	Label will fall off	5	Hole oversize from, machining, stripped thread	4	100% visual check by operators when recording the serial number on audit sheet; work instructions by station describing method of assembly.
Affix label to centre housing of compressor housing	Label missing	Unable to identify unit	5	Operation carried out incorrectly	4	100% visual check by operators'. Serial number recorded on audit sheet; work instructions by station describing method of assem

Figure 6.5 Potential Failure Mode and Effects Analysis (process FMEA).
Source: Allied Signal Automotive

robability tection	Risk priority number	Recommended action(s)	Responsibility and target completion data	Actions taken	Severity	Occurrence	Probability of detection	Risk priority number
				Action results				
	42							
	98	Introduce cleaning process for all the boxes, which the parts are presented to the line. Euroboxes 300mm × 200mm, 400mm × 300 mm and 600mm × 250mm.	LM, DN, PE, BW, mid December 1997	Quotes collected capital approval sanctioned delivery 12 December 1997	7	2	3	42
	120	New poka yoked fixture provided for an 'in process' end of line check. Will pressure test the centre housing and check that the cross-over hole is present. If OK a letter 'T' will be stamped	PC, DC, MB Oct 1997	New end of line test fixture, pressure tests CH and checks for crossover hole, being debugged at supplier to be on stream 1 Dec 1997	8	2	3	48
	100	Design new fixture to mistake proof, by interlocking the fixture to prevent assembly. Will prevent the stick screws from being supplied with air on the detection of incorrect label orientation.	LM, AM, FW, 15 November 1997	Design and detail drawings being modified to suit CI I with backplate assembled	5	2	3	30
	70							
	60							
	40							

FLOW CHARTS

Process mapping (sometimes called 'blue printing' or process modelling) in either a structured or unstructured format, is a prerequisite to obtaining an in-depth understanding of a process, before the application of quality management tools and techniques such as FMEA, SPC and quality costing. A flow chart is employed to provide a diagrammatic picture, by means of a set of symbols, showing all the steps or stages in a process, project or sequence of events and is of considerable assistance in documenting and describing a process as an aid to examination and improvement.

A chart, when used in a manufacturing context, may show the complete process from goods-receiving through storage, manufacture, assembly to despatch of final product or simply some part of this process in detail. What is important is that each 'activity' is included to focus attention on aspects of the process or subset of the process where problems have occurred or may occur to enable some corrective action to be taken or countermeasure put into place.

Traditionally charts (called process charts) have employed conventional symbols to define activities such as operation, inspection, delay or temporary storage, permanent storage and transportation, and are much used by operations and methods and industrial engineering personnel (see Currie 1989 for details).

There are a number of variants of the classical process flow chart, including those tailored to an individual company's use with different symbols being used to reflect the situation under study. What is important is not the format of the chart and/or flow diagram, but that the process has been mapped out with key inputs, value-adding steps and outputs defined and it is understood by those directly involved and responsible for initiating improvements. Analysing the data collected on a flow chart can help to uncover irregularities and potential problem points. It is also a useful method of dealing with customer complaints, by establishing the cause of the break/problems in the customer/supplier chain and rectifying it by means of corrective action. In a number of cases, processes are poorly defined and documented. Also in some organizations people are only aware of their own particular aspect of a process and process mapping helps to facilitate a greater understanding of the whole process, it is essential to the development of the internal customer/supplier relationship. Figure 6.6 is an example of a simple flow chart.

The following are the main steps in constructing a flow chart:

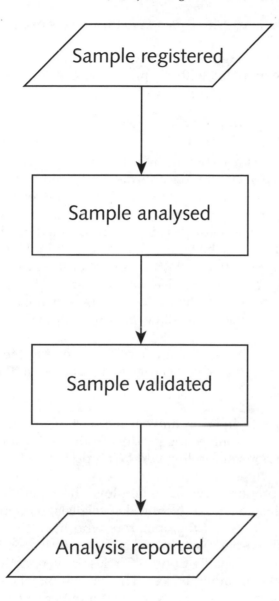

Figure 6.6 Flow chart: laboratory services.
Source: North West Water

- define the process and its boundaries, including start and end points
- decide the type and method of charting and the symbols to be used, and do not deviate from the convention chosen
- decide the detail with which the process is to be mapped

- describe the stages, in sequence, in the process using the agreed methodology
- assess if these stages are in the correct sequence
- ask people involved with the process to check its veracity

MISTAKE PROOFING

Mistake proofing is a technique which is used to prevent errors being converted into a defect. The concept was developed by Shingo (1986). The technique is based on the assumption that no matter how observant or skilled people are, mistakes will occur unless preventative measures are put in place. Shingo argues that using statistical methods is tantamount to accepting defects as inevitable, and that instead of looking for and correcting the causes of defective work, the source of the mistake should be inspected, analysed and rectified. He places great emphasis on what he calls 'source inspection', which checks for factors which cause mistakes, and then using poka-yoke or mistake proofing devices to prevent their reoccurrence.

Mistake proofing has two main steps – preventing the occurrence of a defect and detecting the defect. The system is applied at three points in the process:

1. in the event of an error, prevent the start of a process
2. prevent a non-conforming product from leaving a process
3. prevent a non-conforming part being passed to the next process

The mistake proofing technique employs the ingenuity and skills not only of the engineers and/or technical specialists, who may develop and fit the devices, but also of the operators who have firstly identified the cause for the mistake and participated in the corrective action measures. In Japanese companies, Quality Control Circles are very active in developing and using mistake proofing devices. The devices may be simple mechanical counters which ensure that the correct number of parts are fed into a machine. They may be cut off switches or limit switches or float switches which provide some regulatory control of the process or operation, and thereby stopping a machine or process automatically. They may be devices which prevent a part being incorrectly fed into the machine, assembled incorrectly, fabricated incorrectly, or placed incorrectly into fixturing. In other words the assumption is made that, if the part can possibly be fed in wrongly, etc. it will be unless some preventative measure is taken. This is the essence of mistake proofing. It is usual to integrate the mistake proofing device and signal with some audible, visual display, or warning light to indicate that something has gone wrong.

QUALITY FUNCTION DEPLOYMENT (QFD)

The QFD methodology was developed in Japan at Kobe Shipyard, Mitsubishi Heavy Industries. It arose out of a need to achieve simultaneously a competitive advantage in quality, cost and delivery (QCD). All the leading companies in Japan use QFD. It is based on the philosophy that the 'voice of the customer' drives all company operations.

The technique seeks to identify those features of a product or service which satisfy the real needs and requirements of customers (market or customer required quality). This analysis also takes into account discussions with the people who actually use the product, to obtain data on issues such as:

- what they feel about existing products?
- what bothers them?
- what features should new products have?
- what is required to satisfy their needs, expectations, thinking and ideas?

It is usual to express the customers' needs in their original words and then translate these needs into the technical language of the organization. The superior performing companies are using QFD to identify product and service features (including additional features) which customers will find attractive, and help 'to charm and delight them'. In this way differentiating quality characteristics, features and/or technical advantages can be established between the organization and its competition. These requirements, features and specifications are then translated into design requirements and then deployed through each phase in the 'manufacturing' cycle to ensure that what is delivered to the customer truly reflects his/her wants or needs. It provides the mechanism to target selected areas where improvement would enhance competitive advantage.

QFD is a systematic procedure to help build-in quality in the upstream processes and in the early stages of new product development. In this way it helps to avoid problems in the downstream production and delivery processes and shortens the new product/service development time. It promotes pro-active rather than re-active development.

QFD employs a step-by-step approach from customer needs and expectations through the four planning phases of:

Product requirements — Quality Function Deployment (House of Quality) matrix

Legend:

Importance
- 1 – Minimal
- 2 – Minor
- 3 – Desirable
- 4 – Necessary
- 5 – Mandatory

Correlation
- ● Strong possibility
- ◇ Positive
- × Negative
- xx Strong negative

Relationships
- ● Strong – 6
- ○ Medium – 3
- ▲ Weak – 1

Customer satisfaction — Satisfaction
- 1 – Poor
- 2 – Fair
- 3 – Average
- 4 – Good
- 5 – Excellent

	Customer requirement	Importance rating	Turbine performance	Compressor performance	Product durability	Lube system integrity	Vibration resistance	Actuator durability	CHRA balance	Regulator calibration	Operating noise	Bearing system durability	No coking conditions	Mounting system integrity	T (7)	A (2)	B (4)	C (4)	Disadvantage
Good power	Adequate amount	3	●	●	●			●		●		○		○	3	3	3	3	
Good power	Fast response	5	○	○	●			●		○		○		◇	4	4	4	3	
Good performance	Smooth response	4	●	○	●							○		○	4	4	5	3	Y
Good performance	Low end response	4	●	●	●			●		●		○		◇	4	3	3	3	
Good performance	Low fuel usage	4	●	●				●		○				◇	3	3	3	3	
Good performance	Air/exhaust	4				●	●							●	4	4	4	4	
No leaks	Oil/water	4			●	○	○						○		2	1	2	4	Y
No leaks	Safe product	5	◇	○	●	●	●	●	○	●	○	●	●	○	3	3	3	3	
Reliable product	No breakdown	5	○	○	●		○	●	●	●	●	●	●	●	3	4	2	4	Y
Reliable product	No turbo noise	4					○					●		●	2	4	3	5	Y
Reliable product	No exhaust emissions	5					●			●				●	4	4	4	4	Y

Figure 6.7 Quality Function Deployment: House of Quality: Product Planning Stage.
Source: Allied Signal Automotive

Product requirement (Regulations x cust. need imp.)	122	120	156	69	132	156	39	129	39	102	42	121	Est. cost
Product requirement specifications	Proprietary												
Products					Performance ratings for product requirements								
A-2	3	3	3	4	3	5	1	5	5	3	3	4	360
B-4	5	3	4	4	3	3	2	3	2	5	4	3	285
C-6	3	4	3	5	5	4	4	4	4	4	3	4	345
T-7	3	4	3	4	2	3	5	3	1	4	3	4	330
T-X (improved)	5	5	4	4	5	4	5	4	5	5	4	4	270
Field repairs – quantity/1,000	1.5	1.5	4.0	1.4	0.9	3.4			2.5	5.0	4.0	2.7	
Warranty cost – cost/unit sold	0.22	0.17	0.35	0.24	0.02	0.60			0.32	0.45	0.27	9.18	
Customer rejects – quantity /1,000								2.5					
Internal quality costs/unit sold							0.10	0.05	0.50				
Product requirement importance (1,3,5)	5	5	5	3	5	5	1	5	1	3	1	5	60% Weights
Competitive disadvantage – after improvement actions				Y		Y		Y					
Quality problems (1,3,5)	3	3	5	3	3	5	1	1	5	5	5	3	20%
Technical difficulty (1,3,5)	3	3	5	3	5	5	1	3	5	5	5	1	20%
Overall product requirement importance	4	4	5	3	5	5	4	4	3	4	3	4	

Technical product evaluations

Quality history

Evaluation summary

Rating scale
1 – poor
2 – Fair
3 – Average
4 – Good
5 – Excellent

Relative rank
1 – Low
2 – Medium
3 – High

1. product planning
2. product development
3. process planning
4. production planning through to manufactured products and delivered services

In endeavouring to meet the objective of delighting the customer, conflicting issues often arise and some trade-offs are made in a logical manner.

An example of the 'house of quality' derived from the product planning phase of QFD is shown in figure 6.7. In simple terms, QFD comprises:

*   Translating customer objectives and 'wants' (termed a what) into product or service design 'hows' (i.e. the product planning and design concept – phase 1). This 'voice of the customer' is the starting point for QFD and drives the process. Comparative analysis is performed between competitive products and/or services. This helps to rate the importance of each customer want (the output from this rating process is termed 'whys'). There may be conflicts between customer 'wants' and design requirement 'hows'. The centre relationship matrix of the chart represents the relationship strength of each customer need with each of the design requirement. These conflicts are prioritized and a logical trade-off is made in terms of the addition and/or modification of product requirements. A 'how much' is established for every 'how' and target/specification values set. The design features interactions are analysed in the roof of the house as quality. Technical comparisons are made against the design requirements both from the company's existing product and also from the view point of competitive ones under investigation. This could involve some revision of the target value of the design feature.
*   Design requirements are then deployed to the next phase in the manufacturing cycle (i.e. product development and detail design – phase 2), again any conflicts are prioritized and trade-off agreed and made.
*   The analysis is continued throughout the complete process of manufacture to delivery and even after-sales (i.e. process planning and production planning – phases 3 and 4). In this way technology, restraints are identified and reliability and quality assurance control points identified.

The analysis is progressive and can be stopped at any of the four phases. However, the experience from the Japanese companies is that the greatest benefit is derived when all phases are completed. A multi-disciplinary team is used and again the usefulness of the process flow chart cannot be overstated. A number of the seven management or planning tools (e.g. relationship diagram, affinity diagram, matrix diagram and systematic diagram) are also used to assist with the QFD process .

The following are suggested readings for readers wishing to develop their knowledge of QFD: Akao (1990) and Eureka and Ryan (1988).

SEVEN QUALITY CONTROL TOOLS

It was Ishikawa who advocated the use of the seven tools of quality control: cause and effect diagram (this was created by Ishikawa); histogram; check sheets; Pareto diagram; control chart; scatter diagram; and graph. These are simple tools to be used by everyone in the organization to solve

Check item	Week no						
	Day 1	2	3	4	5	6	7
Warp board							
Board delamination							
Surface defect							
Incorrect board spec.							
Incorrect print density							
Shouldering							
Incorrect ink weight							
Off square feeding							
Print mis-registration							
Split bends							
Deep slots							
Narrow slots							
Ink smudging							

Figure 6.8 Check sheet: gluing/stitching department.
Source: Rexam Corrugated North East Ltd

problems which they encountered. His view was that these tools could solve most problems. The observations of Dale (e.g. Dale 1993) in studying Japanese organizations is that they use these tools together, in an integrated manner, to solve problems. It is also important that these simple tools are used properly before attempts are made to use more complex techniques.

Check sheets

They are a sheet or form used to record data. The check sheet is a simple recording method for determining the occurrence of events such as non-conformities, including the position in which they appear on the non-conforming item (when used in this way they are sometimes referred to as a 'measles' chart or defect position or concentration diagram or areas for concern chart). Check sheets are also used to determine the occurrence of breakdowns of machinery and/or associated equipment, non-value adding activity or, indeed, anything untoward which may occur within a process. They are prepared, in advance of the recording of data, by the operatives and staff being affected by a problem. Check sheets, in table or diagram format, are extremely useful as a data collection device and record to supplement attribute quality control charts. The data from a check sheet provide the factual basis for subsequent analysis and corrective action. There are many different kinds of check sheets, figure 6.8 is an example of a check sheet.

Tally charts and histograms

Tally charts are a descriptive presentation of data and help to identify patterns in the data. They may be used as check sheets with attribute data (pass/fail, present/absent) but are more commonly used with measured or variable data (e.g. temperature, weight, length) to establish the pattern of variation displayed, prior to the assessment of capability and computation of process capability indices. Tally charts are regarded as simple or crude frequency distribution curves.

Statisticians would tend to construct histograms rather than tally charts, but for analysis purposes they are more or less the same. A histogram is a graphical representation of individual measured values in a data set according to the frequency or relative frequency of occurrence. The histogram takes measured data from the tally sheet and displays its distribution using the class intervals or value as a base – it resembles a bar chart with

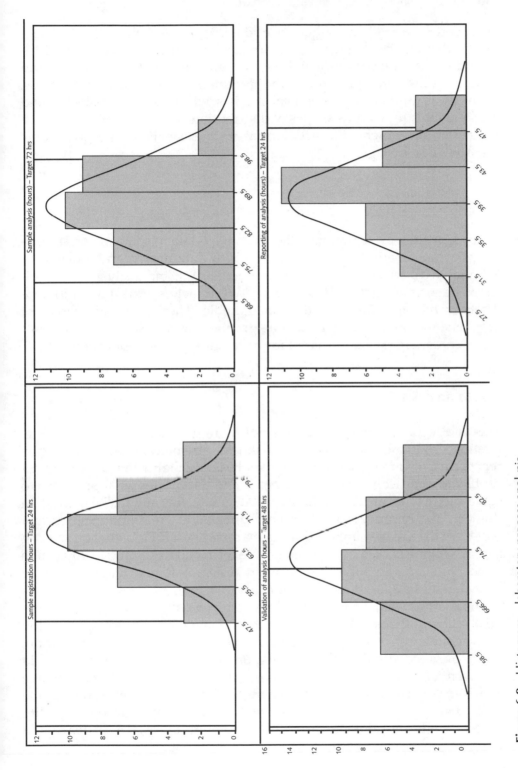

Figure 6.9 Histogram – laboratory process analysis.
Source: North West Water

the bars representing the frequency of data. The histogram helps to visualize the distribution of data. There are several forms of histogram which should be recognized – normal, skewed, bimodal, isolated island, etc. and in this way histograms can reveal the amount of variation within a process. There are a number of theoretical models which provide patterns and working tools for various shapes of distribution. The shape of distribution most often encountered is called normal or Gaussian. Figure 6.9 gives some examples of a histogram.

Graphs

Graphs, be they presentational, (i.e. to convey data in some pictorial manner), or mathematical, (i.e. ones from which data may be interpolated or extrapolated), are used to facilitate understanding and analysis of the collected data, investigate relationships between factors, attract attention, indicate trends and make the data memorable. There is a wide choice of graphical methods available (i.e. line graphs, bar charts, pie charts, Gantt charts, radar charts, band charts) for different types of application.

Pareto analysis

This is a technique employed for prioritizing problems of any type, e.g. quality, production, stock control, sickness, absenteeism, accident occurrences and resource allocation. The analysis highlights the fact that most problems come from a few of the causes and it indicates what problems to solve and in what order (e.g. Juran's (1988), 'vital few and trivial many'). In this way the improvement efforts are directed at areas and projects that will have the greatest impact. It is an extremely useful tool for condensing a large volume of data into a manageable form and in helping to determine which problems to solve and in what order. A Pareto diagram can be considered as a special form of bar chart.

The analysis was labelled 'Pareto' after a nineteenth century Italian economist Wilfredo Pareto who many years ago observed that a large proportion of the country's wealth was held by a small proportion of the population, hence the generalized term or expression, the 80/20 rule. Lorenz, early in the twentieth century, using Pareto's observations, produced a cumulative graph for demonstrating the dominance of the 20 per cent. Juran, in the 1950s, using a similar analogy observed that a large proportion of quality problems were attributable to a small number of causes, (i.e. 80 per cent of the rejections are caused by 20 per cent of the defect types).

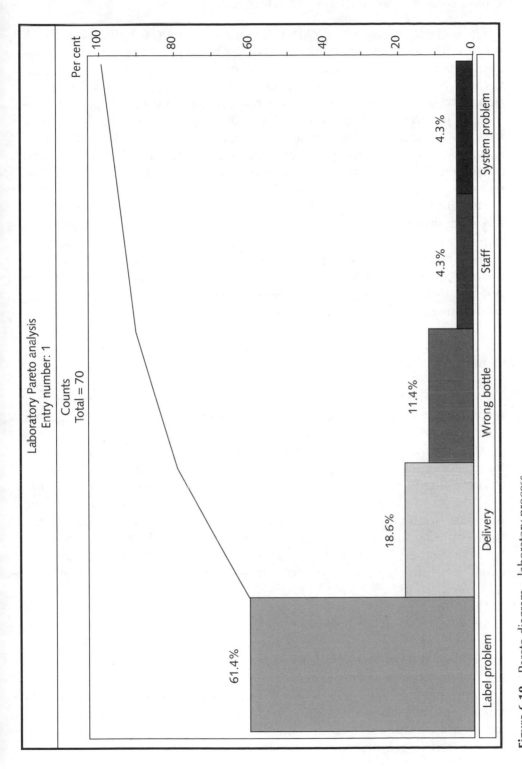

Figure 6.10 Pareto diagram – laboratory process.
Source: North West Water

The technique involves ranking the collected data, usually via a check sheet, with the most commonly occurring problem at the top and the least at the bottom. The contribution of each problem to the grand total is expressed as a percentage, and cumulative percentages are used in compounding the effect of these problems. The ranking of the problems is usually in terms of occurrence and/or cost. Just because one defect type happens more frequently than another it does not necessarily mean that it is the costliest or the one that should be tackled first. The results are often presented in two ways: (i) ranked data as a bar chart and; (ii) cumulative percentages as a graph (see figure 6.10).

Pareto analysis, although a very simple technique, is extremely powerful in presenting data by focusing attention on the major contributor(s) to a quality problem in order to generate attention, efforts, ideas and suggestions to hopefully gain a significant overall reduction in these problems. It is not a 'once and for all' analysis. If used regularly and consistently, the presentational part of the technique is extremely useful in demonstrating continuous improvement over a period of time.

Cause and effect diagrams

These were developed by the late Kaoru Ishikawa (1976) to determine and breakdown the main causes of a given problem. Cause and effect diagrams are often called Ishikawa diagrams and sometimes 'fishbone' diagrams because of their skeletal appearance. They are usually employed where there is only one problem and the possible causes are hierarchal in nature.

The effect (a specific problem or a quality characteristic/condition) is considered to be the head, and potential causes and sub-causes of the problem, or quality characteristic/condition to be the bone structure of the fish. The diagrams illustrate in a clear manner the possible relationships between some identified effect and the causes influencing it. They also assist in helping to uncover the root causes of a problem and in generating improvement ideas.

They are typically used by a Quality Control Circle, quality improvement team, Kaizen team, problem solving team, etc., as part of a brainstorming exercise to solicit ideas and opinions as to the possible major cause(s) of the problem, and subsequently to offer recommendations to resolve or counteract the problem.

It is important to clearly define the problem or abnormality, giving as much detail as possible to enable the identification of potential causes. This can be quite a difficult task, and the team leader must assume responsibility for defining a manageable problem (if it is too large it may need subdividing into a number of sub-problems) to ensure that the team's efforts and contributions are maximized in a constructive manner. There are three types of diagrams:

1. 5M cause and effect diagram

The main 'bone' structure or branches typically comprise machinery, manpower, method, material and maintenance. Often teams omit maintenance, and hence use a 4M diagram, whilst others may add a sixth M (mother nature) and so use a 6M diagram. The 4M or 5M or 6M diagram is useful for those with little experience of constructing cause and effect diagrams and is a good starting point in the event of any uncertainty. In non-manufacturing areas the 4Ps (policies, procedures, people and plant) are sometimes found to be more appropriate. As with any type of cause and effect diagram, the exact format is not so important as the process of bringing about appropriate countermeasures for the identified and agreed major cause(s) for the problem.

2. Process cause and effect diagram

The team members should be familiar with the process under consideration, therefore, it is usual to map it out using a flow chart and seek to identify potential causes for the problem at each stage of the process. If the process flow is so large as to be unmanageable, the sub-processes or process steps should be separately identified. Each stage of the process is then brainstormed and ideas developed using, for example a 4M/5M or 6M format. The key causes are identified for further analysis.

3. Dispersion analysis cause and effect diagram

This diagram is usually used after a 4M/5M/6M diagram has been completed. The major causes identified by the group are then treated as separate branches and expanded upon by the team.

Figure 6.11 shows an example of a cause and effect diagram.

Scatter diagrams and regression analysis (including correlation)

Scatter diagrams or scatter plots are used when examining the possible relationship or association between two variables, characteristics or factors, they indicate the relationship as a pattern – cause and effect. For

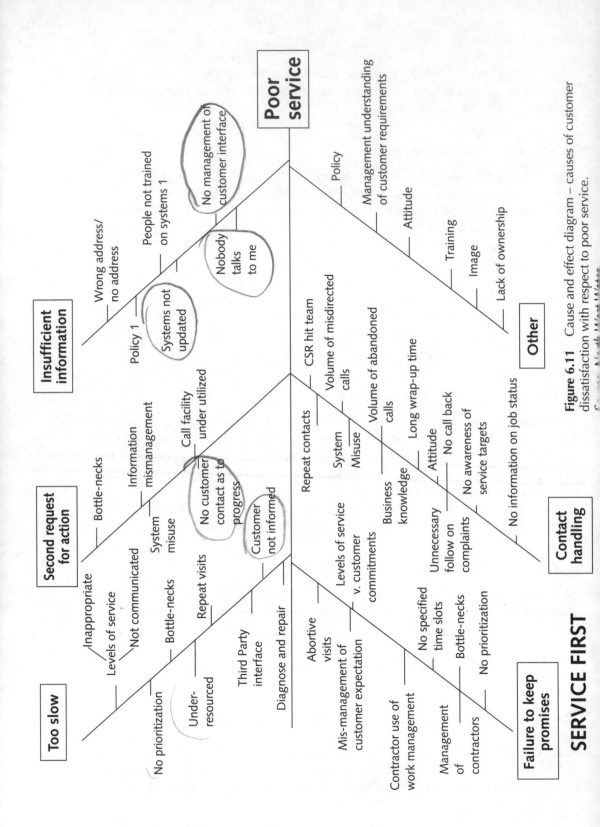

Figure 6.11 Cause and effect diagram – causes of customer dissatisfaction with respect to poor service.

Source: North West Water

example, one variable may be a process parameter (e.g. temperature, pressure, screw speed), and the other may be some measurable characteristic or feature of the product (e.g. length, weight, thickness). As the process parameter is changed (independent variable), it is noted together with any measured change in the product variable (dependent variable), and this is repeated until sufficient data have been collected. The results when plotted on a graph will give what is called a scatter graph, scatter plot or scatter diagram. Variables that are associated will show a linear pattern and those that are unrelated will portray a random pattern.

Analysis should concern itself with the dispersion of the plots and identifying if some linear, or known non-linear, relationship exists between the two variables. In this way the scatter diagram is a valuable tool for diagnosis and problem solving. Regression analysis would subsequently be used to establish not only lines of 'best fit', but provide the basis for making estimates or predictions of, say, the product variable for a given value of the process parameter. In this way, it is possible to reduce the amount of data which are measured, collected, plotted and analysed.

How valid or reliable such estimates are, is largely a function of the degree of correlation which exists between the two variables (if indeed only two variables are under consideration), and whether the estimates are interpolated (i.e. from within the range of collected data) or extrapolated (i.e. outside that range). Where there are more than two variables, multivariate regression analysis should be used, but a good background of statistical knowledge is required to undertake this analysis.

CONTROL CHARTS

This is dealt with in the section on statistical process control.

SEVEN MANAGEMENT OR PLANNING TOOLS

These tools sometimes termed the 'seven new tools' of quality control were developed by the Japanese to collect and analyse non-qualitative and verbal data, in particular, from sales and marketing, and design and development activities. Most of the tools have seen previous use in other than Total Quality Management applications: e.g. value engineering and value analysis, critical path analysis, Programme Evaluation and Review Technique (PERT), organizational analysis. The choice of the term 'new' is unfortunate. In Japanese companies, these seven tools are typically used by Quality Control Circles in sales and design areas and in Quality Function

Deployment. It is usual to find some of the tools used together (esystematic diagram being produced from the data contained in an affinity diagram). A full description of these tools is outside the scope of this chapter. However, they are covered in detail by Mizuno (1988), Ozeki and Asaka (1990) and Barker (1989). In brief, the tools are:

1. Relations diagram method

These are relationship diagraphs or linkage diagrams used to identify, understand and clarify complex cause and effect relationships, to find the causes and solutions to a problem and to determine the key factors in the situation under study. They are also employed to identify the key issues to some desired result. Relations diagrams are used when the causes are non-hierarchic and when there are multiple interrelated problems. They allow the problem to be analysed from a wide perspective as a specific framework is not employed. Relations diagrams can be considered to be a more free and broader version of a cause and effect diagram, see figure 6.12.

2. Affinity diagram method

This is the KJ (Kawakita Jiro) method used to categorize verbal data about previous unexplored issues, problems and themes which are hazy and difficult to understand, helping to create order out of chaos. This diagram uses the natural affinity between opinions and partial data from a variety of situations to help understand and structure the problem. It helps, perhaps in a less logical manner than the relations diagram, to organize data and ideas for decision making and reach solutions about previously unresolved problems, see figure 6.13.

3. Systematic diagram method

This is a tree diagram used to examine, in a systematic manner, the most appropriate and effective means of planning to accomplish a task or solving a problem. Events are represented in the form of a root and branch relationship. It is used when the causes that influence the problem are known, but a plan and method for resolving the problem have not been developed. A systematic diagram is usually used to evaluate several different methods and plans for solving a problem, see figure 6.14.

4. Matrix diagram method

This is used to clarify the relationship between results and causes or be-

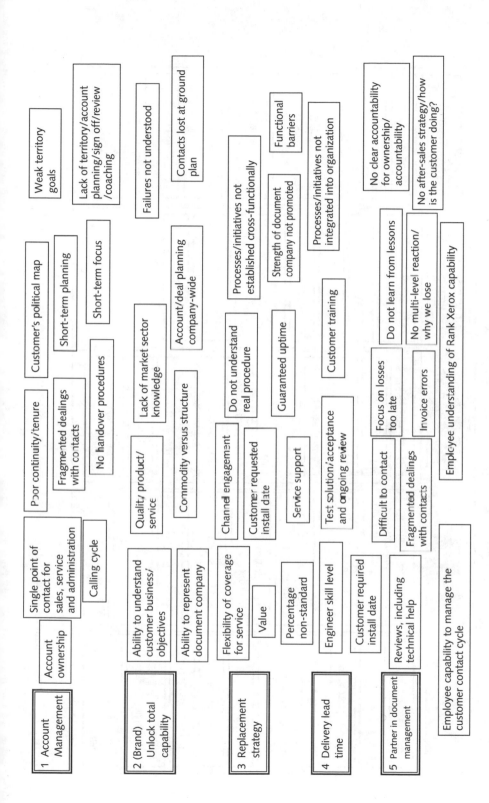

Figure 6.12 Relations diagram: linking issues and ideas from the affinity diagram relating to managing the customer contact cycle.
Source: Rank Xerox

What are the issues involved in losing customers?

1 Contact	2 Needs	3 Negotiation	4 Implement	5 Support
Account ownership	Ability to represent document company/do not unlock total capability	Replacement strategy	Test solution/ acceptance	Difficult to contact
Calling cycle	Quality service Produce	Service support	Engineer skill level	No single point of contact
Handover procedures	Strength of document company brand not promoted	Delivery lead time	Quality service	Invoice/order errors
Point of contact	Lack of market sector knowledge	Functional barriers	Customer training	Focus on losses too late
Ability to represent document company	Lack of integrated team approach	Account/deal, planning company-wide	Lack of reviews including technical support	Fragmented dealings with contacts
Team approach	Weak territory goals	No multi-level reaction	Customer required install date	No multi-level reaction
Short-term planning	Lack of territory/ account planning	Team approach	After-sales strategy	Do not learn from lessons
Fragmented dealings	Short-term planning	Flexibility of coverage for service		Continuity of account management
Reviews including technical help		Guaranteed uptime		
Poor continuity/ tenure		Percentage non-standard		

Figure 6.13 Affinity diagram: grouping of causals against the customer contact cycle evaluation model.
Source: Rank Xerox UK

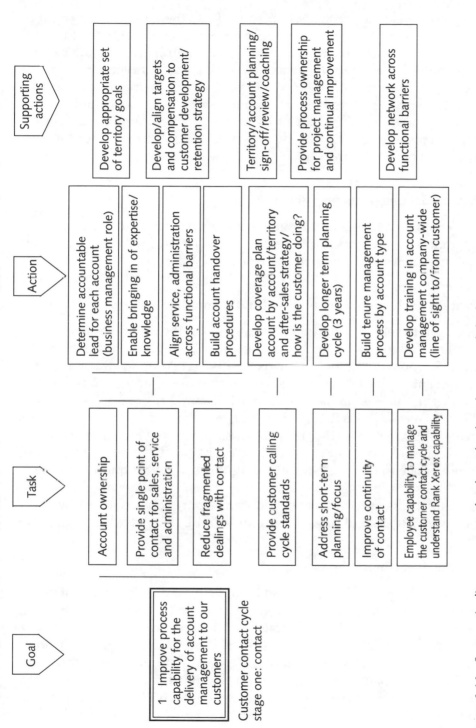

Figure 6.14 Systematic diagram: range of paths and tasks to be accomplished to manage customer retention.
Source: Rank Xerox

tween objectives and methods and to indicate their relative importance. These factors are arranged in rows and columns on a chart with the intersections identifying the problem and its concentration. The intersecting points are the base for future action. By seeing the complete problem and its essential characteristics this is of considerable help in developing a strategy for solving it. Symbols are used to depict the presence and strength of a relationship between sets of data. There are a number of types of matrix diagrams (e.g. L-type, T-type, Y-type), each having a specific range of applications, see figure 6.15.

5. Matrix data analysis method

This method is used to quantify and arrange the data presented in a matrix diagram in a clear manner. It is a numerical analysis method and employs techniques such as multivariate analysis.

6. Process decision program chart (PDPC) method

This is used to select the best processes to obtain the desired outcome from a problem statement by evaluating all possible events and conceivable outcomes. Considering the system as a whole it is used to anticipate unexpected events and develop plans, countermeasures and actions for such outcomes. In this it is similar to Failure Mode and Effects Analysis (FMEA) and Fault Tree Analysis (FTA). However, it is claimed to be more dynamic than these two methods since the relationship between the initiating condition/event and terminating condition/event has been thought out and mapped. It is based on a systematic diagram and uses a questioning technique, for example asking 'What could go wrong?', 'What are the alternatives?' and the listing of actions or countermeasures accordingly. The PDPC has no prescribed set of rules. An example of PDPC is given in figure 6.16.

7. Arrow diagram method

This is used to establish the most suitable plan for a series of activities in a project, and to monitor its progress in an efficient manner. The sequence of the steps involved and their relations to each other are indicated by arrows and in this way a network is developed. This method, its form of construction, calculations and identification of critical path are well known and used in project management in relation to critical path analysis and programme evaluation and review techniques. Figure 6.17 is an example of an arrow diagram.

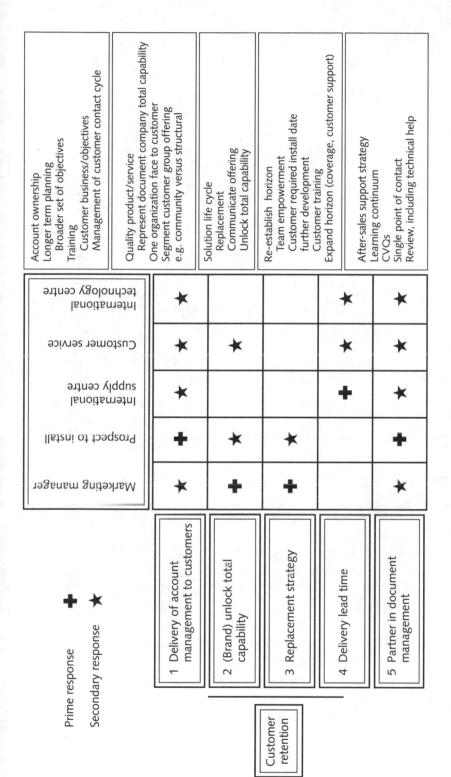

Figure 6.15 Matrix diagram: to show relationship and strength of influence and deploy definable and assignable tasks to the organization.
Source: Rank Xerox UK

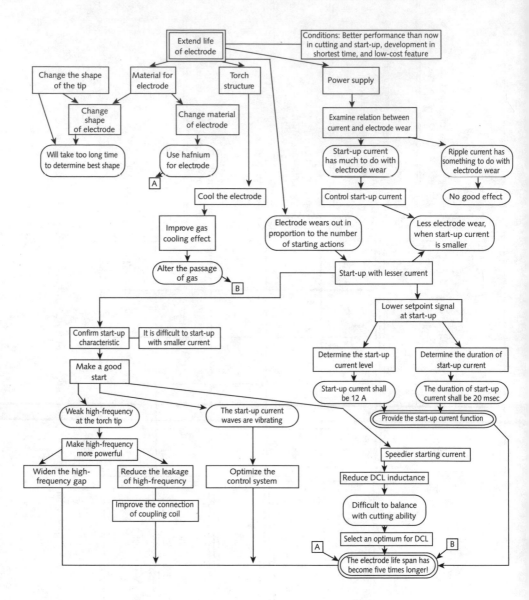

Figure 6.16 The PDPC method: bottleneck engineering problem.
Source: Courtesy of the Daihen Corporation

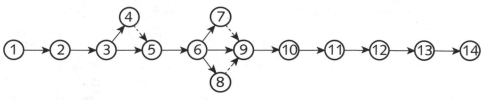

Notes

Activities
- 1–2   Choose locations
- 2–3   Assign responsibilities
- 3–4   Determine size and configuration of displays needed
- 3–5   Consider health and safety implications of potential locations
- 5–6   Establish public relations departments' stock of displays and their availability
- 6–7   Determine method of display (free-standing/wall-mounted)
- 6–8   Determined preferred 'editorial content' of displays
- 6–9   Action update of display contents
- 7–9   Obtain costings for additional/alternative displays
- 9–10 Source initial display items (e.g. graphs, photographs, successes)
- 10–11 Agree format and action the 'design a logo' competition
- 11–12 Arrange for displays to be sited/mounted
- 12–13 Review cost implications
- 13–14 Seek verbal feedback from site employees

Figure 6.17   Arrow diagram: siting of a quality notice board.
Source: Betz Dearborn

STATISTICAL PROCESS CONTROL

Statistical Process Control (SPC) is generally accepted to mean management of the process through the use of statistical methods. Its four main uses are to:

- achieve process stability
- provide guidance on how the process may be improved by the reduction of variation
- assess the performance of a process and identify changes
- provide information to assist with management decision making

SPC is about control, capability and improvement, but only if used correctly and in an environment which is conducive to the pursuit of continuous improvement. It is the responsibility of the senior management team to create these conditions. SPC supports the philosophy that products and services can always be improved upon. However, on its own, SPC will not solve problems. A control chart only records the 'voice of the process' and SPC may, at a basic level, simply confirm the presence of a problem. There are many quality management tools and techniques which support and encourage quality improvement and, in many instances, they should be used both prior to and concurrently with SPC to facilitate analysis and improvement. It is basically a measurement technique and it is only when a mechanism is in place to remove and reduce 'special' and 'common' causes of variation that an organization will be using SPC to its fullest potential.

The first step in the use of SPC is to collect data to a plan and plot the gathered data on a graph called a control chart. The control chart is a picture of what is happening in the process at a particular point in time, it is a line graph. The data to be plotted can be in variable or attribute format. Figure 6.18 shows a typical control chart. Variable data are the result of using some form of measuring system. It is essential to ensure the capability of the measuring system to minimize the potential source of errors which may arise in the data. The measurements may refer to product characteristics, (e.g. length) or to process parameters, (e.g. temperature). Attribute data are the result of an assessment using go/no-go gauges or pass/fail criteria. It is important to minimize subjectivity when using this pass/fail type of assessment. Reference standards, photographs, or illustrations may help and, where possible, the accept/reject characteristics should be agreed with the customer.

The objective of data collection is to get a good overall 'picture' of how a process performs. A data-gathering plan needs to be developed for collection, recording and the plotting of data on the control chart. The data collected should accurately reflect the performance of the process. The factors to be considered are:

- whether the data are to be collected as variables or attributes
- the sample or sub-group size
- the frequency of collection
- the number of sub-groups to be taken
- sampling risks – the risk of a sample indicating that a process is out of control when it is not, and, on the other hand, the risk that the sample fails to detect that a process is out of control
- costs – the cost of taking the sample, the cost of investigation and correction of special causes, and the cost of non-conforming output

Different data gathering plans may give different pictures of a process and there are many economic models of control charts. However, consideration of statistical criteria and practical experience, has led to the

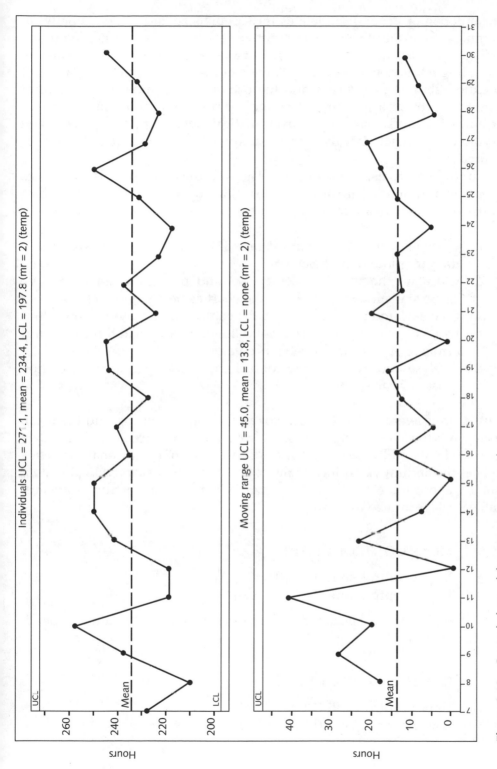

Figure 6.18 Control chart – laboratory process cycle time.
Source: North West Water

formulation of general guidelines for sample size and intervals between samples. For example, in the automotive-related industry it has led to the widespread acceptance (for variables) of a sample size of five, a one-hourly sampling frequency, the taking of between 20 and 30 sub-groups as a test for the stability of a process, and the use of three standard error control limits. To obtain a meaningful picture of process performance from attributes data, and to ensure that the statistical theory supporting the design of the control chart is valid, larger samples (i.e. greater than 25) are required.

Control charts using mean and range are the most popular variables charts in use and they are now used to outline the methods of control chart construction. There are four major steps:

1. Calculate each sub-group average ($\bar{x}$) and range value (R). These data are plotted on the chart.
2. Calculate the process average ($\bar{\bar{X}}$) and process mean range ($\bar{R}$). These statistics are plotted on the chart as heavy broken lines.
3. Calculate and plot on the chart the control limits. These control limits are drawn on the chart as solid lines and are set at three standard errors or $A_2 \bar{R}$ from the reference value.
4. Analyse and interpret the control charts for special and common causes of variation.

The process average $\bar{\bar{X}}$ is the mean of all the sample means, and the mean range, $\bar{R}$ is the average of all the sample ranges. These are used to calculate control limits and are drawn on the chart as a guide for analysis. They reflect the natural variability of the process and are calculated using constants, appropriate to the sample size, which are taken from statistical tables. The formulae used are:

MEAN CONTROL CHART:

Upper control limit (UCL$\bar{x}$) = $\bar{\bar{X}} + A_2\bar{R}$
Lower control limit (LCL$\bar{x}$) = $\bar{\bar{X}} - A_2\bar{R}$

where A_2 is a constant derived from statistical tables and is dependent upon the sample size.

RANGE CONTROL CHART:

Upper control limit (UCL$_R$) = $D_4\bar{R}$
Lower control limit (LCL$_R$) = $D_3\bar{R}$

where D_4 and D_3 are constants derived from statistical tables and are dependent upon the sample size.

The range and mean charts are analysed separately, but the patterns of variation occurring in the two charts are compared with each other to assist in identifying special causes which may be affecting the process. The range chart monitors uniformity and the mean chart focuses on where the process is centred.

Special causes of variation influence some or all the measurements in different ways. They occur intermittently and reveal themselves as unusual patterns of variation on a control chart. They should be identified and rectified, and with improved process and/or product design, their occurrence should in the long term be minimized. Special causes of variation include:

- a change in raw material
- a change in machine setting
- a broken tool or die or pattern
- failure to clean equipment
- equipment malfunction
- keying in incorrect data

Indications of special causes are:

- A data point falling outside the control limits.
- A run of points in a particular direction, consistently increasing or decreasing. In general, seven consecutive points are used as the guide.
- A run of points all on one side of the reference value $\bar{\bar{X}}$ or $\bar{R}$. In general, seven consecutive points are used as the guide.
- If substantially more or less than two-thirds of the points plotted lie within the mid-third section of the chart. This might indicate that the control limits or plot points have been miscalculated or misplotted, or that data have been edited in some way, or that process or the sampling method are stratified.
- Any other obvious non-random patterns.

Common causes influence all measurements in the same way. They produce the natural pattern of variation observed in data when they are free of special causes. Common causes arise from many sources and do not reveal themselves as unique patterns of deviation. Consequently they are often difficult to identify. If only common cause variation is present the process is considered to be stable, hence predictable. Typical common causes include:

- badly maintained machines
- poor lighting
- poor workstation layout
- poor instructions
- poor supervision
- materials and equipment not suited to the requirements

An argument in favour of inspection by attributes is that it is not such a time consuming task as that for variables, so the sample size can be much larger. It is also less costly to undertake. Experience shows that attribute data often exist in a variety of forms in an organization, although it may not be necessarily analysed statistically. There is a variety of charts which can be used to organize attribute data in order to assist with process control. The choice of chart is dependent on whether the sample size is kept constant and whether the inspection criterion is a non-conforming item or a non-conformity within an item. The main types of attributes chart for non-conforming items are proportion/percentage (p) and number defective (np) charts; while for non-conformities they are proportion (u) and number (c) charts.

The collection and organizing of data is almost identical to that described for variables, except that for each sample, the number (or proportion or percentage) of non-conforming items or non-conformities are recorded and plotted. The reference value on attribute charts is the process average. The control limits are again three standard errors from the process average.

Process capability

Because it is easier to understand, the capability of processes using attribute data is discussed first.

With the np chart (number of non-conforming items), it is usual to express the average number of acceptable items per sample as a percentage to quantify capability:

i.e. $\dfrac{(1 - n\bar{p})}{n} \times 100\%$

With the p chart, it is simply the average proportion of acceptable items expressed as a percentage:

i.e. $(1 - \bar{p}) \times 100\%$

With measured data, the use of indices such as C_{pk} and C_p has been in increasing use. The capability of a process is defined as three standard deviations on either side of the process average when the process is normally distributed. The C_p index is found as the result of comparing the perceived spread of the process with the specification width or tolerance band.

$$C_p = \frac{\text{Total specified tolerance}}{\text{Process spread}}$$

As the C_p index compares the 'spread of the process' with the tolerance band, it is primarily concerned with precision. It is for this reason that C_p is often defined as 'process potential'.

The C_{pk} index takes into account both accuracy and precision by incorporating them into the calculations. Because it assesses both accuracy and precision, they are often defined as 'process capability' measures. There are two formulae:

$$C_{pk} = \frac{USL - \bar{\bar{X}}}{3 \text{ standard deviations}}$$

where USL is the upper specification limit and $\bar{\bar{X}}$ is the process average

$$\text{or } C_{pk} = \frac{\bar{\bar{X}} - LSL}{3 \text{ standard deviations}}$$

where LSL is the lower specification limit.

It is customary to quote the smaller of the two values, giving the more critical part of the measurements distribution.

The comments made on capability relate to data collected over a long term from a stable, in-control and predictable process. Often short-term capability needs to be investigated, particularly for new products or processes and as part of a supplier verification programme. In this case the time scale is then reduced to cover only a few hours run of the process. The data are collected in the same manner as for initial control chart study, but the frequency of sampling is increased to get as many samples (of size n) as possible to give a good picture of the process (i.e. about 20 samples of size n). Data are plotted on the control chart with appropriate limits, but the following indices are calculated:

P_p = preliminary process potential
P_{pk} = preliminary process capability

The formulae is exactly as for C_p and C_{pk} but the minimum requirements may be higher.

All capability indices are estimates derived from estimates of the process variation. The reliability or confidence in the estimate of the process standard deviation is a function of:

- the amount of data which have been collected
- the manner in which the data were collected
- the capability of the measuring system, (i.e. its accuracy and precision)
- the skill of the people using the measuring system
- people's knowledge and understanding of statistics

Further details on SPC are provided by Montgomery (1996), Oakland (1996) Owen (1989), and Price (1984).

SUMMARY

To support and develop a process of continuous improvement an organization needs to use a selection of tools and techniques. It is wise to start with the more simple tools and techniques such as the seven quality control tools and to ensure that the tools and techniques which are currently employed are used effectively before attempts are made to introduce other tools.

A planned approach for the application of tools and techniques is necessary. The temptation to single out one tool or technique for special attention should be resisted and to get maximum benefit from the use of tools and techniques they should be used in combination. It should be recognized that tools and techniques play different roles and management and staff should be fully aware of the main purpose and use of the tools and techniques they are considering applying in the organization. If they are not fully aware of the main purpose and use they could well be disappointed if the tools or technique fails to live up to their expectations. It is also important to understand the limitations of how and when tools and techniques can best be used.

The tools and techniques should be used to facilitate improvement and be integrated into the way the business works rather than being used and viewed as 'bolt-on' techniques. The way the tool or technique is applied and how its results are interpreted are critical to its successful use. A tool or technique is only as good as the person who is using it.

Tools and techniques on their own are not enough, they need an environment and technology which is conducive to improvement and to their use. An organization's CEO and senior managers have a key role to play in the effective use of tools and techniques. They should, for example:

- develop their knowledge of the tools and, when appropriate, use them in their day-to-day activities and decision making
- delegate responsibility for their promotion to suitable individuals
- maintain an active interest in the use of tools and the results
- endorse expenditure arising from the education and training required and the improvement activities resulting from the employment of tools
- recognize and reward those employees who utilize tools and techniques in their day-to-day work activities

REFERENCES

Akao Y. 1990: *Quality Function Deployment: Integrating Customer Requirements into Product Design*, Productivity Press, Cambridge, Massachusetts.

Barker R. L. 1989: 'The Seven New Q.C. Tools', *Proceedings of the First Conference on Tools and Techniques for TQM*, IFS Conferences, Bedford, 95–120.

Bendell A., Wilson G. and Millar R. M. G. 1990: *Taguchi: Methodology Within Total Quality*, IFS Publications, Bedford.

Camp R. C. 1989: *Benchmarking: the Search for Industry Best Practices that Lead to Superior Performance*, ASQC Quality Press, Milwaukee.

Currie R. M. 1989: *Work Study*, Pitman, London.

Dale B. G. 1993: 'The Key Features of Japanese Total Quality Control', *Quality and Reliability Engineering International*, 9 (3), 169–78.

Eureka W. E. and Ryan E. 1988: *The Customer Driven Company: Managerial Perspectives on QFD*, American Supplier Institute, Michigan.

Ishikawa K. 1976: *Guide to Quality Control*, Asian Productivity Organisation, Tokyo.

Juran J. M. 1988: *Quality Control Handbook*, (Fourth Edition), McGraw Hill, New York.

Lewis L. 1984: *Quality Improvement Handbook*, IBM, Hants.

Lochnar R. H. and Matar J. E. 1990: *Designing for Quality*, Chapman and Hall, London.

Mizuno S. 1988: *Management for Quality Improvement; the Seven New Q.C. Tools*, Productivity Press, Massachusetts.

Montgomery D. C. 1996: *Introduction to Quality Control*, (Third Edition),

John Wiley, New York.

Oakland J. S. 1996: *Statistical Process Control: a Really Practical Guide,* (Third Edition), Heinemann, London.

Owen M. 1989: *SPC and Continuous Improvement,* IFS Ltd, Bedfordshire.

Ozeki K. and Asaka T. 1990: *Handbook of Quality Tools,* Productivity Press, Cambridge, Massachusetts.

Plackett R. L. and Burman J. P. 1946: 'The Design of Optimum Multi-factorial Experiments', *Biometrika,* 33 1, 305–25.

Price F. 1984: *Right First Time,* Gower Press, Hants.

Shingo S. 1986: *Zero Quality Control: Source Inspection and the Poka Yoke System,* Productivity Press, Cambridge, Massachusetts.

Taguchi G. 1986: *Introduction to Quality Engineering,* Asian Productivity Organisation, Tokyo.

Zairi M. 1996: *Effective Benchmarking: Learning from the Best,* Chapman and Hall, London.

7

Teams and teamwork

INTRODUCTION

The development of people and their involvement in improvement activities both individually and through teamwork is a key feature in a company's approach to TQM. There are a number of different types of teams with different operating characteristics, all of which can act as a vehicle for getting people involved in improvement activities. Some teams have a narrow focus, with members coming from one functional area, whereas others are wider and cross-functional dealing with the deep-rooted problems between internal customers and suppliers. The names given to the teams are varied and include, Quality Circles, Yield Improvement Teams, Quality Improvement Teams, Continuous Improvement Teams, Problem Elimination Teams, Self-Directed Work Teams, Process Improvement Groups, Task Groups, SPC Teams, Error Cause Removal Teams, Corrective Action Teams, Kaizen Teams and Cross-Functional Teams, in areas such as design, quality assurance, costs, standardization, delivery and supply. There are also groups of people already working together with colleagues and customers and suppliers, who are also committed to making improvements and form hybrids between two or more types of teams.

Japanese companies and their people are much more comfortable with the use of teams as part of their continuous improvement efforts than is usually the case in European companies. This may be because of the divisive nature of Western industry with 'them and us', 'management and unions', 'staff and hourly paid', 'headquarters and operating locations', etc. It is often the case in European organizations that management will decide to launch some form of team activity as part of an improvement initiative, put the members together and expect the team to work in an effective manner without any form of training, coaching, direction, management attention, counselling or teambuilding. In such circumstances it is little wonder that the team starts to flounder within a few months of its inception.

This chapter, which is based on the UMIST research on teams (e.g. Dale and Lees 1986, Manson and Dale 1989, Briggs et al. 1993, Boaden et al. 1991 and Dale and Huke 1996) and practical experience of working with teams in many different types of organization, examines the role of teamwork in a process of continuous improvement and outlines the operating characteristics of project teams, quality circles and quality improvement teams. The key constituents of teams in terms of sponsor, facilitator, leader and member are outlined. A method for evaluating the health of teams is described. Some guidelines are also given which should help to ensure that teams are both active and effective.

THE ROLE OF TEAMS IN CONTINUOUS IMPROVEMENT

Teams have a number of roles to play as a component in a process of continuous improvement. Teams can:

- aid the commitment of people to the principles of TQM
- provide an additional means of communication between individuals, management and their direct reports, across functions and with customers and suppliers
- provide the means and opportunity for people to participate in decision making about how the business operates
- improve relationships, develop trust and facilitate co-operative activity
- help to develop people and encourage leadership traits
- build collective responsibility and develop a sense of ownership
- aid personal development and build confidence
- develop problem solving skills
- facilitate awareness of improvement potential, leading to behaviour and attitude change
- help to facilitate a change in management style and culture
- solve problems
- imbue a sense of accomplishment
- improve the adoption of new products to the production line
- improve morale
- improve operating effectiveness as people work in a common direction through interaction and synergy

The American Society for Quality Control (ASQC) commissioned the Gallup Organisation to assess employee attitudes on teamwork, empowerment and quality improvement. The survey of 1,293 adults focused on a variety of topics: including, extent of participation in quality teams, employee feelings of empowerment, and effects of technology and teamwork on empowerment. The report (Gallup Organisation 1993) shows a high level of employee participation in improvement-related teamwork and there was considerable evidence which pointed to the positive effects of quality and teamwork on employee empowerment. It was also found that employees are very clear on the purpose of quality-related teamwork, under its multitude of names and that those employees participating in such teamwork are also more likely to receive training than those who do not participate.

TYPES OF TEAMS

In the superior performing organization teamwork is second nature. For example, the senior management work together as an effective team, managers of the various operating and functional units act as a team, people from different functions co-operate in the team activities which are needed in FMEA, SPC, simultaneous engineering, benchmarking, supplier development, ISO 9000 quality management series registration and internal audits. In addition to teamwork within functions it is common to find teams working together across the business. In some cases (e.g. Crosby methodology 1979) teams are hierarchal in nature – a corrective action team is formed on a directive from a quality improvement team. Unless effective teamworking and cohesion is seen at the top of an organization, it is unlikely that the managers will be able to encourage their employees to work effectively in teams. The superior performing organizations use a variety of ways to facilitate teambuilding, improve relationships and reinforce the teamwork ethic. For example Dale and Huke (1996) writing about their experiences in Hong Kong give examples such as carnivals, team competitions, social and recreational activities, and entry into the dragon boat race competition.

There are a variety of types of teams with differing characteristics in terms of: membership, mode of participation, autonomy, problem selection, scope of activity, decision making authority, access to information, problem solving potential, resources and permanency which can be used in the continuous improvement process. It is important that the right type of team is formed for the project, problem, activity under consideration and a working definition of the team is decided upon. The following four types of teams are amongst the most popular.

Project teams

As discussed in chapter 3 (in section called 'Why senior executives should become involved in TQM) the drive to improve originates at the top of an organization. If senior management identify the main problems facing the organization, key improvement issues can be developed which are then allocated amongst their membership for consideration as a one-off project. The project owner then selects employees to constitute a team which will consider the improvement issue. The owner can either lead the team personally or act as 'foster parent', 'sponsor' or 'guardian angel' to the team. Through participation in project teams, managers better understand the problem solving process and become more sensitive to the problems faced by other types of teams. The senior management project team is one example of this type of team, but there are others. The typical characteristics of such teams are:

- the objective has been defined by senior management
- the team is led by management
- it is temporary in nature
- the project is specific and significant, perhaps addressing issues of strategic change and will have clear deliverables within a set time scale
- the team is organized in such a way to ensure it employs the appropriate talents, skills, and functions which are suitable in resolution of the project
- the scope of activity tends to be cross-functional
- participation is not usually voluntary – a person is requested by senior management to join the team and this is done on the basis of their expertise for the project being tackled
- team meetings tend to be of long rather than of short duration, although they occur on a regular basis

Quality Circles

Quality Circles (QCs), when operated in the classical manner, have characteristics which are different from other methods of teamwork. They have been the subject of many books (e.g. Hutchins 1985, Mohr and Mohr 1983 and Robson 1984) and the focus of much research (e.g. Bradley and Hill 1983, Hayward et al. 1985 and Hill 1986) almost to the exclusion of research on other types of team activity. However, QCs, in the classical sense, have not been too 'successful' in Western organizations. The UMIST research (e.g. Hayward et al. 1985) indicates that this is because they were introduced at a time in the West when organizations did not fully understand the principles and practices of TQM. A vast amount of experience was however acquired in the operation of QCs, much of which has been well documented. It is suggested that any organization wishing to develop effective teamwork and resolve some of the issues which arise in the operation of teams should consult the written wisdom on QCs. There they will find many clues on facilitation, problem solving skills, organization of meetings and maintaining the momentum.

A Quality Circle is a voluntary group of between six to eight employees from the same work area. They meet usually in company time, for one hour every week or fortnight, under the leadership of their work supervisor, to solve problems relating to improving their work activities and environment.

The typical characteristics of Quality Circles are:

- Membership is voluntary and people can opt out as and when they wish.
- Members are usually drawn from a single department and are doing similar work.
- All members are of equal status.
- They operate within the existing organizational structure.
- Members are free to select, from their own work area, the problems and projects which they wish to tackle – these tend to be the ones they have to live with every day; there is little or no interference from management.
- The QC members are trained in the use of the seven basic quality control tools, meeting skills, facilitation, teambuilding, project management and presentation techniques, etc.
- Appropriate data collection, problem solving skills and decision making methods are employed by QC members to the project under consideration.
- Meetings are generally of short duration, but a large number are held.
- There is minimum pressure to solve the problem within a set time frame.
- A facilitator is available to assist the QC with the project.
- The solutions are evaluated in terms of their cost-effectiveness.
- The findings, solutions and recommendations of the QC are shown to management for comment and approval, usually in a formal presentation.

- The QC implements management's recommendations, where practicable.
- Once implemented, the QC monitors the effects of the solution and considers future improvements.
- The QC carries out a critical review of all its activities related to the completed project.

Fabi (1992) has carried out a wide ranging analysis and review of the literature published between 1982 and 1989 on QCs and from this has analysed 40 empirical studies undertaken on QCs. From examination of this work, using contingency factors, he has identified the following factors which are critical to the success of QCs:

- management commitment and support
- involvement and support of employees and unions
- training of members and leaders
- organizational and financial stability
- personal characteristics of the facilitator
- individual characteristics of members
- external and organizational environments
- organization readiness and implementation

There have been a number of derivatives of QCs resulting in teams operating under a variety of names but with very similar characteristics to QCs.

Quality improvement teams

Teams of this type can comprise members of a single department, be cross-functional, and include representatives of either or both customers and suppliers. The objectives of such teams range across various topics but fall under the general headings of: improve quality; eliminate waste and non-value-added activity; and improve productivity.

The characteristics of quality improvement teams are more varied than any other type of team activity but typically include:

- Membership can be voluntary or mandatory and can comprise of line workers, staff or a mixture of both. Some teams involve a complete range of personnel from different levels in the organizational hierarchy.
- Projects can arise as a result of: a management initiative, a need to undertake some form of corrective action, a high incidence of

defects, supplier/customer problems and an opportunity for improvement. It is usual to agree the project brief with management.
- The team is usually formed to meet a specific objective.
- In the first place, the team leader will have been appointed by management and briefed regarding objectives and timescales.
- The team is more permanent than project teams but less so than QCs. In some cases teams disband after a project, in others they continue.
- Members are usually experienced personnel and well versed in problem solving skills and methods.
- The team is self contained and can take whatever action is required to resolve the problem and improve the process.
- The assistance of a facilitator is sometimes required to provide advice on problem solving, use of specific tools and techniques and keeping the team activity on course. In most cases a facilitator is assigned to a number of teams.

At Chesterfield Cylinders (a manufacturer of steel cylinders who are owned by United Engineering Forgings) the procedure and responsibilities for setting up a Quality Improvement Team is as follows:

- The Total Quality Steering Group (TQSG) agrees the project for the team.
- The TQSG appoints one of its members to act as mentor for that team.
- The TQSG discusses possible candidates for team leader. The mentor then approaches the proposed team leader and invites him to lead the project.
- The mentor clearly identifies the problem to be addressed with the team leader.
- The mentor and the team leader agree the team.

From this point, the mentor's role is as follows:

- To guide the team leader when required.
- To monitor the team progress and ensure that the team is addressing the identified and agreed project.
- To give support to the team leader when problems arise that cannot be resolved by the team leader.
- To introduce outside expertise when required.
- To report back to the Steering Group on team progress.

High-performance teams

Many companies are discovering what may be the productivity break-through of the 1990s. Call the team a self-managed work group, a cross-functional team or a high-performance work team. To quote Corning Chief Executive Officer Jamie Horton, whose company has 3,000 teams, 'If you really believe in quality, when you cut through everything it's empowering your people, and it's empowering your people that leads to teams'

Teamwork can be working with your colleagues or it can be working with your customers and suppliers. This is not about working harder and longer to achieve improved results, but about obtaining those results by improving the way in which we work or by finding new ways to work. Essentially high-performance teams focus on the customer and whether the customer is internal or external. Performance is about satisfying or exceeding expectations. Importantly the key to productivity is how effectively, efficiently and economically this can be done. Management and organizational support are essential:

Management support   Teams cannot reach their full potential unless management is prepared to commit to nurturing and supporting team and individual development. This is not about abdicating power. It is about releasing authority and accountability and gradually developing the team into competency. Management style and leadership needs to change to create an environment of openness and trust, providing direction when needed. Managers need to act as facilitators to work groups, coaching and developing, setting boundaries and recognizing and rewarding team efforts. They need to encourage empowerment and allow the teams freedom to fail. The teams need to learn from each failure to improve performance through self-inspection. The teams take ownership of goals, are accountable for decisions, assign roles and are results- and team-orientated.

Organizational support   High-Performance Work Teams (HPWT) must have the right organizational support structure to enable it to function properly. Systems support should provide the necessary information to make the right decisions at the right time. Flattening the organization to ensure optimum upward and downward communication, together with a more flexible control structure is an essential ingredient for successful implementation of HPWTs.

The benefits that team members share are:

Personal growth by taking responsibility for improving performance. This can be stimulating and rewarding, as individuals and teams get better at what they do. The vital ingredients follow below.

Involvement As members of a high-performing team people become more active in the company's decision making process. They could be setting their own workload, deciding how to use their own efforts on a daily basis.

Work smarter Teams are free to decide the best way to work to meet their customers' requirements.

Employability Being involved by participating in decision making and developing personal and team skills and knowledge of the business helps to increase both personal and company value and motivation.

The stages of group formation after Tuckman (1965) (see figure 7.1) are:

Forming Getting to know each other, formal and structured.

Storming Airing and resolving differences, building relationships and agreeing group goals.

Norming Establishing group norms, working together, knowing each other. Defining individual and team goals. Developing the meeting process, communication process and work processes.

Performing Effective teamworking.

To quote Shaun Pantling, Director Customer Service, Rank Xerox:

Empowerment through High Performance Work Teams is a simple concept. In a large organization it needs considerable thought, the highest levels of

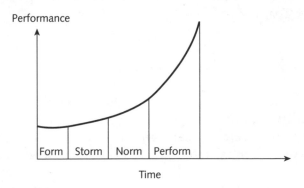

Figure 7.1 Stages of team formation.

Figure 7.2   A model for team development.

commitment and a significant time-frame to make it work. But if customer and employee satisfaction are driving the business, the gain definitely justifies the gain.

Figure 7.2 demonstrates the typical stages of development for a High Performing Work Team.

DIFFERENCES BETWEEN TEAMS

Manson and Dale (1989) have carried out research on the differences between Quality Circles and Yield Improvement Teams (YITs) (one type of quality improvement team) in one of the UK's largest printed circuit board manufacturers, table 7.1, overleaf, has been developed from their work.

It is recommended that when a company uses more than one type of team activity they clearly identify the characteristics and operation of each

Table 7.1   Differences between Quality Circles and Yield Improvement Teams

Feature	Quality Circle	Yield Improvement Teams
Purpose	<ul><li>Involve employees</li><li>Increase employee participation</li><li>Teambuilding</li><li>Develop people</li></ul>	<ul><li>Improve process yields</li><li>Reduce scrap</li><li>Solve quality-related problems</li></ul>
Teambuilding	<ul><li>Will only solve problems if an effective team has been developed</li><li>Members work together</li><li>Operate by consensus</li></ul>	<ul><li>Formed around a problem</li><li>Members are given specific tasks</li><li>Onus is on the individual</li><li>Peer pressure to perform</li><li>Goals, targets and achievements are established and assessed</li><li>Team develops around its achievements</li></ul>
Leadership	<ul><li>Section members/first line supervisor</li><li>Members lack authority and power</li><li>Lack of access to functions, people, and information</li><li>Dependent on others for data and advice</li></ul>	<ul><li>Production/Section managers</li><li>Members are relatively senior</li><li>Independent</li></ul>
Problem solving potential	<ul><li>Limited</li><li>Minor problems</li><li>Limited skills</li></ul>	<ul><li>Considerable</li><li>Major problems</li><li>Highly skilled</li></ul>
Project resolution rate	<ul><li>Low</li></ul>	<ul><li>High</li></ul>
Infrastructure	<ul><li>Steering committee</li><li>Infrequent meetings</li><li>Lack of regular reporting of individual circle progress</li></ul>	<ul><li>Steering committee</li><li>Monthly reports to Managing Director</li><li>Weekly reporting of leaders to steering committee</li></ul>

type of team. For example, at Betz Dearborn Ltd Widnes (manufacturer of speciality chemicals), in deciding which improvement approach to adopt, the following three factors are taken into account (Bunney 1996):

- where the idea for the improvement originated
- the strategic significance of the improvement
- whether the improvement affects more than one major area of the company's operation

COMMONALITIES BETWEEN TEAMS

In relation to the operating characteristics of any type of team used in the improvement process the following two points should be noted.

1. The key issue is not the name of the team activity, but rather the structure of the team, its operating characteristics, remit, account-ability, and ability to resolve problems.
2. If management initiates any form of team activity it has an implicit responsibility to investigate and evaluate all recommendations for improvement, implement all feasible solutions, demonstrate interest in the team's activities, recognize and celebrate success – otherwise there is de-motivation of team members.

Any type of team is composed of a number of key constituents, and requires more than an enthusiastic membership if it is to be successful. The following is adapted from guidelines developed by Betz Dearborn and Chesterfield Cylinders (Bunney 1996):

1. Team Sponsor

- Quality Steering Group (QSG) member and a senior manager
- actively supports the team in its task, especially by contributing to the removal of road-blocks
- helps resolve priority conflicts
- mentor to the team leader
- ensures that the team leader has the skills and training required to lead the team
- communications link between the team and QSG and also with de-partments who are affected by the project
- ensures that the team's activities are accepted by the department in which it is working (e.g. hold meetings with the area management,

staff and operator to help to generate a total understanding of the project and the reasons for it)
- the sponsor agrees a charter with the team, this charter should include:

  - objective
  - deliverables/outcomes
  - resources (team)
  - boundaries
  - timeframe

- ensures that other people and teams are not addressing the same project as the team
- ensures that the team and its leader are responsible for the processes which interface with the chosen project
- holds regular meetings with the team's facilitator

2. Team Facilitator

- helps the team mentor and team leader in establishing the team
- ensures that the right balance of skills is on the team and available to the team
- acts as coach to the team leader and assists with tasks as requested by the leader
- responsible for team progress and direction
- ensures all team members contribute
- responsible for communication from the team to the world outside the team
- communicates team road-blocks to team sponsor and help remove
- identifies training needs of the team and provides and implements, as appropriate
- assists the team in preparing recommendations and presentations to management
- helps sponsor resolve external resource/priority conflicts
- celebrates success with the team

3. Team Leader

- organizes and sends out agenda
- ensures the team members are familiar with the protocol of team meetings
- ensures the team does have a convenient place to meet
- consults with line managers on suitable times for team meetings

LIVERPOOL
JOHN MOORES UNIVERSITY
AVRIL ROBARTS LRC
TITHEBARN STREET
LIVERPOOL L2 2ER
TEL. 0151 231 4022

- starts the meeting on time and adheres to the agenda
- takes minutes
- collates data
- at the end of the meeting, agrees the date and agenda for the next meeting
- communicates minutes and follow-up actions
- needs to be an active contributor and listener
- ensures that team members know what is expected of them
- leads the definition and implementation of team processes
- prepares to commit time to the project
- responsible for team progress and direction
- understands and is sympathetic to the various stages of development that teams go through (e.g. the forming-storming-norming-performing cycle developed by Tuckman 1965) and outlined in figure 7.1
- identifies any training needs of the team and its members
- provides regular verbal reports and copies of team minutes to the mentor about the progress of the team

4. Team Member

- needs to be clear on why he/she wishes to become a member of a team (e.g. wish to solve problems and resolve concerns, improved access to information, increased involvement in decisions)
- needs to be enthusiastic about the project (its resolution must be of direct benefit to him/her)
- must be a willing team member who was not coerced into joining the team
- should contribute relevant experience
- needs to be prepared to commit time outside of team meetings to collect data and carry out agreed actions
- needs to take responsibility, as requested, for follow-up actions
- should respect the role of team leader
- needs to be an active contributor
- needs to be an active listener
- should never be afraid to say 'I don't understand'
- needs to be able to follow through actions
- should respect the ideas and views of other members
- should take minutes as and when requested by the team leader

EVALUATION OF TEAMS

It is not easy to evaluate the effectiveness of teamworking, other than by the effectiveness of the actual solutions produced and improvements made. It is, however, important that the 'health' of a team is regularly assessed. The observable characteristics of an effective team are:

- everyone is participating, making a contribution and is involved in actions
- relationships are open
- team members trust and respect each other
- members listen closely to the views of other members of the team and have an open mind and maintain a positive attitude
- everyone expresses their views, ideas and problems and all available means are used to support ideas
- members respect the operating procedures and principles of the team
- there is clarity of focus on the project being tackled and members know what is expected of them
- the TQM team leader has the ability to translate ideas into action

On the other hand, the usual characteristics of an ineffective team are:

- poor leadership
- cliques, defensiveness, and closed minds within the team membership
- downright hostilities, conflict and lack of tolerance between team members
- members are not all participating in the activities of the team
- limited communications between team members
- insufficient attention to the team process
- there is no pride displayed in the team activity

Briggs et al. (1993) describe the aims of an audit, based on a semi-structured interviewing methodology, undertaken of the quality improvement teams operating at Staffordshire Tableware Ltd in relation to:

- what teams were involved
- who comprised the membership
- how teams were operating
- what projects were being tackled
- how participants felt about the programme

Briggs et al. (1993) go on to say that the information gathered 'was used to create a picture of team activity for use as: an historical record, prior to an expansion of the programme, a feedback tool to improve team effectiveness and to plot a course for future development of the team programme.'

UMIST, in conjunction with Chesterfield Cylinders Ltd, have developed a 'team fitness check' which consists of a questionnaire completed by each member, the leader and the mentor of the team and then discussed and acted on by the team (and the management, if necessary). The idea for this team fitness check came from a Quality Circle Health Assessment developed in the mid-1980s by Eric Barlow at Philips (Hazel Grove). The questionnaire considers the following factors:

1. Is your team meeting regularly?

Has not met for 6 months	Has not met for 3 months	Has not met for 6 weeks	Meets every 3 weeks			
1	2	3	4	5	6	7

If you have scored 5 or less:

- Is it due to pressure of work?   Yes/No
- Is it due to a lack of resources?   Yes/No
- Is it due to company reorganization?   Yes/No
- Is it due to the non-availability of the leader?   Yes/No
- Is it due to the apathy of team members?   Yes/No
- Is it due to the meeting time?   Yes/No
- Is it due to shift patterns?   Yes/No
- Is it due to the team comprising of people from different shifts?   Yes/No
- Is it due to the availability of a convenient place to meet?   Yes/No
- Is the project too large?   Yes/No
- Is the project too difficult?   Yes/No
- Is it due to some members of the team not identifying with the project?   Yes/No

2. Is the level of attendance at meetings satisfactory?

Less than 50% of members attend	Less than 60% of members attend	Less than 80% of members attend	All members attend			
1	2	3	4	5	6	7

If you have scored 5 or less:

- Is it due to work pressure?   Yes/No
- Is it due to members being off site?   Yes/No
- Is it due to people being instructed not to attend?   Yes/No

- Is it due to people having nothing to report?   Yes/No
- Is it due to people being involved in other committees, projects
  and teams?   Yes/No
- Is it due to a lack of interest in the project?   Yes/No

3. Are all members of the team involved in making decisions about the project
    and committed to resolving it successfully?

None committed		Less than 30% committed		Less than 50% committed		All committed
1	2	3	4	5	6	7

If you have scored 5 or less:

- Is it the nature of the project?   Yes/No
- Is it the size of the project?   Yes/No
- Is it due to all members of the team not being associated with
  some elements of the project?   Yes/No
- Is it due to a lack of commitment?   Yes/No
- Is it due to personality clashes within the team?   Yes/No
- Is it due to the size of the team?   Yes/No
- Is it due to lack of appreciation and recognition?   Yes/No

4. Is the team operating effectively?

Very ineffective						Very effective
1	2	3	4	5	6	7

If you have scored 3 or less:

- Is it due to the leader?   Yes/No
- Is it due to the team?   Yes/No
- Is it due to one member of the team?   Yes/No
- Is it due to one member of the team dominating the meeting?   Yes/No
- Is it due to a clique?   Yes/No
- Is it due to personality clashes between the leader and
  members?   Yes/No
- Is it due to decisions based on opinion and not fact?   Yes/No
- Is it due to not all members of the team being involved in its
  activities and associated decision making?   Yes/No
- Is it due to members not feeling part of the team?   Yes/No
- Is it due to a lack of structure and procedure?   Yes/No
- Is it due to the size of the team?   Yes/No
- Is it due to lack of skills?   Yes/No
- Is it due to a lack of adherence to team rules?   Yes/No
- Is it due to a lack of a periodic review?   Yes/No

5.   Are inter-meeting actions carried out satisfactorily?

Not at all   Very
satisfactory   satisfactory

1   2   3   4   5   6   7

If you have scored 3 or less:

- Is it due to a lack of leader co-ordination?   Yes/No
- Is it due to a failure to set priorities?   Yes/No
- Is it due to workload priorities?   Yes/No
- Is it due to lack of member commitment?   Yes/No
- Is it due to poor definition of activities?   Yes/No
- Is it due to lack of support from the mentor?   Yes/No
- Is it due to a lack of support from people outside the team?   Yes/No

6.   Is the team receiving support from departments?

No support   Complete
whatsoever   co-operation

1   2   3   4   5   6   7

If you have scored 3 or less:

- Is it due to one or more departments?   Yes/No
- Is it due to management?   Yes/No
- Is it due to supervisors?   Yes/No
- Is it due to technical specialists?   Yes/No
- Is it due to lack of support from the mentor?   Yes/No
- Is it due to departments viewing the team as outside
  interference?   Yes/No
- Is it due to a lack of publicity about the team's activities?   Yes/No

7.   Does the team require further training?

Yes   No

If YES, in which areas is training required?

8.   Has the team received proper recognition of its activities?

No recognition   Complete
whatsoever   recognition

1   2   3   4   5   6   7

If you have scored 3 or less:

- Is it due to a lack of a personal 'thank you' from management   Yes/No
- Are the current methods not sufficient?   Yes/No
- Are the current methods not suitable?   Yes/No

9. Do the members of the team regard the team as successful?

Not at all successful						Very successful
1	2	3	4	5	6	7

10. Summarize what actions you are going to take.

TEAM COMPETITION

To formally recognize and celebrate team activity and encourage role model behaviour a number of organizations hold an annual team competition/conference, usually held off-site, in which those team activities considered to be the best are presented. The judging committee of internal staff and external experts assess the team projects in terms of: theme selection, problem analysis and solution, members' participation and contribution, results and benefits, and presentation.

With respect to the RHP Bearings (manufacturer of industrial, precision and aerospace bearings) annual team competition, each site holds its own internal competition to decide which team will represent them at the annual competition. At the formal event each team submits a project brief detailing issues such as: team members; project objective and details; how the data were analysed, problem solving approach used; results and outcomes; future opportunities. The team of judges makes assessment of each team using the following scoring guideline.

Teamwork   35 points

Did all the team members get involved?
Did they think and work outside the meeting time?
Did they share, care, support and develop?
Did they have regular meetings and reports?
Did they involve others when required?

Tackling the Problem   30 points

How was the project selected?
Did they consider people impact, complexity, company benefit?

Did they set clear and challenging objectives?
Were the objectives in line with company policy?
Did they use a systematic approach, e.g. PDCA?
Did they use appropriate tools and techniques?

Solution/results   20 points

What was the degree of originality used?
Were all possible options considered?
Was an action plan shown for implementing the solution?
Are the objectives/plan being met?
Are results expressed in terms of objectives?
Are there other spin-off benefits?
Are the results relevant to the customer – internal or external?
Was the result verified as effective and permanent by monitoring
the implementation?

Presentation   15 points

Was it well planned and structured?
Did it emphasize the key points and justify the solution?

It is usual to award a commemorative certificate to each member of a team
making a presentation and a small financial reward (e.g. vouchers) to be
spent together as a team activity such as a dinner, attendance at a sports
event or theatre, holding of a picnic, attendance at a training event, to
improve the working environment, etc. The winning team receives a similar certificate and reward but, in addition, an annual trophy of some kind.

Writing in the RH Bearings' Spring 1996 newsletter, Paul Monk (Chief
Executive) the made the following comments regarding the 1995 Team
Competition (Anon 1996):

> The standard of entries to the competition gets better each year. This year
> surpassed what has gone before.

> The Team Competition is symbolic. It is the crowning event in a year of good
> work and it represents the total quality ethic we embrace through involving
> all our people, in order to improve the business results of our company and
> make it a better place to work.

> As a result of team working, scrap rates across the NSK-RHP group have
> halved in 2 years and productivity has increased by between 35% and 40%.

GUIDELINES FOR DEVELOPING EFFECTIVE TEAMS

A continuous improvement process will encounter periods of stagnation when nothing appears to be moving. This phenomenon is mirrored by teams but with more frequent troughs of inactivity.

To ensure that teams work effectively and efficiently the following factors should be taken into account:

- Management must commit itself to nurturing and supporting teams. Management needs to release, on a gradual basis, authority and accountability and put in place a suitable organizational support structure to assist the team to develop.
- Prior to launching any form of team activity in relation to the introduction and development of TQM, it must be ensured that the appropriate awareness and education with regard to TQM has been undertaken.
- Each member must be clear about the aims and objectives of the team and its potential contribution to the day-to-day operations. The team should have specific goals, and an action plan and milestone chart for the project in hand, with completion dates related to the objective. This not only assists in setting boundaries on the project but helps the team to stay focused on the project in-hand. All members of the team should benefit from the resolution of the project. The project must not be too large to discourage team members; an early success is vital.
- The team members must be trained in appropriate data collection, problem solving, experimental and decision making methods and the team must ensure that it uses the taught skills and methods effectively. The team members should be confident in the use of the tools they have been taught to use and also be aware of any relevant new tools. Training should include project planning, teambuilding and team dynamics in order to provide an understanding of the behavioural needs which may determine team effectiveness and to assist members to feel part of the team. Team members must also be aware of which type of tools and methods work best for specific problems or situations.
- Special coaching and counselling should be provided to the team leaders since they are critical to a team's success.
- The team mentors must be seen to be actively supporting and contributing to the team. This applies, in particular, to requests for resources and support from key organizational functions.
- The team should be disciplined and should have and utilize a set method of problem solving based on fact and not opinion, along the

lines of classic project management. Some companies have developed a process which they recommend their teams should follow. However, it is recognized that some teams prefer a less structured approach to retain flexibility.

- There should be a set of rules and operating procedures that guide the meetings of the team. A project monitoring system also needs to be set-up to ensure that the team is operating in an effective manner.
- Teams should meet on a regular basis and work to an agenda. Each meeting should be constructive, with a purpose, an aim and an achievable goal. The team must be led effectively in terms of direction, support, feedback encouragement, participation and keep minutes and record actions. The team must never leave a meeting without agreeing future actions and the date and time of the next meeting.
- Once a team meeting has been agreed by the team members, only in exceptional circumstances should the leader and any team member fail to attend the meeting.
- Periodic reports to management and the 'mentor' on team activities must be prepared. The results and decisions should be communicated accurately to the rest of the workforce.
- People who are likely to be affected by the results of the project should be involved in the team activity.
- The team should receive appropriate recognition for successful improvements.
- The performance of the team on completion of a project should be evaluated and reviewed to see what worked and what did not, including the identification of training needs. This feedback should be constructive. It is recommended that team members are counselled on how to give and receive feedback in order to learn from each of their failures. It is sometimes useful to use someone from outside the company to evaluate team activity and provide added impetus to the team. The following are the type of improvements made to the team process at Betz Dearborn through this team performance evaluation (Bunney 1996).

    - re-specifying the role of sponsor and facilitator
    - formalizing the team initiation process
    - preparation of action based minutes
    - preparation of team fact sheets
    - standardized team report format
    - implementation report
    - team training provided by facilitator
    - facilitator communication
    - recognition and reward system

SUMMARY

Teamwork is a key element of any TQM approach. There are a variety of teams with different operating characteristics which can be used in TQM. The superior performing organizations employ a number of different types of teams. Different types of teams can be used at different stages of an organization's development of TQM. Some teams are drawn from one functional area of the business and have a narrow focus with perhaps limited problem solving potential. Other types of teams are wider and tend to be cross-functional. This chapter has concentrated on three types of teams – project teams, quality circles and quality improvement teams – and describes their operating characteristics.

It is surprising how many organizations make a number of fundamental mistakes in establishing teamwork as part of their TQM approach. For example, teams not given any training, the wrong type of team established for the project being tackled, the team is structured in such a way that team members discuss their views on the cause of the problem and these ideas are then passed over to technical personnel and engineers to come up with a solution – the end result is team members feel they have achieved nothing and become disaffected with the team process, too many teams introduced at one time which the infrastructure cannot support, and the leader is unaware of the importance of his/her role to the success of the team.

The setting-up of teams usually occurs within the first 6 months of introducing TQM. To help organizations avoid some of the common mistakes, guidelines are outlined which should be considered prior to setting-up any form of team activity. However, even if the guidelines are followed, teams are likely to encounter periods of stagnation when nothing appears to be happening. A means of assessing the health of teams is proposed to help team members overcome these periods of inertia and maintain their performance and effectiveness. It is vital that teams learn from experience.

Dale and Huke (1996) quote the Director of Materials of Maxtor (HK) Ltd who likens teamwork to sport in making the comment:

> In our business, team is of the essence with product life cycles getting shorter and shorter, if any individual or department is not fully co-operating it is akin to a player in a sports team game dropping the ball.

REFERENCES

Anon 1996: *RHP News*, Spring.
Bradley K. and Hill S. 1983: 'After Japan: The Quality Circle Transplant

and Production Efficiency', *British Journal of Industrial Relations*, 21 (3), 291–311.

Briggs R., Palmer J. and Dale B. G. 1993: 'Quality Improvement Teams: An Examination', *Proceedings of the Quality and Its Applications Conference*, University of Newcastle-upon-Tyne, September, 101–5.

Bunney H. 1996: 'Sustaining quality improvement: a study', MSc Thesis, Manchester School of Management, UMIST, Manchester.

Crosby P. B. 1979: *Quality is Free*, McGraw Hill, New York.

Dale B. G. and Barlow E. 1984: 'Facilitator Viewpoints on Specific Aspects of Quality Circle Programmes', *Personnel Review*, 13 (4), 22–9.

Dale B. G. and Huke I. 1996: Quality Through Teamwork, Booklet 0.7, Hong Kong Government Industry Department, Hong Kong.

Dale B. G. and Lees J. 1986: *The Development of Quality Circle Programmes*, Manpower Services Commission, Sheffield.

Fabi B. 1992: 'Contingency Factors in Quality Circles: a Review of Empirical Evidence', *International Journal of Quality and Reliability Management*, 9 (2), 18–33.

Gallup Organisation Inc. 1993: *Employee Attitudes on Teamwork Empowerment and Quality Improvement*, American Society for Quality Control, Milwaukee.

Hayward S. G., Dale B. G. and Frazer V. C. M. 1985: 'Quality Circle Failure and How to Avoid it', *European Management Journal*, 3 (2), 103–11.

Hill F. M. 1986: 'Quality Circles in the U.K.: a Longitudinal Study', *Personnel Review*, 15 (3), 25–34.

Hutchins D. 1985: *Quality Circles Handbook*, Pitman, London.

Manson M. M. and Dale B. G. 1989: 'The Operating Characteristics of Quality Circles and Yield Improvement Teams: a Case Study Comparison', *European Management Journal*, 7 (3), 287–95.

Mohr W. L. and Mohr H. 1983: *Quality Circles: Changing Images of People at Work*, Addison Wesley, Reading, Massachusetts.

Robson M. 1984: *Quality Circles in Action*, Gower Press, Aldershot.

Tuckman, B. W. 1965: 'Development sequence in small groups', *Psychological Bulletin*, 63 (6), 384–99.

8

Assessment of progress

INTRODUCTION

If a process of continuous improvement is to be sustained and its pace increased it is essential that organizations assess and monitor on a regular basis which activities are going well, which have stagnated, what needs to be improved and what is missing. Self-assessment provides this type of framework in generating such feedback about an organization's approach to continuous improvement. It helps to satisfy the natural curiosity of management as to where its organization stands with respect to the development of TQM. This method is now being given a considerable amount of attention by organizations throughout the world. The main reason for this increasing interest is the Malcolm Baldridge National Award (MBNQA) which was introduced in America during 1987 and the European Quality Award (EQA) introduced in Europe during 1991. These provide the mechanism for putting a score on the organization's current state of TQM development. The criteria of each award encapsulate a comprehensive business management model. There are many definitions of self-assessment provided by writers such as Conti (1993), (1997) and Hillman (1994) but an all-embracing definition is provided by the EFQM (1998):

> Self-assessment is a comprehensive, systematic and regular review of an organization's activities and results referenced against a model of business excellence.
>
> The self-assessment process allows the organization to discern clearly its strengths and areas in which improvements can be made and culminates in planned improvement actions which are monitored for progress.

Self-assessment implies the use of a model on which to base the evaluation and diagnostics. There are a number of internationally recognized models, the main ones being the Deming Application Prize in Japan, the MBNQA in America and the EFQM Model for Business Excellence in

Europe. Although there are some differences between the models they have a number of common elements and themes. In addition there are many national quality awards (e.g. the British Quality Award, Irish National Business Excellence Award and the Australian Quality Award) and regional quality awards (e.g. North West Quality Award). Most of the national and regional awards are more or less duplicates of the international models, with some modifications to suit issues of national or local interest. In America alone there are over 60 state and regional award schemes. Sometimes an organization will adjust the criteria of one of these models to cater for its own specific situation. The models on which these awards are based comprise definitions of TQM in a broad sense; they are comprehensive considering the whole organization and its various activities, practices and processes. Since the establishment of these awards there has been an explosion in published material describing them (e.g. Brown 1996, Cole 1991, Conti 1993, 1997, Hakes 1998, Lascelles and Peacock 1996, Nakhai and Neves 1994 and Steeples 1993).

The models on which the awards are based and the guidelines for application are helpful in defining TQM in a way in which management can easily understand. This is one of the reasons behind the distribution of thousands of booklets outlining the guidelines and award criteria. The majority of companies requesting the booklets have no intention, in the short term, of applying for the respective awards. These organizations are simply using the criteria of the chosen model to assist them to diagnose the state of health of their improvement process and provide indications of how to achieve business excellence. The criteria help organizations to develop and manage their improvement activities in a number of ways. For example:

- They provide a definition and description of TQM which gives a better understanding of the concept, improves awareness and generates ownership for TQM amongst senior managers.
- They enable measurement of the progress with TQM to be made, along with its benefits and outcomes.
- Year-on-year improvement is encouraged and this provides the basis for assessing the rate of improvement.
- Forces management to think about the basic elements of the organization and how it operates.
- The scoring criteria provide an objective fact based measurement to gain consensus on the strengths and weaknesses of the current approach and thereby help to pinpoint improvement opportunities.
- Benchmarking and organizational learning is facilitated.
- Training in TQM is encouraged.

A full listing of the benefits which have been found to result from the self-assessment process are given in the EFQM Self-Assessment Guidelines for Companies (1998). There is little doubt that the MBNQA and EQA have helped to raise the profile of TQM in America and Europe.

To use any self-assessment method effectively, various elements and practices need to be in place and management needs to have had some TQM experience to understand the questions underpinning the concept. What has not been implemented cannot be assessed. The decision to undertake self-assessment needs to be fully considered from all angles and management must be fully committed to its use. In the view of the authors the use of self-assessment methods based on quality award models are best suited to those organizations that have had a formal improvement process in place for at least 3 years, although there is a clear need to assess progress before this time has elapsed. This view is supported by Sherer (1995) the Managing Director of Rank Xerox (Germany) who in explaining how the Corporation won the EQA says 'Do not use the Award Programme, your application for the EQA, as an entry point into your quality journey. It is something you should do after you have been on the road for a long time.' He also goes on to comment 'Do not try to run for the award too early'. A similar point is made in the *Deming Prize Guide for Overseas Companies* (JUSE 1996): 'It is advisable to apply for the Prize after two to three years of company-wide TQM implementation efforts or after top management has become fully committed and has begun to assume a leadership role'. Having made this point the TQM models underpinning the Quality Awards are also helpful in demonstrating what is involved to those managers in organizations inexperienced in TQM. However, they must understand the potential gap that can exist between where they currently stand in relation to TQM and the model of the award being used to make comparisons.

AWARD MODELS

Deming Application Prize, the Deming Prize and the Quality Control Award

The Deming Prize was set-up in the honour of Dr W. E. Deming, back in 1951. It was in recognition of his friendship and achievements in the cause of industrial quality. Deming through the royalties received from the text of his 'eight day course on Quality Control' contributed to the initial funding of the Deming Prize. Dale has led four Missions of European manufacturing executives to Japan to study how they manage quality. It is clear from the evidence collected during these Missions that the Deming

Application Prize criteria have produced an almost standard method of managing quality. Compared to the West, there is much less company-to-company variation in the level of understanding of TQM and in the degree of attainment. This has helped to promote a deep understanding of TQM amongst all employees. Rather than argue about the merits of a particular approach, system, method or technique, the Japanese tend to discuss how to apply the TQM approach more vigorously through a common core level of understanding. JUSE (1996) outline the following results which have been achieved in applying for the Deming Application Prize:

- quality stabilization and improvement
- production improvement/cost reduction
- expanded sales
- increased profits
- thorough implementation of management plans/business results
- realization of top management's dreams
- participation and improvement of the organizational constitution
- heightened motivation to manage and improve as well as to promote standardization
- converged large power from the bottom of the organization and enhanced morale
- establishment of various management systems and the total management system

The original intention of the Deming Application Prize was to assess a company's use and application of statistical method. Later, in 1964, the intention was broadened out to assess how TQM activities were being practised. The award is managed by the Deming Application Prize Committee and administered by JUSE. It recognizes outstanding achievements in quality strategy, management and execution. There are three separate divisions for the Award. The Deming Application Prize, the Deming Prize for individuals and the Quality Control Award for factories. The Deming Application Prize is open to: individual sites; a division of a company; small companies; and overseas companies. It is awarded each year and there is no limit on the number of winners. On the other hand, the Committee reserves the right not to award the prize in any year. It is made to those 'companies or divisions of companies that have achieved distinct performance improvement through the application of company-wide quality control' (JUSE 1996). Data collected by Dale (1993) suggest that it has become customary in Japan for organizations wishing to improve their performance to apply for the Deming Application Prize. This arises from the continuous improvements which are necessary to qualify for the award, along with the considerable prestige associated with winning the prize.

The Deming Application Prize is comprised of ten primary categories (see table 8.1) which in turn are divided into 66 sub-categories. Each primary category has 6 sub-categories apart from the quality assurance activities which has 12 categories. There are no pre-designated points allocated to the individual sub-categories. It is claimed that the reason for this is to maintain flexibility. However, discussions with JUSE indicate that the maximum score for each sub-category is 10 points. This checklist is prescriptive in that it identifies factors, procedures, techniques and approaches that underpin TQM. The examiners for the Deming Application Prize are selected by JUSE from quality management experts from not-for-profit organizations. The applicants are required to submit a detailed document on each of the Prize's criteria. The size of the report is dependent upon the number of employees in each of the applicant company's business units, including the Head Office. The Deming Prize Committee examines the application document and decides if the applicant is eligible for on-site examination. The Committee chooses the two or more examiners to conduct this examination. Discussions between Dale and JUSE suggest that considerable emphasis is placed on the on-site examination of the applicant organization's practices. It is also evident that the applicant organization relies a great deal on advice from the JUSE consultants. JUSE would also advise an organization when it should apply for the prize.

The Malcolm Baldrige National Quality Award

The Malcolm Baldrige National Quality Improvement Act of 1987, signed by President Reagan on 20 August 1987, established this annual US quality award, some 37 years after the introduction of the Deming Prize. The award is named after a former American Secretary of Commerce in the Reagan Administration, Malcolm Baldrige. The MBNQA programme is the result of the co-operative efforts of government leaders and American business. The purposes of the Award are to promote an understanding of the requirements for performance excellence and competitiveness improvements and to promote sharing of information on successful performance strategies. The MBNQA guidelines contain detailed criteria that describe a world-class total quality organization. The US Department of Commerce and the National Institute of Standards and Technology (NIST) are responsible for administering the Award scheme.

Up to two awards can be given each year, out of the average number of 100 applicants in each of three categories: manufacturing companies or

Table 8.1   Quality award criteria

(a)   Deming Application Prize

Category

Policies
Organization
Information
Standardization
Human resources focus
Quality assurance activities
Maintenance/control activities
Improvement
Effects
Future plans

Total

(b)   Malcolm Baldrige National Quality Award

Category	Max
Leadership	110
Strategic planning	80
Customer and market focus	80
Information and analysis	80
Human resource development and management	100
Process management	100
Business results	450
Total	1,000

(c)   European Quality Award

Category	Max
Leadership	100
People management	90
Policy and strategy	80
Resources	90
Processes	140
People satisfaction	90
Customer satisfaction	200
Impact on society	60
Business results	150
Total	1,000

sub-units, service companies or sub-units, and small business (defined as independently owned, and with not more than 500 employees). Since its inception in a single year there has never been less than two and no more than five awards. Any for-profit, domestic or foreign organization located in the US that is incorporated or a partnership can apply. The applicant can be a whole firm or a legitimate business unit. The award is made by the President of the United States, with the recipients receiving a specially designed crystal trophy mounted with a gold plated medallion. The recipients may publicize and advertise their awards provided they agree to share information and best practice about their successful quality management and improvement strategies with other American organizations.

Every Baldrige Award application is evaluated in seven major categories with a maximum total score of 1,000 (United States Department of Commerce 1998). The seven major categories are: leadership (110 points); strategic planning (80 points); customer and market focus (80 points); information and analysis (80 points); human resource focus (100 points); process management (100 points); and business results (450 points), see figure 8.1. Each of the seven categories is sub-divided into 20 items and the items are further defined by 29 areas to address. The criteria and processes are reviewed each year to ensure that they remain relevant and reflect current thinking and, based on experience during the intervening period, their

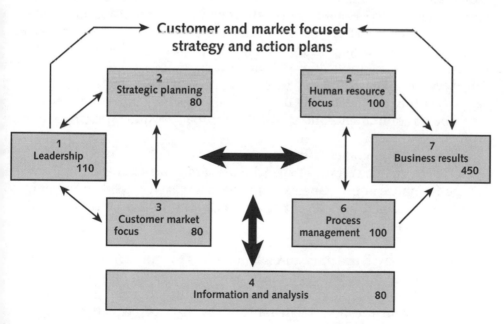

Figure 8.1 Baldrige criteria for performance excellence framework.
Source: US Department of Commerce (1998)

wording and relative scores are updated. It should be mentioned that like the EFQM model the MBNQA criteria were developed originally by the business fraternity, management consultants and academics.

The framework (see figure 8.1) has three basic elements: strategy and action plans, system, and information and analysis. Strategy and action plans are the set of customer and market focused company-level requirements, derived from short- and long-term strategic planning, that must be done well for the company's strategy to succeed. They guide overall resource decisions and drive the alignment of measures for all work units to ensure customer satisfaction and market success. The system is comprised of the six Baldrige categories in the centre of figure 8.1 that define the organization, its operations and its results. Information and analysis (category 4) is critical to the effective management of the company and to a fact-based system for improving company performance and competitiveness.

The evaluation by the Baldrige examiners is based on a written application of up to 50 pages. (This summarizes the organization's practices and results in response to the criteria for performance excellence) and looks for three major indications of success:

Approach Appropriateness of the methods, effectiveness of the use of the methods with respect to the degree to which they are: systematic, integrated and consistently applied; embody evaluation/improvement/ learning cycles; and are based on reliable information and evidence of innovation and/or significant and effective adaptions of approaches used in other types of applications or businesses.

Deployment The extent to which the approach is applied to all requirements of the item, including use of the approach in addressing business and item requirements and use of the approach by all appropriate work units.

Results The outcomes with respect to factors such as: current performance; performance relative to benchmarks; rate, breadth and importance of performance improvements; demonstration of sustained improvement and/or sustained high-level performance and linkage of results of key performance measures.

The assessors will use these three dimensions to score an applicant. Most entrants tend to score within a fairly narrow range on 'approach', and a few fall down on 'deployment', but it is 'results' that separates the real contenders from the rest. High scoring on 'results', which are heavily weighted towards customer satisfaction, requires convincing data that demonstrate steady improvement over time, both internally and externally.

Experience has shown that, even with a good internal approach and deployment strategy, it takes time for results to show.

Following a first stage review of the application by quality management experts (i.e. leading consultants, practitioners and academics), a decision is made as to which organizations should receive a site visit. The site visit takes between two to five days from a team of between six to eight assessors. The assessors have to be fair, honest and impartial in their approach. A panel of judges review all the data both from the written applications and site visits and recommend the award recipients to the National Institute of Technology (NIST). Quantitative results weight heavily in the judging process, so applicants must be able to prove that their quality efforts have resulted in sustained improvements. The thoroughness of the judging process means that applicants not selected as finalists get valuable written feedback on their strengths and areas for improvement. The detail of the report is related to the scores achieved and this is considered by many organizations to be valuable consultancy advice.

The European Quality Award

The European Quality Award was launched in October 1991 and first awarded in 1992. According to the EFQM it was intended to: 'focus attention on business excellence, provide a stimulus to companies and individuals to develop business improvement initiatives and demonstrate results achievable in all aspects of organizational activity'. Whilst only one European Quality Award is made each year for Company, Public Sector and SME, several European Quality prizes are awarded to those companies who demonstrate excellence in the management of quality through a process of continuous improvement. The EQA is awarded to the best of the prize winners in the categories of companies and public service organizations (i.e. healthcare, education and local and central government), that is the most successful exponent of TQM in Europe. The winner of each of the three awards gets to retain the EQA Trophy for a year and all prize winners receive a framed holographic image of the trophy. The winners are expected to share their experiences of TQM at conferences and seminars organized by the EFQM.

The EFQM model is intended to help the management of European organizations to better understand best practices and to support them in their leadership role. The model provides a generic framework of criteria that can be applied to any organization or its component parts. The EQA is administered by the EFQM with the support of the European Organization for Quality (EOQ) and the European Commission. The EFQM in developing the Model of Business Excellence and the EQA drew upon the experience in use and application of the MBNQA. The model is structured on the following nine criteria which companies can use to assess and measure their own performance:

Leadership: 100 points (10%)   The behaviour of all managers in driving the company towards business excellence. How the executive team and all other managers inspire and drive excellence as the organization's fundamental process for continuous improvement.

People management: 90 points (9%)   The management of the organization's people. How the organization releases the full potential of its people to improve its business continuously.

Policy and strategy: 80 points (8%)   The organization's values, vision and strategic direction and the manner in which it achieves them. How the organization incorporates the concept of excellence in the determination, communication, implementation, review and improvement of its policy and strategy.

Resources: 90 points (9%)   The management, utilization and preservation of resources. How the organization improves its business continuously by optimization of resources, based on the concept of excellence.

Processes: 140 points (14%)   The management of all the value-adding activities within the organization. How key and support processes are identified, reviewed and if necessary revised to ensure continuous improvement of the organization's business.

People satisfaction: 90 points (9%)   What the people's (employees) feelings are about the organization. The organization's success in satisfying the needs and expectations of its people.

Customer satisfaction: 200 points (20%)   What the perception of the external customers, direct and indirect, is of the organization and of its products and services. The organization's success in satisfying the needs and expectations of customers.

Impact on Society; 60 points (6%)   What the perception of the organization is among the community at large. This includes views of the organization's approach to quality of life, the environment and to the preservation of global resources. It is about the organization's success in satisfying the needs and expectations of the community at large.

Business Results; 150 points (15%)   This deals with what the organization is achieving in relation to its planned business performance. The organization's continuing success in achieving its financial and other business targets and objectives and in satisfying the needs and expectations of everyone with a financial interest in the organization.

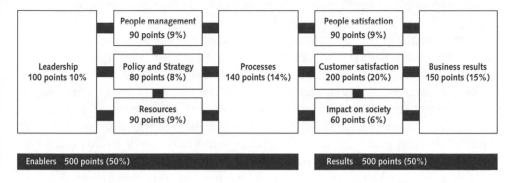

Figure 8.2 The EFQM model for business excellence.
Source: EFQM (1998)

The criteria which are shown in table 8.1 are split into two groups: 'Enablers' and 'Results' and illustrated in figure 8.2. The nine elements of the model are further divided into 32 criteria parts. For example, leadership is divided into four parts and people management into six parts. The model is based on the principle that processes are the means by which the organization harnesses and releases the talents of its people to produce results. In other words, the processes and the people are the enablers which provide the results. The results aspects of the award are concerned with what the organization has achieved and is continuing to achieve and the enablers with how the results are being achieved. The rationale for this is that customer satisfaction, people satisfaction, and impact on society are achieved through the leadership driving policy and strategy, people management and the management of resources and processes leading to excellence in business results. Each of these nine criteria can be used to assess the organization's progress to business excellence.

The enablers (i.e. the 'hows') are scored in terms of approach and deployment. The approach is concerned with how the requirements of a particular item are approached and met. This will take into account:

- the appropriateness of the methods, tools and techniques used
- the degree to which the approach is systematic and prevention based
- the use of review cycles
- the implementation of improvements
- the degree to which the approach has been integrated into normal operations

The deployment is the extent to which the approach has been deployed and implemented vertically and horizontally in all relevant processes and to all relevant products and services within the organization. The results (i.e. the 'whats') criteria are evaluated in terms of degree of excellence and the scope or breadth (i.e. all relevant areas, full range of results and understanding) of the results presented. They include: positive trends; performance against trends; understanding of negative results; comparison of results with competitors, similar organizations and best-in-class organizations and the ability to sustain performance. The results criteria do not cover just financial performance. The scoring framework consists of 1,000 points with 500 points each being allocated to Enablers and Results (i.e. existence of positive trends, comparison with both internal targets and external organizations, and the ability to sustain performance).

A revised model, (The EFQM Excellence Model) is in the process of being launched as this book goes to press.

The EFQM model does not stipulate any particular techniques, methods or procedures which should be in place. The organizations that put themselves forward for the award are expected to have undertaken at least one self-assessment cycle. Following this a 75-page report is written and once the application has been submitted to the EFQM headquarters, a team of six fully trained independent assessors examine each application and decide whether or not to conduct a site visit. The assessors comprise mainly practising managers, but also include academics and quality professionals. Irrespective of whether or not the company is subject to a site visit, a feedback report is provided to the company that gives a general assessment of the organization, a scoring profile for the different criteria and a comparison with the average scores of other applicants. For each part-criterion the key strengths and areas for improvement are listed. A jury, comprising of seven members, reviews the findings of the assessors to decide who will win the award.

THE SELF-ASSESSMENT PROCESS

Self-assessment was defined in the introduction to this chapter. In short, it uses one of the models underpinning an award to pinpoint improvement opportunities and identify new ways in which to encourage the organization down the road of business excellence. On the other hand, audits, with which self-assessment is often confused by the less advanced organizations with respect to their development of TQM, are carried out with respect to a quality system standard such as the ISO 9000 series. Audits are, in the main, looking for non-compliances and are assessing to see if the system and underlying procedures are being followed. In ISO 8402 (1994) audits are defined as:

Systematic and independent examination to determine whether quality activities and related results comply with planned arrangements and whether
these arrangements are implemented effectively and are suitable to achieve
objectives.

After gaining the commitment of management to the self-assessment
process and carrying out the necessary education and training, the following are the main steps which an organization should follow in setting
about self-assessment against a Business Excellence Model:

- assess what the organization has done well
- identify what aspects could be improved upon
- pinpoint gaps and what elements are missing
- develop an action plan to pick up the pace of the improvement process

A key aspect of the process is take a good hard and honest look at the
organization in order to identify its shortcomings, keeping in mind at all
times a golfing analogy 'You will never become a better golfer by cheat-
ing'.

There are several methods by which an organization may undertake
self-assessment. Each method has advantages and disadvantages and an
organization must choose the one(s) most suited to its circumstances. These
methods are outlined in detail in the EFQM *Self-Assessment Guidelines for
Companies* (EFQM 1998). The broad approaches which can be used separately or in combinations are:

Award simulation   This approach, which can create a significant workload for an organization, involves the writing of a full submission document (up to 75 pages) using the criteria of the chosen quality award
model and employing the complete assessment methodology including
the involvement of a team of trained assessors (internal) and site visits.
The scoring of the application, strengths, and areas for improvement are
then reported back and used by the management team for developing
action plans.

Some organizations have modified and developed the criteria of the
chosen award model to: suit their own particular circumstances, provide
more emphasis on areas which are critical to them, make the criteria
easier to understand and use, and to reduce some of the effort in preparing the application document. In some cases a Corporation or Holding
Company has set a minimum score which each of its facilities has to
achieve within a set timeframe. Once an internal award has been achieved

its continuation will require the successful completion of a subsequent assessment, usually within 2 years after the initial award has been granted.

Peer involvement This is similar to but less rigid than the award simulation approach in that there is no formal procedure for data collection. It gives freedom to the organization undertaking the self-assessment to pull together all relevant documents, reports and factual evidence in whatever format they choose against the appropriate model being used.

Pro forma In this approach the criterion is described and the person(s) carrying out the assessment outlines the organization's strengths, areas for improvement, score and evidence which supports the assessment in the space provided on the form. It is usual to use one or two pages per assessment criterion.

Workshop This approach is one in which managers are responsible for gathering the data and presenting the evidence to colleagues at a workshop. The workshop aims to reach a consensus score on the criterion and details of strengths and areas for improvement identified and agreed.

Matrix chart This involves rating a prepared series of statements, based on the appropriate award model on a scoring scale. The statements are usually contained within a workbook which contains the appropriate instructions. The person(s) carrying out the assessment finds the statement which is most suited to the organizations and notes the associated score.

Questionnaire This is usually used to carry out a 'quick and dirty' assessment of the organization's standing in relation to the award model being used. It involves answering a series of questions and statements, which are based on the criteria of the award model being used, using a yes/no format or on a graduated response scale.

In recent times a number of self-assessment packages, based on software have come onto the market which claim to simplify the self-assessment process and provide a benchmark of progress against other organizations. Typical examples are the British Quality Foundation's Assess Rapid Score and Assess Valid Score.

Assessment against a model, whether by internal or external assessors, has three discrete phases:

Phase 1   The gathering of data for each criterion
Phase 2   The assessment of the data gathered
Phase 3   Develop plans and actions arising from the assessment and monitoring the progress and effectiveness of the plan of action

There are a number of flow diagrams which outline the self-assessment

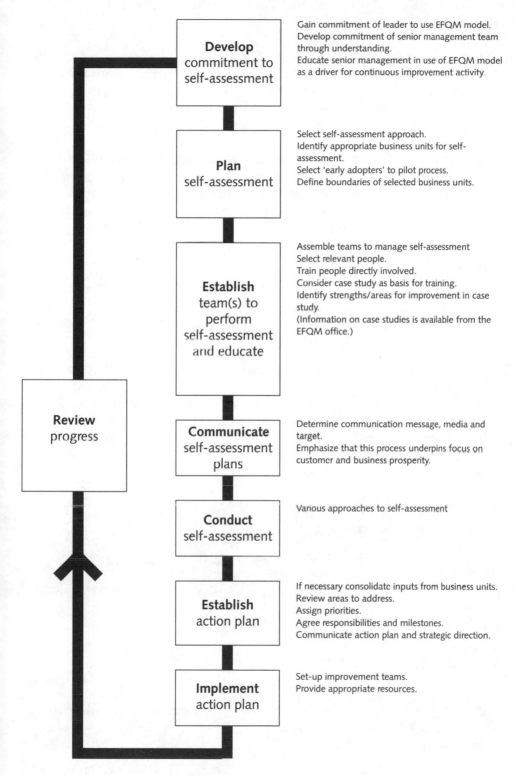

Figure 8.3 Self-assessment: general process.
Source: EFQM (1998)

process. The flow diagram in figure 8.3 is from the EFQM *Self-Assessment Guidelines for Companies* (1998). It is not the purpose of this chapter to regurgitate the details of a self-assessment process but simply to list the key issues which need to be considered by those organizations undertaking self-assessment for the first time:

- Senior management must be committed to the self-assessment process and be prepared to use the results to develop improvement plans.
- The people involved in the process need to be trained.
- Communicate within the business the reasons for and what is involved in self-assessment.
- Decide the self-assessment method(s) to be used.
- Plan the means of collecting the data:
  - decide the team and allocate roles and responsibilities for each criteria of the model
  - develop a data collection methodology and identify data sources
  - agree an activity schedule and manage as a project.
- Decide the best way of organizing the data which have been collected
- Present the data, reach agreement on strengths and areas for improvement and agree the scores for the criteria.
- Prioritize the improvements and develop an action plan.
- Regular review of progress against the plan.
- Repeat the self-assessment.

Case study: Betz Dearborn

The primary objectives for the initiation of the self-assessment process within this Global Speciality Chemical company were threefold:

1. to develop potential improvement areas
2. to prioritize resources
3. to give a common understanding to the term world class

All of the above were achieved by the process detailed below and in addition there was a fourth and very important objective realized. This was that all managers had an opportunity to become familiar with and understand the implications of the business line strategy.

The process initially involved communicating to the European senior management team the model to be used (in this case it was the MBNQA), its history, the benefits realized by its winners and a suggested process for company-wide deployment. Following this all European managers were invited to attend one of six 3–day workshops at various European locations hosted by the regional Vice-President and facilitated by the European Quality Director and UK Quality Manager. During the workshop delegates had an opportunity to discuss the company strategy and operating guidelines with the Vice-President and begin to decide on the best possible route towards world class, using the MBNQA model. Syndicates were asked to rate the company on both a 'Where are we now?' and 'Where do we need to be in 5 years time to achieve the Strategic Objective?' basis. The scores were depicted using a radial diagram shown in figure 8.4 which depicted the areas in which the greatest effort needed to be employed.

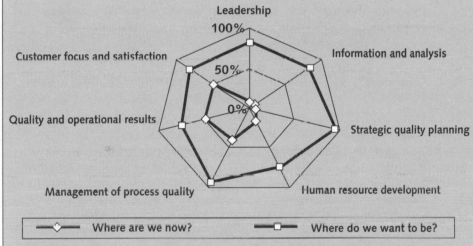

Figure 8.4   MBNQA scores: current and 5 year projection.

The improvement areas were identified on the final day of the workshop and action plans were discussed but no individual responsibilities were assigned. On completion of the six workshops improvement areas (115 in total) were grouped and prioritised by the European Management Team and the appointed European Project Sponsors. The projects were then progressed at the local business unit level and reviewed quarterly by the European Steering Group. These projects proceeded at different rates at each location and to avoid repetition of work and prevent the proliferation of new approaches it was finally agreed to pilot each project at a single site and then use the expertise developed to provide best practice throughout the company.

The approach to self-assessment proved to be successful and was later adopted on a global scale. The following is a list of strengths and possible improvements that could be made with this approach.

Strengths

- Wide audience.
- Company-wide goals developed.
- Proliferation of 'what' we can do to improve.
- Common TQM Framework – which amalgamated six unique approaches which had been previously used on a country-by-country basis.
- Excellent vehicle for communicating the company strategy.
- Internal networks established.

Areas for Improvement

- Varying previous experience of TQM had a significant effect on perception of current status and the respective scores.
- Very few 'hows' developed.
- Unhealthy business unit competition developed when emphasis was placed on initial scores rather than the areas for improvement.

Case study: North West Water

Shortly after privatization, the then NWW part of United Utilities set out on the journey towards being world class. A number of major initiatives were put in place to address the required changes. However, there was no measuring process to check the progress being made. In early 1993, a presentation was made by a management consultant to a group of managers interested in TQM. The presentation described the EFQM model and how it gave a 'score' out of one thousand points for the degree of excellence of an organization. Senior management became convinced that this was the means of enabling them to measure progress to the goal of world class.

The model was piloted in the IT Department by use of a quick report. In practice the model was found to be simple, quick and not requiring management consultants to interpret its use and results. The IT Director announced the department's score which was a mere 198 to the Board with targets for improvement and an action plan. Other directors immediately took notice, particularly as the Chief Executive became interested in their scores. Furthermore, the effect on the IT Department from the action plan was quickly noticeable. For example, employee and customer satisfaction was measured and improved, a help desk was introduced and procedures and measures for processes established and process improvement teams were created and these produced immediate benefits. By the end of 1994, an additional six departments were being assessed against the model. At the beginning of 1995, the average score for the assessed departments had risen to 316 and the benefits of the self-assessment process were clearly recognizable. The Board started a Business Quality Initiative, one of the targets of which was that all areas of the business would have annual self-assessments to be centrally facilitated by the Business Quality Group.

Three different types of assessment have been used by NWW. Initially perception assessments based on questionnaires were used. This was followed by an assessment workbook and finally a full formal assessment of each department of the organization was carried out. The advantages and disadvantages of the various methods are now described.

The Perception Method

This became known as the A3 method after the size of the sheet of paper from Excellence North West which contained details of the matrix and questions. These types of assessments were carried out at half-day workshops. Initially, a presentation on TQM was given together with an explanation of the EFQM model. This was followed by the attendees from a particular department individually filling in the scoresheet, which took about 20 minutes. Whilst the attendees enjoyed a coffee break the sheets were collected in and the scores noted to calculate an average and note the extreme ranges on each criterion of the model. When this was done the sheets were handed back to the owners and for each criterion 10 minutes was spent with the lowest scorer challenging the highest score to justify his/her score. The main quality issues quickly materialized from these discussions.

The advantages of the perception method were:

- it was very quick and cheap
- it was an excellent training aid to ensure people understood the model by undertaking a scoring activity
- working groups were set up to look at the issues and report back on their progress to management meetings

The disadvantages were:

- the scores were usually hopelessly overoptimistic, even when averaged. The results were not comparable with any other department or organization and indeed varied wildly even between groups from the same department
- the working groups were sometimes effective in getting something changed but generally fizzled out as the issues were described in rather woolly terms

However, a considerable number of people were made aware of the self-assessment process and some of the working groups made improvements to particular areas of activity. This led the company to investigate a more objective means of measuring against the model. The managers who had run the workshop set about developing a workbook which had hard objective questions and a prescriptive scoring system.

The Workbook Method

The workbook was developed by interpreting the model for a water company and for each of the points in the model putting a measure in place on how it related to processes in the business. For instance with impact on society the point on noise was measured by how many complaints about noise the department had received while carrying out their operations. In departments where a question was irrelevant (e.g. noise did not usually apply to the finance function), the score for noise was reallocated to questions that were relevant.

During October 1995, all of the 20 departments which at that time comprised NWW were assessed using the workbook. The process involved a 1-day meeting with a representative group of employees from the department, usually about ten in number but from different levels of the organization and different geographical locations when the department was not centrally located. Each of the questions in the workbook asked for evidence. The workbook then assigned points based on the response, (e.g. the deployment of communication points score was based on how many employees in the department replied positively to the employee survey question on whether or not they were team briefed).

The workbook allowed notes to be made on improvement actions where the points score on a question was low. These actions were then written up and passed to the General Manager of the department. With the help of their management group the general managers then assigned priorities, owners, success criteria and target dates to the actions and monitored their progress at their regular management meetings. Around 600 actions were raised at these assessments and during the next 9 months about 30 per cent of them were completed. It is not reasonable to expect all actions to be addressed but there was clear progress in quality improvement. Interestingly, the department that recorded the lowest score replaced its manager and completed over 60% of the recommended improvement actions. In the 1996 assessment it had moved up to mid-table.

The advantages of the workbook method were:

- it could be completed for each department in about 12 man-days of effort and produced 180 completed quality improvement actions in the next 9 months
- for the first time there existed an objective measure across the business of the level of business excellence and it gave a straightforward way of identifying internal best practice

The disadvantages were:

- it was not externally comparable – the company did not really know how good, or bad, they were in comparison with other companies
- the score was highly prescriptive and sometimes good improvement initiatives which had been recently implemented and had not yet shown results did not add to the score
- it gave an overestimation of the score although not as high as the perception score – this confused a lot of people, especially directors who had briefed the perception score to their employees and now had to explain why it had dropped

In spite of these disadvantages, the Board recognized what a useful process self-assessment was and agreed to fund the training of internal employees to become fully qualified EFQM assessors so that in the next cycle, each department would be assessed as if it had entered for the EQA. This was referred to as formal self-assessment.

Formal Self-Assessment

In the spring of 1996, 25 employees (termed Quality Support Managers), were trained as EFQM assessors. These 25 represented the 20 departments of the Regulated Utility Division (at this time the merger with Norweb had taken place) and after training it was their job to ensure that a report was written about the achievements of their departments in relation to the EFQM model. The reports were sized at 1 page per sub-criterion of the model, approximately 35 pages.

After the report had been written, three assessors from other departments scored it against the model individually and then came together for a consensus meeting. For each sub-criteria they agreed a score, three strengths and three areas for improvement. Where there was insufficient information in the report, a site visit was organized and any issues resolved by discussion and inspection. The results of the assessment were then written up by the lead assessor in the form of a scorebook which included all the sub-criteria scores, the areas for improvement and the strengths. The lead assessor and the assessor from the department concerned then visited the General Manager and discussed the improvement actions to be completed in the next year, agreeing measures and owners where possible.

To ensure that the improvement actions were carried out, the actions were included in the business plans for 1996–7. The standard format of the departmental business plans was changed to move them from a financial focus to a total quality focus. This was done by aligning the four main sections in the plan to the four results criteria of the model so that there were clear targets in the plan for customer satisfaction, employee satisfaction, impact on society and both financial and non-financial business results. To ensure every employee understood what the company was trying to achieve a newspaper called 'The Plan' was sent to their homes with the targets and how the company was achieving them.

The advantages of the formal self-assessment method were:

- there was an objective and highly accurate measure of the excellence of the department which was comparable both internally and externally with other organizations
- the improvement actions were fully integrated with the business planning process and were integrated into the work of the department

The only disadvantage of formal assessment is that it takes a lot longer than most people anticipate. The planning estimates which are used are outlined below:

Initial writing of the report	10 days
Scoring the report	3 days per assessor
Consensus meeting	1 day for the three assessors
The site visit	1 day
	3 days for the assessor of the department being assessed
Writing up the scorebook	1 day
General manager meeting	1 day for the manager, lead assessor and department's assessor
Building into the business plan	2 days
Total for each department	32 days

Where the department has a dedicated quality role this is not excessive. However, most quality support managers performed the job in addition to their current workloads.

The Business Quality Group has a database which records all the improvement actions and has key fields of the department where the improvement action is taking place and the sub-criteria of the model to which the action relates. This allowed the group to ensure that any two or more departments that are engaged in improvements linked to a certain area of the model can be put in touch with each other to ensure avoidance of duplication of effort.

Lessons Learned

Keep the scores quiet
While the scores act as a measure of progress towards world class it is important not to make the scores of individual departments public to other departments. Whilst some competition is healthy, issuing a league table resulted in a lot of 'rubbishing' of the process and argument over why a department had scored more than another based on anecdotal evidence and the perception of individuals. In addition the change in assessment process lowered the score in some areas and no matter how detailed the explanation this did not stop disappointment amongst people who had worked hard on improvements.

Do not link score to bonus
One department tried setting a target score in the bonus for all managers to encourage team working. All it succeeded in doing was to develop a culture of point-seizing within the department. Before any improvement action was done the question of 'how many points does it get us?' was inevitably raised and priorities for improvement became badly warped. Setting objectives based on individual process targets is much better.

Improvement actions are not the responsibility of the Quality Support Manager
In some departments the Quality Support Manager had most of the improvement actions imposed on him/her by the General Manager. It is crucial to ensure the improvement actions are evenly spread amongst the employees of a department. Some departments use a matrix to ensure that there is a one-to-one relationship between the improvement actions and individuals or teams.

Process improvement teams
Initially most of our improvement teams were focused in the department to which they belonged. However, the real benefits of these teams came when they tackled end-to-end processes which cross departmental and/or company boundaries.

SUMMARY

Self-assessment by an organization against one of the models described in this chapter can prove extremely useful in assisting it to improve its business performance. However, if used in an artless manner by organizations just starting out on the quality journey and without an adequate vision of TQM by the senior management team it will not provide the necessary results and may even push the organization down blind alleys. When used in such a naïve way the emphasis tends to be on training staff as assessors, assembling data, preparing long reports and assessment and annual points scoring, without the development of the all important action plans and the solving of the day-to-day quality problems. The focus tends to be on meeting a minimum set standard of points for an internal award and which activities should be concentrated on to increase the score, rather than what are the priorities to increase the velocity of the improvement process. As a consequence the ongoing day-to-day quality problems which beset the organization are not resolved. It is also observed that senior management become obsessive about gaining some form of award (regional or national) within a set time frame. In using self-assessment it is important that management attention is focused on the identification and implementation of improvements and not on the mechanics and techniques of the assessment process and with the obsession of the scoring of points. If this is not done management will run into the problems of self-deception. The commitment and support of senior management to self-assessment is crucial to its success.

The benefit of using self-assessment against one of the recognized models is not the winning of the award but its adoption as a methodology to assess progress, using appropriate diagnostics, and identifying opportunities for improvement, not forgetting the need to satisfy and delight customers. This measurement of progress on a regular basis and comparison of scores from assessments is a confirmation to the management team that real improvement and achievement has taken place. The quantification of performance in terms of numbers is important for senior management. It is also important that the management team of the organization buys-in to the self-assessment process and is enthusiastic about its use. This applies, in particular, to developing action plans to address the outcomes from the self-assessment. Senior management must also be clear on its objectives for self-assessment. When used in the correct manner, the challenge, effort and involvement helps to generate an environment in which it is enjoyable to work.

It would appear that the MBNQA and EQA have generated an industry of its own in running training courses and advising how to understand the assessment process and detail requirements of the award criteria. In organizations this often creates an internal expert who, after intensive external training, applies the knowledge gained in providing advice to the local management team as to how each of the individual criterion can be interpreted and applied to its own particular area of activity. A danger inherent in this is that the 'expert' keen to demonstrate his/her knowledge ends up in keen discussion on the details of the mechanics of self-assessment and consequently the purpose of self-assessment can be lost in the ensuring debate. Another worrying trend is that some organizations seem to believe that using one of the models as the standard and almost as a checklist approach will automatically lead them to TQM. In such organizations people will continually use the term 'business excellence model' in their language almost as a comfort factor that all will be right with their continuous improvement efforts.

REFERENCES

Brown G. 1996: 'How to Determine Your Quality Quotient: Measuring Your Company Against the Baldrige Criteria', *Journal for Quality and Participation*, June, 82–8.

Cole R. E. 1991: Comparing the Baldrige and Deming Awards, *Journal for Quality and Participation*, July-August, 94–104.

Conti T. 1993: *Building Total Quality: A Guide to Management*, Chapman and Hall, London.

Conti T. 1997: *Organizational Self-Assessment*, Chapman and Hall, London.

Dale B. G. 1993: The Key Features of Japanese Total Quality Control, *Quality and Reliability Engineering International*, 9 (3), 169–78.

European Foundation for Quality Management (EFQM) 1998: *Self-Assessment Guidelines for Companies*, EFQM, Brussels.

Hakes C. 1998: *Total Quality Management: The Key to Business Improvement*, (Third Edition), Chapman and Hall, London.

Hillman P. G. 1994: 'Making Self-Assessment Successful', *The TQM Magazine*, 6 (3), 29 31.

ISO 8402 1994: *Quality Management and Quality Assurance – Vocabulary*, International Organization for Standardization, Geneva.

JUSE 1996: Deming Prize Committee, *The Deming Prize Guide for Overseas Companies*, Japanese Union of Scientists and Engineers (JUSE), Tokyo.

Lascelles D. M. and Peacock R. 1996: *Self-Assessment for Business Excellence*, McGraw Hill, Berkshire.

Nakhai B. and Neves J. 1994:, 'The Deming, Baldrige and European Quality Awards', *Quality Progress*, April, 33–7.

Sherer F. 1995: 'Winning the European Quality Award: a Xerox Perspective', *Managing Service Quality*, 5 (2), 28–32.

Steeples, M. M. 1993: *The Corporate Guide to the Malcolm Baldrige National Quality Award*, ASQC Quality Press, Milwaukee.

United States Department of Commerce 1998: *Malcolm Baldrige National Quality Award 1998 Criteria for Performance Excellence*, United States Department of Commerce, National Institute of Standards and Technology Gathersburg.

ACKNOWLEDGEMENTS

Heather Bunney wishes to thank Lee Robinson, Business Quality Manager (Utility Division), for his contribution to the material depicting the North West Water approach to self-assessment.

9

The introduction of Total Quality Management

INTRODUCTION

There are a number of approaches which can be followed in the introduction of TQM, these include: (i) a listing of TQM principles and practices in the form of a generic plan along with a set of guidelines; (ii) prescriptive step-by-step approaches; (iii) methods outlining the wisdom, philosophies and recommendations of the internationally respected experts on the subject (i.e. Crosby, Deming, Feigenbaum and Juran); (iv) self-assessment methods such as the MBNQA Model for Performance Excellence and the EFQM Model for Business Excellence (see chapter 8) and; (v) non-prescriptive methods in the form of a framework or model. With all this available advice and prescriptions it is not surprising that there is sometimes inertia on the part of senior management teams who are faced with the task of introducing TQM in their organizations.

It is up to the management team of each organization to identify the approach which best suits its needs and business operation. Indeed, it is not unusual for an organization to find that its TQM approach is not working out as planned and switch to another approach. Some of the main ways of starting TQM are examined in this chapter along with a summary of the approaches adopted by Betz Dearborn and North West Water Ltd. The chapter opens up by examining why organizations decide to embark on TQM.

THE NEED FOR CHANGE

Lascelles and Dale (1989) report that the improvement process is often triggered by one or more change agents, or opportunities:

- the Chief Executive
- competition

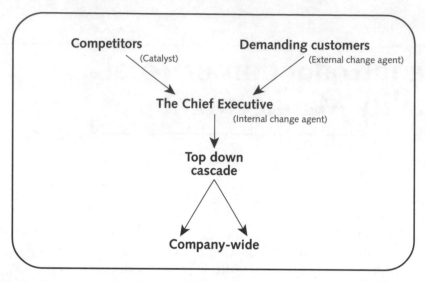

Figure 9.1 Market-led paradigm of TQI.
Source: Lascelles and Dale (1993)

- demanding customers
- 'fresh-start' situations

In a later paper (Lascelles and Dale 1993) they argue that these can be viewed as links in a chain, with competition acting as a catalyst setting off a chain reaction which enhances quality awareness in the market, resulting in demanding customers and the Chief Executive Officer (CEO) behaving as external and internal change agents respectively, (see figure 9.1). Drawing on this work these forces are now described.

The Chief Executive Officer

Most writers on the subject of TQM are agreed that unless the CEO of an organization takes the lead in TQM, attempts and gains made by individuals, functions and departments will be short-lived. However, most CEOs want tangible proof of the need for their own involvement. Thus other forms of change agent must be present, of which market pressure (e.g. competition, demanding customers) have the greatest impact. A restart situation or 'greenfield' opportunity may also help by eliminating some of the barriers to change or reducing their effects.

Competition

There is little doubt that quality is an essential part of the marketing mix as companies seek ways to differentiate their products and/or services from competitors. Many successful companies (in market share terms) now advertise their products and/or services on the basis of quality rather than price. There are numerous well-publicized cases in which intense competition has been the change agent compelling companies to improve quality. The options may be to go out of business, to lose market share, or withdraw from a particular market. The motivation is provided by the need to stay competitive, and the change agent is the customer whose awareness of quality has been enhanced. As a result of such pressures, organizations have, in turn, themselves become demanding customers and sought improvements from their own suppliers.

Demanding customers

Demanding customers with high expectations and an established reputation for quality can be very effective change agents. This also applies to regulatory bodies in those organizations operating in regulated supply situations. In addition to providing tangible evidence of the value of reputation and standing, they have the potential for bringing about radical and permanent changes in attitudes towards quality among their suppliers through contractual requirements. Many major purchasers have policies which outline what is required of suppliers. These documents describe fundamentals that must be incorporated into a supplier's quality planning methods and quality management system to control and improve quality. Each supplier is responsible for building on these fundamentals to develop an effective quality management system and products and services which are defect free. Many purchasers assess and evaluate supplier performance and also provide resources to help suppliers implement tools and techniques, and give guidance on problem solving. Lascelles and Dale (1993) make the point that companies that take an active interest in their suppliers are likely to provoke a far-reaching effect on the way in which they manage quality.

Fresh-start situations

The degree of entrenchment of attitudes and hence the difficulty of changing them, is related to the length of time an organization has been established, its size, length of staff service, product and market stability and managerial mobility. A fresh-start situation therefore provides an excellent opportunity to make rapid and fundamental changes to attitudes and relationships.

A greenfield venture may be the setting up of a new company, a new operational direction for an existing company (e.g. creation of a new strategic business unit as part of a diversification programme), an established company relocating to a new factory, or a company establishing a new operation in existing premises after rationalizing plant, product lines and manpower. It may be argued that most greenfield ventures are in areas where growth expectations are high and where demanding customers are at their most influential. Furthermore, most greenfield companies tend to be small at the outset so that the purchasing power of individual customers is considerable. A greenfield venture provides an opportunity for the introduction of TQM in a situation where there is no prior history of excuses, blame acceptance of mediocrity, shipping non-conforming products in order to meet production targets, providing and accepting a poor level of service, poor delivery performance, and where 'we have always done it this way', 'it will not work here' and other unhelpful attitudes are absent. In a greenfield venture there is an opportunity to start from scratch without any vested interest or inhibiting procedures to overcome. It is an opportunity for senior management to try to do all the things that should be done to engender TQM.

An interruption of a company's operations may present the same kind of opportunity. Intentional temporary dislocation or cessation of normal activities (e.g. moving to a new site, a take-over, management buy-out and large scale refurbishing of premises or equipment) may be another way of breaking with tradition and removing the barriers to change.

APPROACHES TO TOTAL QUALITY MANAGEMENT

The main approaches are now examined in brief.

Applying the wisdom of the quality management experts

The writings and teachings of Crosby, Deming, Feigenbaum and Juran (see chapter 2) is a sensible starting point for any organization introducing TQM. These four men have had a considerable influence in the development of TQM in organizations throughout the world. The usual approach is for an organization to adopt the teachings of one of these experts and attempt to follow his programme. The argument for this is that each expert has a package which works, the package gives some form of security, it provides a coherent framework, gives discipline to the process and provides a common language, understanding and method of communication. To facilitate this some companies have purposely opted for the simplest package; that of Crosby is generally recognized as being the easiest to follow. Dale (1991) found that Crosby followed by Juran and then Deming were the most frequently used experts. Observations of organizations setting out to employ the methods advocated by one of these experts is that sooner or later they will start to pull into their improvement process the ideas of others. This is understandable because none of them has all the answers to the problems facing an organization, despite the claims made about the exclusivity of approach.

Whichever programme or approach is being followed, it should be used to focus on the improvement process and not treated as an end in itself.

Applying a consultancy package

Some companies (usually large concerns) decide to adopt the programme of one of the major management consultancies on the grounds that it is a self-contained package which can be suitably customized for application in their organization. Some companies are very comfortable with consultants, others not so. It should also be noted that most of the 'gurus' have their own consultancy activities to help organizations implement their ideas and principles.

It is important for a company to understand that the use of a consultant organization does not relieve the senior management team of its own responsibilities for TQM (e.g. to demonstrate commitment and give direction to the improvement). Executives should never allow the consultant to become the 'TQM champion' or the company expert on TQM. A key part of consultancy is the transfer of skills and knowledge and when the project is complete the training and guidance, provided by the consultant must remain within the organization in order that TQM can progress and develop. The consultant should be perceived by the organization as an asset to assist with implementation and not as an initiator of TQM. It may be that the consultant is also learning on the job and any ideas, proposals and decisions should always be scrutinized carefully by senior management and/or the TQM steering committee for their applicability to the company's operations.

Management consultancies bring their expertise to the company and provide the resources, experience, disciplines, objectivity and catalysts for getting the process started. The consultants are usually involved in a wide range of activities from planning through to training and project work and implementation of specific improvement initiatives. There are a myriad of consultancies offering a variety of TQM products and packages and not all of them will suit every organization. It is likely that organizations, in particular large ones, will use more than one consultancy as they make progress along the TQM journey.

A company intending to use a consultancy must carefully consider its selection so as to ensure that the one chosen is suited to its needs. This also applies to the individual consultant(s) who will actually carry out the work. There are a number of factors to be taken into consideration in the selection process including:

- presentation of the TQM approach used by the consultancy to senior management and other interested parties
- personality of the consultant(s) and the perceived interaction he/she will be working with
- proposal details
- previously published material
- availability of educational material and supporting systems, programmes and tools
- reputation and track record of the consultancy and individual consultant(s), with existing clients
- knowledge of TQM and its application in practice in similar or related companies – not just in consulting, research and/or teaching
- rapport and ability to communicate with staff at all levels in the organization
- training skills and ability
- grasp of the client organization's culture and management style
- the extent to which the consultancy is prepared to assist in carrying out a diagnosis of the business and tailor the package to suit the needs of the client

The decision to use a consultant organization is usually made by the CEO with support from the Quality Director. It is dangerous for the consultant to assume that other board members will contribute more than vocal support.

The company needs to understand clearly what it is buying from a consultancy. It is often difficult to define in precise detail what is required in a TQM assignment with the consequence that the terms of reference are vague. This sometimes results in a difference between what was ordered and delivered; wrangling over the products and services delivered from a

TQM contract can be a major detractor. The company should also take care that a TQM assignment is not used to open the door for other consultancy work in problem areas such as manufacturing management, business process re-engineering, logistics, human resources, organization development, accountancy and business management. The easiest way of selling consultancy is on the back of a short-term successful assignment. This might have a negative influence on the long-term success of TQM.

A major complaint that organizations make about consultancies is the use of 'off-the-shelf' packages and prescriptive solutions that fail to maximize client involvement, do not reflect the client's business processes and business constraints, and the use of prescriptive words and terms which do not suit the culture of the organization.

For those considering the utilization of an external consultant, the main issues to be addressed and agreed on can be summarized as follows:

- Clear terms of reference specifying the expected benefits to the organization of the consultancy project, with tangible objectives, milestones and timescales.
- The precise nature of the relationship between the client management team and the consultancy. The management team will need to consider the precise form of consultancy input required, and identify success criteria for the project.
- The mechanism for implementing the strategy and managing the change process, together with the resources required. The issues involved include the role of the senior management team, the amount of time and energy individual senior managers are able or prepared to commit, and who might assume the day-to-day role of project co-ordinator.

Frameworks and models

A framework or model is usually introduced to present a picture of what is required in introducing TQM. They are the means of presenting ideas, concepts, pointers and plans in a non-prescriptive manner and are usually not considered to be a 'how-to' guide to TQM introduction and its subsequent development. They are guides to action and not things to be followed in a slavish manner. Step-by-step approaches have a set starting point and usually follow one route and, in general, are rigid. They are more concerned with the destination than the route to get there. A framework allows the users to choose their own starting point, course of action and build gradually on the individual features and parts at a pace which suits their business situation and available resources. Aalbregtse et al. (1991) provide an excellent description of what a framework should consist and its objectives. A number of writers (e.g. Burt 1993, Chu 1988, Dale and Boaden 1993, Flero 1992 and Johnson 1992) have proposed a range of TQM/ improvement frameworks.

A typical framework is the UMIST improvement framework which is described by Dale and Boaden (1993). The framework is divided into four main sections, all of which need to be addressed once the motivation for starting TQM has been identified and the overall strategic direction set. The foundation of the framework is 'organizing' and the two pillars which form its structure are the use of 'systems and techniques' and 'measurement and feedback'. 'Changing the culture' is the fourth section of the framework and is something which must be considered at all stages. Central to the whole process are people, both as individuals and working in teams, without whose skills and commitment TQM will not occur. A diagrammatic representation of the framework is given in figure 9.2 and a summary of its features are found in table 9.1.

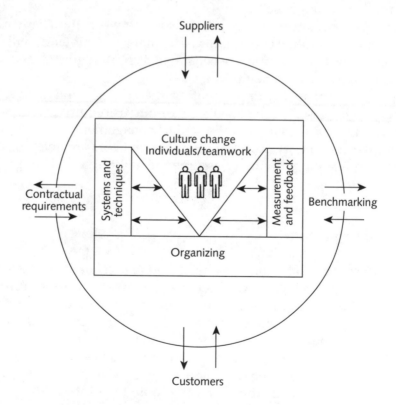

Figure 9.2   The UMIST TQM framework.
Source: Dale and Boaden (1993)

The framework provides an indication of how the various aspects of TQM fit together and is particularly useful for those organizations who:

- are taking their first steps towards TQM
- have got ISO 9000 quality management series registration and require some guidance and advice on what to do next
- are attempting to develop improvement plans and controls across a number of sites
- have less than 3 years of TQM operating experience

Developing a tailor-made organizational route map

A variation on the previously described approaches is to absorb the 'received wisdom' and the experiences of other companies and extract the ideas, methods, systems and tactics which are appropriate to the particular circumstances, business situation and environment of the organization. Organizations starting with any of the popular approaches to TQM will eventually use this method.

In this approach management has to think through the issues and develop for itself a vision, values, objectives, policy, approach, a route map for TQM and the means of deploying the philosophy to all levels of the organization. A feature of organizations following this approach is that senior management will have visited other companies with a reputation for being 'centres of excellence' to see at first hand the lessons learned from TQM. Senior management will have become involved in meetings relating to TQM with executives of like minds from different companies. Senior management members are also frequent attendees at conferences and are generally well-read on the subject.

When getting started on TQM it is always beneficial for organizations to establish contacts with others that have a reputation for excellence in systems, products and services. There is much to be said for learning by association and sharing information through networks. In our experience, companies working with or competing directly against companies with advanced management processes, develop their knowledge of TQM at a fast rate. A case in point is the influence which the resident Japanese automotive and electronic companies have had on the development of improvement practices of the UK supply base.

From the outset, organizations must accept that TQM is a long and arduous journey, which has no end. Unfortunately, there are no short cuts and no-one has a monopoly of the best ideas. Furthermore, once started, the

Table 9.1 UMIST TQM framework: a summary

Organizing	Systems and techniques	Measurement and feedback	Changing the culture
Formulation of a clear long-term strategy for the process of continuous improvement, integrated with other key business strategies, departmental policies and objectives.	Identification of the tools and techniques applicable at different stages of the continuous improvement process.	Identification and definition of key internal and external performance measures to assess the progress being made and to ensure customer satisfaction.	Assessment of the current status of organizational culture, before developing and implementing plans for change.
Definition and communication of a common organizational definition of quality, TQM and continuous improvement.	Development of the appropriate type of training in the use of tools and techniques, targeted at the right people.	Discussion with customers, about expected performance, needs and expectations, using a variety of techniques.	Recognition of the ongoing nature of culture change, rather than a prerequisite for TQM.
Selection of an approach to TQM.	Consideration of the use of a formal quality system, if one is not in place.	Consideration of benchmarking, once the organization has taken some steps down the continuous improvement journey.	The development of plans for change that enable it to take place in a consistent and incremental manner.
Identification of the organizations and people (internal and external) who can be sources of advice on aspects of TQM.	Identification and implementation of other systems and standards that may be required by customers, legislation or in order to compete.	Consideration of various means for celebration and communication of success, and the development of methods for recognizing the efforts of teams and individuals.	The recognition of the role of people within the organization.

Identification of stages of improvement activity, taking into account the starting point of the organization, the motivation for continuous improvement and the tools that may be applicable.

Recognition of executive leadership, tangible commitment and support as being crucial at all stages.

Development and communication of vision and mission statements that are concise and understandable to all employees.

Establishment of a formal programme of education and training.

Establishment of an organizational infrastructure that will ultimately facilitate local ownership of the continuous improvement process.

Establishment of teamwork that is designed to become part of the organization's method of working.

Adoption of process analysis and improvement as a continual part of the organization's continuous improvement process.

Consideration of linking rewards to quality improvement activities and results.

Utilization of some means of assessing the progress toward world-class performance.

Identification of the interrelationships of all activities, and the way in which they contribute to quality within the organization in order to minimize conflict.

Identification of factors that indicate that TQM has started to change culture.

Consideration of the culture of a country and its people in planning for change.

momentum needs to be maintained, otherwise even the gains may be lost. Even the most successful organization has periods when little headway is made. The method of getting started on TQM is less important than management commitment to its ideals and the leadership management is prepared to demonstrate. This is the key determinant of long-term success.

TRAINING FOR QUALITY

Quality products and services depend on a quality workforce. As David Kearns (1997) says, 'we can't have a world-class economy without a world-class workforce'. As discussed in the earlier chapters of this book, the involvement of employees in TQM is critical to its success. An organization does not want to have compliant employees who are not naturally curious and do not challenge the status quo and do not want to learn and relearn. Total quality management requires hard work and continued effort over the entire life of an organization. A business cannot expect improved performance in any area of its activities by doing the same things the same way as it has always done them and it must endeavour to change the status quo. Details of how this may be done is given by Provost and Langley (1998). Change must take place and well planned and executed training is a key element in leading this process. Behavioural changes and performance improvement require training specific to the needs of each individual. Training that is not Just-in-Time wastes time and assets and usually demotivates those people receiving it.

This section of the chapter examines the different types of training and their characteristics and uses two case studies of a speciality chemical manufacturer and a water supply services organization to outline the issues which need to be considered in developing a training programme to facilitate an organizational culture which is conducive to continuous improvement.

Types of Training

There are three major types of quality training undertaken in organizations who are committed to the successful introduction and development of TQM.

1. Awareness

This is used to launch TQM. Its main purpose is to gain commitment, communicate the plan and helps to answer questions such as: 'what

Table 9.2   Advantages of internal and external training

Benefits of in-house programme	*Benefits of external programme*
Cost	Knowledge and skills
Focus on internal objectives	Core activity
Demonstrates commitment	Development work
Self-education	A 'new' voice
Leadership	External comparison
Known quantity	Time resources and capacity
Standardization	
Personal growth	
Specific	

does TQM mean to me and what value will it provide to me in my job?'
The typical content of such training includes:

- TQM and the benefits
- the quality vision
- outlining the infrastructure
- employee surveys/perception and issues output

2. Education

This provides employees with the technical skills, tools and techniques
necessary to gain their involvement in TQM. The typical content includes:

- teams and teamwork
- quality environment
- customer focus
- process
- audits
- problem solving process
- tools and techniques
- self-assessment against a recognized model of business excellence

3. Specific/specialist training

This relates the training to the needs of individuals. Each employee
needs to know his/her overall process and how this effort fits into the
overall plan and his/her personal development. The training includes:

- management behaviour
- project management
- communications skills
- presentation skills
- decision making
- managing change
- empowerment
- self-directed work teams

The approach and deployment of the three types of training should be considered by analysing the following:

Why is the training required ?	awareness/education/specific
Who is to be trained?	how many and over what time period
Who will the training be done by?	who is to do the training; the advantage of using internal and external training inputs are outlined in table 9.2.
How	cross-functional, peer groups, departments, functions, volunteers
Delivery	lectures, distance learning, self-study, video-conferencing, etc.
Cost	£

The ultimate goal of course is for there to be no quality training. Quality should be integrated into everything which every employee of an organization does as a natural part of his/her job.

Case study: Betz Dearborn

The quality training carried out within this organization was centrally organized around the use of tools and techniques and whilst a management development programme did exist, the two elements were kept separate. This case study outlines the training involved in launching and utilizing tools and techniques.

The tools and techniques were applied in the organization at different periods during 1987 to 1997. In the early stages, they were used in a haphazard manner, without serious thought to their implications on the long-term development of TQM. The choice of tools and techniques was also affected by the available resources to facilitate their successful introduction. On several occasions they were viewed as a 'quick-fix' and lacked senior management commitment to their use and these managers often did not indeed understand what was involved in their successful application. By the end of 1992 a wide range of tools and techniques were being applied, for variety of reasons, in different parts of the organization, but the major utilization was by the quality facilitators, operating in conjunction with improvement teams.

The use of tools and techniques was initially dependent on the involvement of the quality function. The reason for this was the initial SPC training, given to all European Managers in 1987 by external management consultants, was incorrectly focused on complex statistical techniques and delivered prematurely to the wrong group of people. This resulted in a group of senior managers being able to construct a control chart but not knowing how to interpret the data or indeed choose which areas of the business to apply the technique. There was also a lack of real activity and value in the use of SPC and the situation existing in the organization mirrored that as typically described by writers such as Wise and Fair (1998) and Dale and Shaw (1990). In parts of the organization, for some years later, there was considerable resistance to the application of SPC. Dale et al. (1990) state that SPC is essentially a tool used to control and manage a process through the use of statistical methods and on its own will achieve little, although it may cause the right type of questions to be asked and facilitate greater understanding of the process.

There is little doubt that the senior management team had great expectations of SPC. It was initially used when the seven basic quality control tools (as described in chapter 6) would have been more applicable. Initially, a project team was established to determine how the company could use SPC rather than to assess how SPC could help it improve the quality of its products and services. No infrastructure was established to facilitate the introduction of the technique and its application became the sole responsibility of an improvement facilitator.

The initial training of all European managers in the application of SPC was carried out at a very early stage in the development of TQM. With hindsight, SPC was introduced far too early, due to overselling from a management consultant and before the company had developed its approach to TQM. There was also a subsequent lack of follow-up training and application at the operating end of the organization. Consequently, the introduction of other tools and techniques to the rest of the organization was confined to groups working through particular projects as a means of helping them define and identify root causes of the problem and decide on correction action.

In 1992, in order to overcome the problems with SPC, the training of the

Quality Facilitators in a set of simple tools and their application facilitated the necessary improvement team training which enabled them to solve the problems given to them by the management team. The use of the seven basic quality control tools to identify problems which contributed to customer dissatisfaction and quality costs resulted in a number of improvements being recommended by the improvement teams and more importantly being implemented by management. They also provided the senior management team with the information it needed to justify further corporate investment in the site whilst other sister sites were closed and divested.

The success of the use of seven basic quality control tools in improvement team meetings and departmental briefing sessions enlightened the management team to believe that there was a need to first promote those tools before moving onto more complex process control and process capability studies. There is little doubt that the development of in-house training courses, based on company examples, accelerated the general understanding and application of the tools by employees at all levels of the organizational hierarchy.

The change of focus in the improvement activities in 1991 and the development of the Quality Facilitator role accelerated the use of the basic tools throughout the company and they became cornerstones of involving employees in the improvement process. The creation of multi-functional teams which received the same type of tools and technique training

Table 9.3 Introduction of tools and techniques

Tools and techniques	1987	1988	1989	1990	1991	1992	1993	1994	1995
Cause and effect analysis			●						
Pareto analysis			●						
Control chart	●								
Quality costing		●							
Departmental purpose analysis		●							
Q-mapping/flowcharting				●					
Process modelling								●	
FMEA						●			
QFD							●		
Checksheet				●					
Histogram			●						
Scatter diagram			●						
Graphs			●						
Seven planning tools									●
Mistake proofing									●

also helped to engender a sense of common approach to resolution of problems.

Whilst the tools and techniques outlined in table 9.3 were being utilized somewhere in the organization by the end of 1992, there was still a lack of consistency in approach and deployment. This was addressed by the improvement team training which was introduced at the beginning of 1993, administered by the team facilitator and sponsor and focused on the use of four key tools, namely brainstorming, flowcharting, cause and effect diagrams and Pareto diagrams.

Case study: North West Water

The organization developed a business quality strategy to develop the culture of the organization into one that is customer focused and results driven, utilizing the talents and skills of all its employees (see chapter 8, Case study: North West Water). In June 1995, a review was undertaken to identify the existing training within those areas upon which the success of the business quality implementation plan was dependent.

A list of 'Quality Topics' needed to support implementation was developed from Dale (1994, Second Edition) and other similar texts, together with study of the literature of leading quality management consultants so that a comparison of the 'current' versus 'desired' training support could be achieved. The topics given in table 9.4 were considered to be a critical element in developing a quality culture and also to provide the tools and techniques required to successfully Implement the business quality plan.

The data gathering was conducted by circulating the list of topics to the training department and to the network of quality champions and facilitators to determine if any appropriate information currently existed and who would be

Table 9.4 Quality topics

Quality concepts	Customer focus
Problem solving	Seven quality tools
Process improvement	Measures for quality
Quality inspection	Statistical tools
Manager as a facilitator	Teamwork
Interpersonal skills	Empowerment
Reward and recognition	Assessment against the EFQM model
Benchmarking	

Table 9.5   Quality training: course outline

Quality concepts (quality in action) and customer focus	To create an awareness of what is TQM and how it can improve business results through a customer focused and results orientated business. To emphasize that quality is the responsibility of everyone.
Problem solving and seven control quality tools	To provide a process for problem solving, common across all functions and used by all levels of the business. The seven quality control tools are used to display the data used for analysing the problems.
Process improvement and measures for quality	To provide a methodology common across all functions for identifying and selecting the key processes. Documenting the processes and applying in-process measures to determine areas for improvement.
Quality inspection	To help management and staff to gather information, understand what is happening and agree improvement actions and plans.
Manager as a facilitator	To provide managers with the necessary skills to improve communication and productivity. To encourage participation in team decision making and commitment through consensus.
Teamwork	To develop a greater understanding of what the purpose of the team is, its roles and responsibilities and the consequential impact on the business in the broader sense of teamwork.
Interpersonal skills	To improve communication skills for all staff to develop a clear understanding of information requirements, both internal and external.
Empowerment	To help managers understand the behavioural changes that need to take place to maximize the benefits of empowerment. Changing from directing tasks and activities to achieving results through empowering people and facilitating the work process.
Reward and recognition	To understand the power of recognition and how it can be used in both financial and non-financial ways to reinforce the desired quality behaviours of all employees.
EFQM assessment	To understand what is self-assessment, what are the benefits to be gained, the model used and the method of scoring and inspection.
Benchmarking	To understand what is benchmarking, how to use the benchmarking process and where it fits into the strategic planning process.

the best person to speak to on each subject. Meetings were arranged and structured as follows:

- introduction and purpose outlined
- subject material reviewed for relevance
- actions agreed

The 'Quality Topics' were listed sequentially. They could be described as a quality tool kit each having a specific function and yet a complementary value when used with other tools with a problem solving and process improvement methodology. This provided a common approach across all functions in the support of business quality. The details of this are summarized in table 9.5.

The conclusions from the review included the following:

The integration of quality principles, tools and techniques into all current and future training workload required further planning

All employees need to have been previously trained in the principles, tools and techniques of continuous improvement. To integrate these into training in the first phase would require a project team to define the core training and then work together with representatives from the quality network/business quality group to validate the material. Once the training department had the requisite knowledge then validation could take place.

The introduction to a quality company through induction training for new employees requires further planning

When new employees commence working in their respective roles and find that their colleagues do not emphasize the behaviour and attitudes that depict a quality company then the new employees receive mixed messages. The timing of this type of training is crucial. Concepts, problem solving and process improvement need to be included in this programme.

Following this review, the Quality Manager with a responsibility for training was appointed. The quality training support matrix given in figure 9.3 was used, in the first instance, to hold discussions with the line managers in the business, later followed by discussions with quality support managers to determine the breadth and depth of requirements. Each person with whom these discussions were held reviewed the matrix in light of his/her own business circumstances in order to assess if the split between managers, staff and quality support managers was appropriate. Training of the quality network focused on three main areas, namely, problem solving, process simplification and benchmarking. These three courses run for 1 day each and are identified as essential for quality support managers.

Needs	Managers	Staff	Quality support management
Quality in action concepts	Understanding	Understanding	Expert understanding
Problem solving	Understanding	Understanding	Expert understanding
Process simplication	Understanding	Understanding	Expert understanding
Statistical tools	Awareness	Awareness	–
Teamwork/facilitation	Understanding	Understanding	Expert understanding
EFQM assessment	Understanding	Awareness	Expert understanding
Benchmarking	Awareness	Understanding	Expert understanding

Figure 9.3 Quality training support.

The basic problem solving course involves low risk, simple, cheap, and 'business as usual' activities. These require minimal management commitment, low resources and provide a relatively small return on investment. On the other hand, with benchmarking, complex, expensive, breakthrough improvements are being considered. This requires considerable management commitment, high resources and delivering a high return on investment. There are obviously a number of permutations in-between these two extremes.

At the end of the 1996–97 financial year a further review was carried out to determine the deployment of quality training throughout the organization. The results of this review demonstrated that in general, training was permeating throughout the organization and as a consequence, quality training was handed over to the existing training department later that year.

Case study: The introduction of TQM at Betz Dearborn (Widnes site)

This case study is described in detail in Dale (1994 Second Edition).

In early 1986 one of the company's major customers requested that they be registered to the then BS. 5750: Part 1 (1987). (At this time the company was Grace Dearborn and became Betz Dearborn in 1996 with the purchase of the Dearborn business by Betz.) Once registration was achieved several companies approached them for advice on how to meet the requirements of this system series standard. One of these companies was Kodak who, at that time, had a number of years of TQM experience. Kodak is a major customer and from the resulting discussions on various issues relating to TQM, it became increasingly clear to senior management that customers were becoming more demanding with respect to their requirements from suppliers. Requests from other customers for statistical evidence of process capability maintained an impetus for change towards TQM. In order to retain the company's status as a market leader, the Managing Director decided that TQM was the only route to continually meeting the increasing needs and expectations of the marketplace and ensuring long-term business growth and continued success.

The Key Events

A firm of major management consultants was contracted to assist in the introduction of TQM. Under its guidance the introduction took place in four phases:

Phase 1   Diagnosis and preparation
Phase 2   Management focus and commitment
Phase 3   Intensive improvement
Phase 4   Review and reinforcement

Phase 1 – Diagnosis and Preparation

This phase was used to collect and interpret the general culture of the organization. This involved a number of activities:

- a TQM briefing workshop for senior management
- an internal survey of employee attitudes, perceptions and concerns
- a survey of customers to obtain their views on the strengths and weaknesses of the Company
- a quality costing exercise to identify the scale and major areas of wastage and non-value adding activities

The information collected from this series of activities was analysed and presented to the senior management team, who in turn disseminated the key findings and resulting actions to employees. The diagnostic phase highlighted four main areas of concern: leadership; communication; knowledge of the business; and teamworking. The ways in which the company addressed these concerns are now described.

The managing director was instrumental in developing a management development programme for all existing and potential managers. This 10 day programme included a 1 day management stance section administered by the

MD and focused on the way in which he believed managers should behave. The objectives of the programme were to:

- increase awareness of what is involved in TQM and the appropriate managerial behaviour and attitudes
- improve managerial skills
- understand the company's vision and mission
- understand the importance of leadership
- increase awareness of the challenges of change and how this should be handled

Knowledge of the business

The diagnostic phase revealed a need for all employees to have a thorough understanding of the business. The initiatives included:

- team briefings
- our business/our department presentations
- customer visits
- more personnel visits to customers
- communication of strategies
- communication of work/business plan

Teamworking

This final area of concern was the lack of teamworking throughout the company. To overcome this a quality team process was established and two types of team formalized: quality project teams and quality improvement teams.

Phase 2 – Management Focus and Commitment

By early 1989 the diagnostic phase had been completed and phase two commenced.

The purpose of this phase was to focus TQM. A top team workshop chaired by the Managing Director was held to discuss the outcomes of the diagnosis and preparation phase. A number of issues identified from the diagnosis were converted into projects led by members of the senior management team. The senior managers also committed themselves to personal action plans which not only demonstrated their commitment to TQM but endeavoured to ensure that their behaviour was commensurate with the principles.

A TQM steering group consisting of the Managing Director and his senior management team was also established to meet on a quarterly basis.

The next step was the introduction of DPA. A project team, consisting of the Sales Manager, Technical Manager and a Technical Services Administrator, was established to identify the most appropriate way of applying DPA. Each member of the team carried out a pilot DPA in their own department to test out the concept and highlight potential problems. This team made a presentation to the TQM Steering Committee on its experiences, and developed an implementation guide which was submitted to all managers.

One of the major findings from the diagnosis phase was the perceived lack of internal communication. To this end several initiatives were undertaken to improve the internal communication. These included:

- A Key Issues series of conferences took place. The purpose of these was to have representatives from all departments and levels of the organization hierarchy address issues which, by common consent, were key to the future of the company and its employees.
- In 1989 the 'our' department/business presentations were launched. These were held on a regular basis to inform employees of the functions of other departments and the businesses within which the company operated.
- In 1989, a TQM presentation, based on the Chemical Industries Association handbook (Chemical Industries 1989) and video, was developed. This presentation, which was administered by a senior manager, was given to groups of employees. This series of presentations was used as the main vehicle for introducing new company employees to the principles of TQM and also acted as a positive enforcer to existing personnel.
- The introduction of DPA as a means of identifying clearly the purpose and total contribution of a department and to provide a department with the opportunity to examine its internal/customer relationships.
- Business plan presentations were introduced in early 1990. The aim of these presentations was to communicate the financial plans for the forthcoming year including the departmental managers' own plans and measures.
- Quality Action Days, introduced in mid 1990, gave all employees the opportunity to meet the Managing Director to express their views on the company's progress. These days were based on a presentation by the Managing Director followed by workshop sessions to explore relevant issues. These resulting actions were communicated in further feedback sessions.
- In mid 1990 a second employee attitude survey was undertaken. The survey, which was designed, administrated and analysed by the TQM project group, was used to identify what progress had been made since the initial 1988 survey.
- Quality Process Improvement Days were introduced which gave internal customers and suppliers the opportunity to identify and resolve common areas of concern.

Phase 3 – Intensive Improvement

The first action in this phase was to identify facilitators to act as champions. Some 16 people were nominated to act in this role. They represent different levels of the organizational hierarchy and all functions of the business.

The facilitators were given basic training which identified their role and provided an appreciation of TQM and its importance to the future success of the company. However, in the middle of 1990 it was realized, mainly through the introduction of Quality Action Days, that the quality improvement facilitators training was inadequate. Consequently, an intensive training course in some of the more well known quality management tools and techniques (e.g. seven original quality control tools, SPC and flowcharting) was given to the facilitators, and their role redefined.

The identification and action on quality improvements are addressed by:

- management action
- quality project teams
- quality improvement teams

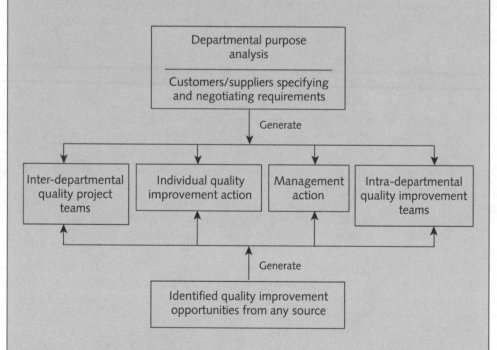

Figure 9.4 Relationship between quality improvement initiatives and team activity.

In deciding which of these three quality improvement approaches/routes to use, the following factors are taken into account:

- where the idea for the improvement originated
- the strategic significance of the improvement
- whether the improvement affects more than one major area of the company's operation

These three approaches (see figure 9.4) coupled with those improvements brought about by individual employees, provide the basis for continuous improvement.

Phase 4 – Review and Reinforcement
This phase was not followed through by the consultants.

Case study: The introduction of TQM at North West Water

United Utilities is an international company primarily involved in the supply of drinking water, treatment of wastewater, electricity distribution and supply. The Company was formed in January 1996 following the merger of North West Water and NORWEB.

The Motivation for Change
After privatization it was anticipated that there would be a rise in customer expectations and the standards expected from NWW. It was also expected that the demands of shareholders would lead to a need to reduce operating costs and increase profits. With this perceived challenge in mind the senior management team set about transforming the culture of NWW into a company that displays the values and characteristics of an aggressive and enterprising private sector firm. The Chief Executive's impression of NWW was largely of a company that had grown stale in ideas and stuck in a public sector mentality. He decided that attitudes and training would have to be dramatically improved. The strategic vision – NWW 2000 – was set up to direct this process. The vision was for North West Water to become a low-cost operator, the most efficient water and wastewater firm in the UK and a world leader in providing high quality products and customer service.

The principles underpinning the North West Water 2000 vision, were taken progressively through the organization by presentations and a number of roadshows. The principles outlined in the vision stressed that NWW would strive to build a high performance culture based on an individual's commitment to producing results in terms of service and quality.

Following the development of the strategy each of the current departments was, in turn, reviewed with the involvement of all staff. The focus of the review was on the way in which activities were carried out and the reason for each activity, seeking at every opportunity to identify those in-house activities that could be out sourced at considerable savings. The objective was to be selective about the things a water company should do. From this analysis it was also found that training, information systems and the organizational culture required considerable attention if the vision was to be achieved.

The mission of managing change in the organization fell to a team called the Change Management Group, headed by the then Group Personnel Director and operated by a mix of NWW personnel. The effort was directed at transforming the culture, skills and abilities of the workforce to meet the vision of NWW 2000, to minimize the disruption to the business and quality of service, and to maximize the benefits of the changes by ensuring that the organization and systems supported the business. The vehicles used by the Change Management Group to implement this change revolved around training, communications and alterations to existing personnel practices.

Key Milestones in the Transformation Journey
The following were some of the activities undertaken to assist with the process of change.

The establishment of a quality infrastructure
The structure consisted of the Customer Steering Group (CSG), Business Quality Group (BQG), Quality Champions and Quality Forum members.

The CSG, chaired by the Customer Services Director and attended by the Managing Director, was set up to provide strategy and direction. It managed customers, communications and quality, including the Customer Charter. The group members included all the directors and the representatives of these three initiatives. The BQG was a support group, headed by the Business Quality Manager and responsible for co-ordinating TQM. The responsibility of the BQG was to ensure the effective implementation of the business quality improvement plan, develop the plan through new quality initiative and to support all the employees in their improvement activities. The objectives of the implementation plan, which had four key strands – communication, training, performance improvement and breakthrough improvement (see figure 9.5) – were to:

- improve internal and external customer satisfaction
- show clear improvements in efficiency and levels of service
- ensure that NWW was viewed as a 'quality' company by its customers, employees and industry

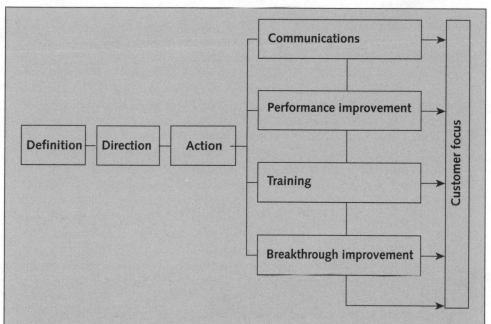

Figure 9.5 Business quality programme.

The effectiveness of the initial plan, which had a five year time scale, was measured against the following metrics:

- percentage of employees who were satisfied that NWW was customer focused
- percentage of employees who were satisfied that NWW was a 'quality' company
- percentage of employees who understood how to use quality in their day-to-day activities
- number of benchmarking projects completed and delivering of break-through service/profitability improvement
- financial savings made as a consequence of costed improvement activity
- score achieved against the EFQM model

In addition seven Quality Champions were appointed for each function and had the responsibility to lead and co-ordinate quality in each function. They also provided an initial point of contact for cross-departmental improvement initiatives. There was also a 'Quality Forum' consisting of 25 people. The forum members (quality support managers) were responsible for supporting and encouraging the implementation of quality in the company and for the review and transfer of best practice from one function within the company to another.

People development
Starting from the 1990 management conference 'Investing in Quality' senior management had emphasized the importance of people in achieving the strategic view of NWW. There was a clear belief that all employees could do an extraordinary job given appropriate and timely training and the right leadership from management. At this conference the then Managing Director challenged line managers to take ownership for TQM and to work with their people to fully utilize their potential.

A considerable amount of training had been given to assist with developing the skills of people in order that they might better serve their customers. This initiative had been co-ordinated by the Employee Development Department. For example, in April 1992 some 500 managers participated in a 2 day workshop and in June 1993 each employee in the new Customer Service Centre was given 2 days of training. Customer service representatives in the centre were multi-functional, handling questions on individual accounts, problem logging, work management and correspondence retrieval, in addition to having the ability from their workstations to call up maps, account histories and local information on work in progress or incidents.

A number of special training models had also been created. For example: a half day course on quality suitable for anyone in the company; a half day course for managers on how to deliver the introduction of quality to their team; a 2 day course on problem solving; a 1 day workshop for managers to produce business plans based on the results arising from self-assessment; and a 1 day course on benchmarking and a series of courses on self-assessment using the EFQM model. In addition quality-related themes appeared in all training courses. This was to help ensure that quality was perceived as integral to the way in which NWW ran its business and to sustain the necessary culture change throughout the organization. It would also encourage employees to identify and build on best practice wherever they found it.

Establishing quality values and attitudes
The 'Strategy for Success' initiative encouraged line managers to take ownership for TQM and develop an environment in which employees would be committed to producing results. Employees were encouraged to identify their internal and external customers and develop ways of satisfying them. They were also empowered to challenge processes, procedures and instructions which did not add value to NWW and/or result in customer satisfaction. Using initiatives such as performance measurement and benchmarking, managers and employees were educated to measure the performance of the processes for which they were the owners and to share their achievements with other teams and departments.

NWW had invested a considerable amount of effort to build 'quality' values into its day-to-day operations, including:

- Ensuring that its employees became and were seen to be more customer-focused, not only in terms of domestic and business customers who pay for services, but people inside the company. The values stressed to every employee were; defining who your customers were; finding out what they wanted then delivering these wants; and identifying ways of improving how these requirements were satisfied.
- Setting up awards and rewards for groups and individuals in order to convey the message that the company meant what it said about achieving its dual objectives through continuous improvement. The following means were employed to recognize the contribution of individuals:

  - a Quality Award for a department, function or geographic location that was either the best exponent of a quality approach to business or that had done the most in improving itself toward becoming a quality role model;
  - an annual improvement day/team competition, with £100 going to each of the teams reaching the final and £500 to the top team;
  - special recognition awards of around £50 or equivalent could be made by managers at a certain level in the organization to recognize special contributions to quality.

- The 'voice' of the employees was taken seriously through an annual employee opinion survey and the implementation of suggestions and proposals to drive the improvement process forward. A suggestion was assessed by the person's manager and valued according to both operational and capital expenditure savings. In addition, there were £5 awards for adopting best practice from elsewhere and the idea of the year competition which was valued at £500.
- Educating its employees to practise the value of continuous improvement through self-assessment and benchmarking.

The detail of this is summarized in figure 9.6.

Organizational structure and operation processes

As mentioned earlier departments and facilities that did not directly contribute to the core businesses of water supply and wastewater services were contracted out, resulting in a large number of employees leaving the organization. These changes in the management structure and the creation of new posts changed the lines of accountability and the links between the employees in the field and those serving as customer services representa-tives.

Communication

Management believed that communication between NWW and external customers, among its employees and between the departments all needed to be

LIVERPOOL
JOHN MOORES UNIVERSITY
AVRIL ROBARTS LRC
TITHEBARN STREET
LIVERPOOL L2 2ER
TEL. 0151 231 4022

WHAT WE ARE TRYING TO DO:

Communication

* Employees understand what business quality means.
* Employees perceive the business quality strategy as cohesive and vital to the achievement of our business goals.
* We are perceived, both internally and externally, as driving continuous customer focused improvement

Performance improvement

* A systematic management process (based on the EFQM model) is implemented across the whole business.
* This management process is used to determine operational priorities, identify best practices and areas of weakness and drive business improvement
* Formal annual assessment of this management process is carried out (based on EQA assessment).
* A healthy spirit of competition is promoted by comparing and contrasting the relative performance improvement management of each part of the business.

Training

* All employees have an understanding of what taking a quality approach to business means and apply this understanding to their day-to-day activity.
* Quality principles are included in all training to help sustain the necessary cultural change throughout the organization.
* Specific training will be provided to ensure that, where appropriate, specialist knowledge and skills are made available (e.g. team working skills, problem solving skills, facilitation, EFQM awareness, process simplification, etc.).

Breakthrough projects

* Significant breakthrough improvement in both customer service and profitability is delivered in major business areas.
* Suitable benchmarks and business processes are selected as project areas.
* Project staff are appropriately trained.
* Recommendations are integrated into the business.
* These projects are used as show-case examples of quality driving bottom line business improvement.

HOW WE WILL KNOW WE ARE SUCCESSFUL:

UK Utility Division 1996–7 Targets

STATUS	Target	
G	60% (51%)	of Employees satisfied that the UK Utility Division is customer focused.
Y	50% 40%	of Employees satisfied that the UK Utility Division is a quality company.
G	75% (7%)	of Employees that understand how to use quality in their day-to-day activities.
G	5 (2)	Benchmarking projects completed and delivering breakthrough service/profitability improvement.
G	£1.5m (£1m)	in financial savings made as a consequence of costed improvement activity.
G		('95 results in brackets)

UK Utility Division 1996–7 Milestones

STATUS		
G	Feb.	Quality conference
G	Mar.	Process Improvement Training
G	Jun.	Utility wide EFQM Assessments
G	Nov.	Improvement Day(s) – Top Team
G	Dec.	Communication of Dept. Business Plans
Y	Dec.	Quality In Action/Managing for Success Workshops complete

Date 28 August 1996

HOW WE ARE CONTRIBUTING:

Communication Actions
(i) Water and Wires Scheme
(ii) Improvement Day and Quality Award
(iii) Best Practice Newsletter
(iv) Customer Satisfaction Handbook and Guide
(v) Management Brief of '96-97 Programme
(vi) Div/Dept Business Plan communications

Performance Improvement Actions
(i) Facilitation of Divisional Business Plan
(ii) Employee Survey management
(iii) Business Improvement Reviews
(iv) Provision of trained EFQM assessors
(v) Co-ordination of EFQM assessments
(vi) Tracking of improvement actions

Training Actions
(i) Quality Action/Success Workshop roll-out
(ii) Quality Principles in training design
(iii) Benchmarking training and guide
(iv) Process Improvement training and guide
(v) Problem Solving training and guide
(vi) Project Management Guide

Breakthrough Project Actions
(i) Review of internal best practice sharing
(ii) Support of Empl. Comms. benchmarking
(iii) Support for Cust. Strategy benchmarking
(iv) Support for Maint. Perf. Measures project
(v) Support for Mains Refurb. Comms. project
(vi) Support for Discoloured Water project
(vii) Support for Meter Connections project
(viii) Support for NORWEB Productivity project
(ix) Support for Plant Stock Control project

Figure 9.6 Business as usual: Business Quality Group – UK Utility Division.

improved. Efforts were made by managers to communicate management decisions and ideas through letters, seminars and briefings to ensure that the employees understood what was required of them. Leaflets and documents stating the customer charters, guarantee standards and how to complain were sent to the customers assuring them of NWW commitment in providing a quality service.

Listening to customers

Measurements of customer satisfaction using the customer opinion survey was now a regular feature of NWW. In addition, NWW listened to customers using a wide range of different measures, including:

- customer contact surveys
- listened and consulted initiatives using TV and the press
- qualitative business customer research
- kept regular track of representative views of customers who were affected by asset maintenance work

Self-assessment

In 1993 after considering the benefits claimed for self-assessment by superior performing organizations, senior management decided to begin the practice of self-assessment using the EFQM model. The two main reasons for this decision were to:

- identify strengths and weaknesses and highlight areas for improvement by comparing its own performance against the model criteria.
- merge the self-assessment process with the business planning cycle, that is, to plan, implement the business plan and review the performance

Benchmarking

By comparing itself with the best companies NWW aimed to deliver significant improvements in key business areas. Each year the company intended to choose three key company-wide projects to benchmark. In 1995 they were in the customer function, operations and regulatory services, as follows:

1. Call handling in Customer Services.
2. Customer communication before, during and after major refurbishment which caused major disruptions in service to customers.
3. Laboratory Services: this dealt with the flow of information and materials into and out of the laboratory.

These benchmarking projects were used as showcase examples of quality driving bottom line business improvement and are described in detail by Love et al. (1998).

SUMMARY

This chapter has argued that a formal approach to TQM is triggered by one or more of four factors, namely the CEO, competition, demanding customers and fresh-start situations.

The point has been made that there is no 'right' way of introducing and developing TQM. There are a number of approaches and these have been examined in this chapter. It is senior management's responsibility to select the approach which best suits the business and operating environment and any constraints which may exist. The approach should always be tailored to the organization and 'off-the-shelf' packages avoided. Senior management have much to gain by networking with its counterparts in different businesses and this exchange of ideas and concerns and discussion of common issues can help to fine-tune the approach which is being used and to advance the development of TQM.

The way that Betz Dearborn and North West Water set about the introduction and development of TQM has been presented. There are a number of reasons why these two organizations approaches to TQM have been successful. However, three reasons stand out. Firstly, the visible commitment and leadership of senior management. Senior management has been prepared to invest its time and resources in thinking through some of the crucial issues involved with TQM and then steering the issues through the organization. Secondly, the establishment of an appropriate and robust infrastructure to support the improvement process. Thirdly, the skills and abilities of staff at all levels in the organization.

Quality training or training for quality is discussed in many articles/publications as a means of initiating, maintaining and developing any continuous improvement initiative. Whilst training certainly is not the primary driver on the TQM journey it is the critical fuel which enables the organization to adopt many of the values (i.e. empowerment, management by fact and reward and recognition). The authors are of the view that before an organization embarks upon any quality training it needs to evaluate the type of training required with respect to awareness, education and technical content.

This chapter has outlined two very different case study examples of the deployment of quality training both of which have merit to the differing circumstances. However, there is one clear message: quality training must be Just-in-Time and job specific if it is to influence the hearts and minds of employees.

REFERENCES

Aalbregtse R. J., Heck J. A. and McNeley P. K. 1991: 'TQM: How Do You Do It?' *Automation*, 38 (8), 30–2.

BS 5750 Part 1 1987: *Specification for Design/Development, Production, Installation and Servicing* (ISO 9001, 1987, *Quality Systems – Model for Quality Assurance in Design/Development, Production, Installation and Servicing*), British Standards Institution, London.

Burt J. T. 1993: 'A New Name for a No-so-New Concept', *Quality Progress*, 26 (3), 87–8.

Chemical Industries Association 1989: *Total Quality Management*, Chemical Industries Association, London.

Chu C. H. 1988: 'The Pervasive Elements of Total Quality Control', *Industrial Management*, 30 (5), 30–2.

Dale B. G. 1991: 'Starting on the Road to Success', *The TQM Magazine*, 2 (6), 321–4.

Dale B. G. (ed.) 1990: *Managing Quality*, Prentice Hall, Hertfordshire.

Dale B. G. (ed.) 1994: *Managing Quality* (Second Edition), Prentice Hall, Hertfordshire

Dale B. G. and Boaden R. J. 1993: 'Improvement Framework', *The TQM Magazine* 5 (1), 23–6.

Dale B. G. and Shaw P. 1990: 'Some Problems Encountered in the Construction and Interpretation of Control Charts', *Quality and Reliability Engineering*, International, 6 (1), 7–12.

Dale B. G., Shaw P., Owen M. 1990: 'SPC in the Motor Industry: an examination of implementation and use', *International Journal of Vehicle Design*, 11 (2), 115–31.

Flero J. 1992: 'The Crawford Slip Method', *Quality Progress*, 25 (5), 40–50.

Johnson J. W. 1992: 'A Point of View: Life in a Fishbowl: A Senior Manager's Perspective on TQM', *National Productivity Review*, 11 (2), 143–6.

Kearns D. T. 1997: 'A CEO's View of Training', *Training and Development Journal*, May, 41–50.

Lascelles D. M. and Dale B. G. 1989: 'Quality Improvement: What is the Motive?', *Proceedings of the Institution of Mechanical Engineers*, 203 (B1), 43–50.

Lascelles D. M. and Dale B. G. 1993: *The Road to Quality*, IFS Publications, Bedford.

Love R., Bunney H. S., Smith M and Dale B. G. 1998: 'Benchmarking in Water Supply Services: the Lessons Learnt', *Benchmarking for Quality Management and Technology*, 5 (1), 59–70.

Provost L. P. and Langley G. J. 1998: The Importance of Concepts in Creativity and Improvement, *Quality Progress*, 31 (3), 31–7.

Wise S. and Fair D. 1998: 'The Control Chart Dilemma', *Quality Progress*, 31 (2), 66–71.

ACKNOWLEDGEMENTS

Barrie Dale wishes to thank Dr David Lascelles for the use of the material in the 'Need for Change' section.

Heather Bunney wishes to thank Mark Smith for the use of his material in the NWW Case Study section. She also wishes to thank Roy Hudson, Fielden-Cegas Box Ltd for his contribution to the material contained in this chapter.

10

Total Quality Management: summary

INTRODUCTION

This concluding chapter of *Total Quality Management* drawing together the main themes running through the book and using research carried out in European business during the last decade as reported by Dale et al. (1998), makes some observations on present and future events which are related to the advancement of TQM.

THE PRESENT

Organizations without an ISO 9000 series certificate of registration will find it increasingly difficult to do business in the world marketplace. This trend will be reinforced by the exponential interest of American industry in the series which to some degree is fuelled by QS 9000. However, this series of quality management system standards should be regarded by organizations as the minimum and the objective should be to surpass the specified requirements. In particular, the current challenge is to develop effective preventive action disciplines and mechanisms and ensure that these drive continual improvements and broaden the vision from merely a paperwork system audit.

Many small and medium enterprises (SMEs) have got ISO 9000 series registration and remain stuck on this quality management foundation stone. They require simple, effective and pragmatic advice on what steps to take next on the improvement journey. The challenge is to provide this in appropriate and easily understandable stages, which can move them from ISO 9000 series registration to EQA prize winner status. However, the gap between the requirements of the ISO 9000 series and the holistic nature of the EFQM Model for Business Excellence cannot be bridged just by taking another list of criteria by which an organization can be measured. More of the basics need to be put in place before the EFQM model can be effectively used for assessing an organization, see van der Wiele et al. 1997).

A current challenge is to evaluate and examine the extent to which TQM philosophy and values are present in the organization, including asking the following questions:

- How does an organization develop its culture so that everyone is committed to continuous improvement?
- What is the best means of managing the change process?
- Did those companies who are successful with TQM have a culture, prior to introduction, different from that typified by the more traditionally managed companies and what was the predominant management style?
- What is the best means of facilitating such changes in traditionally managed organizations, in particular those in public ownership, monopoly and regulated supply situations and also in government departments?
- How, when, where and at what pace does culture change take place?
- What are the best means of measuring change?
- How can the attitudes of middle management be changed?
- How can the organization ensure that production/operations personnel think quality as well as numbers and value, not just costs?
- What are the best means of empowering people to take ownership for their own quality and its improvement?
- What is the effect of national and industry cultures on TQM?
- Are the impediments to progress common across different cultures?
- How can TQM be developed in a downsizing situation?
- How can you engender a need to change when there is no perceived business threat?

In this current age of privatization, contracting-out of government services and pressure for value for money services, government departments, public services and service providers are coming under increasingly competitive pressures for the pursuit of excellence. In these organizations the challenge is how to effectively apply the principles and mechanisms of continuous improvement and change the typical 'civil service' mentality which exists in such environments.

Continuous improvement initiatives must reach every part of an organization and each employee and function need to be involved if TQM is to become total. Quality needs to be seen and treated as an integral part of each department's activities. However, some functions and staff are more resistant to the concept than others. How to convert the cynics, 'blockers' and 'resistors' is a major problem and the same can be said for ensuring that improvement becomes a daily issue in situations when resources are fully stretched and people feel overworked. A related issue which needs attention is how a company can measure the 'conversion' of cynics – who just pay lip service and comply with norm to individuals who are committed to the change.

There is a set of issues relating to employee relations including: what is the role of employee representation in TQM and will it have a diminishing or increasing influence?; what are the effects of the democratizing process in TQM and the increasing values placed on the workforce and their skills on the traditional balance of power in the workplace?; and what, if any, effects will European labour laws have on TQM? Revitalizing the continuous improvement process after a period of stagnation is a key issue. Typical issues with which organizations are wrestling include: why has stagnation occurred?; is stagnation a natural phenomenon?; and what are the best means of revitalizing the process? Most people in an organization will know why the process has stagnated but of more immediate concern is what is the best means of getting it going again and sustaining its momentum. This will continue in the future, with management coping with the effects of organizational restructuring, outsourcing, downsizing and changes in senior management, products, services and processes and attempting to minimize the effects of these changes on TQM.

Some organizations are facing a situation which is more difficult to deal with than TQM stagnation. This is when all the improvement initiatives have collapsed and nothing more than ISO 9000 series registration remains. They require guidance on the best means of rekindling the process. This needs to take into account the conditions which caused the current conditions and have they changed, the views from different levels of the organizational hierarchy on the reasons for the failure, current attitudes, what initiatives to take-up, and how they should be approached, etc.

A key concern of major organizations is how to develop effective working relationships with their supplier base and pursue joint improvement initiatives. Whilst there have been a number of attempts at this, doubts still remain amongst major purchasers about their ability to convert all suppliers to TQM and, where it is possible, the most effective means of achieving it and integrating them into the improvement process. One clear principle for success is that the purchaser must be a good role model. There is also evidence that some organizations talk partnership but, in practice, do not act in this way. There are also different kinds of partnerships and organizations must decide what best suits them and their suppliers (see Burnes and Dale 1998 for details of approaches).

In spite of all the quality propaganda, many production/operations people still view their first priority as meeting the production schedule, quota and cost targets and only after achieving these objectives will they give some consideration to quality. Habits of a lifetime are slow in dying. Having said this there is an increasing realization that whilst meeting the schedule may pay salaries, shipping products which do not conform to the customer's requirements is self-defeating. This change in view is more likely to take place in organizations where the Chief Executive Officer and members of the senior management team act as role models.

Total Quality Management is now being given more attention in the European higher educational system and courses featuring it are on the increase (see van der Wiele and Dale 1996). This trend needs to be encouraged because until TQM is recognized as a subject in its own right, the brightest young people will be deterred from studying it and the best graduates will not be attracted into the quality profession. An issue which is currently under debate is whether TQM should be taught as a separate subject in relation to undergraduate and postgraduate degrees awarded in quality management or be treated as an essential component of all courses, in particular, at postgraduate level. Another debate which is starting to surface is whether Universities and Business Schools should be restructuring their MBA courses around the nine elements of the EFQM Model for Business Excellence.

Organizations, in the main, have some difficulty in seeing the need for TQM research undertaken by the academic fraternity, its relevance to their immediate requirements, how they might use the findings and what is the starting point for collaboration. One of the challenges facing both business and academia is how they can develop a closer working relationship with each other so that businesses can be used as the academics' laboratory.

Self-assessment against the EFQM Model for Business Excellence is currently popular. The model makes clear that quality has a meaning for every activity in the organization. As is the case with the ISO 9000 series there are positive and negative views of self-assessment. The negative stresses:

1. that the EFQM model and the respective EQA is only a standard to measure and assess progress and should not be used as the primary drivers to change and develop the organization
2. there can be a focus on criteria to increase the overall points score and these may not be the most important ones to which a business needs to give attention if it is to develop the improvement process in the most effective and efficient manner for its specific market situation
3. a preoccupation with the scoring mechanism and scores to the

detriment of developing improvement plans, and quality professionals relying too much on the model's criteria as a simplistic check
list to solve basic weakness with their organization's improvement
process

The positive aspects are:

1. the meaning of quality, in a holistic sense, given to managers and
   employees alike by the model
2. the setting of quality in a business framework, the measurement
   system which forces management to give specific criteria more
   attention (e.g. people management)
3. the organizational learning arising from carrying out the self-
   assessment
4. the model's universal acceptance and credibility

Self-assessment against the EFQM model is a booming market for consultancy firms, in the provision of training, guidance on use, facilitating
self-assessment, giving guidance on the preparation of a written report,
and external assessment and scoring, etc. This is not always a good thing
since consultants inexperienced in continuous methodologies and mechanisms are jumping on the bandwagon and this can only tarnish the
self-assessment process. With this readily available consultancy facility
it is all so easy for management to abdicate its responsibility for the
self-assessment process.

THE FUTURE

A number of companies who have received considerable publicity because
of their perceived success with TQM have built-up myths supported by
considerable and readily available documentation of how good they are.
The rhetoric surrounding this is perpetuated both inside and outside the
organization. At the operating level of these businesses the reality often
does not live up to the communicated word and what senior and some
middle management believe to be the situation, in particular, at corporate
headquarters. For example: (i) there is a detailed and fully documented
procedure for policy deployment but it is all top-down cascade with little
'catchball', bottom-up feedback and little audit of the agreed plans and
targets and; (ii) it is a requirement that every business unit carries out a
self-assessment which is subject to peer review but the plans to address the
chosen areas for improvement are only given serious attention prior to

such a review. A challenge facing the senior managers of these organizations is to have the courage to stop believing their own self-perpetuating story of success (i.e. group-think), understand why things have not happened at the grass roots of the business as was intended by the corporate headquarters and to address the deficiencies to ensure that the message gets through to the operational level of the business. This requires real and committed leadership.

Quality will continue to permeate every function of an organization and become more integrated with business activities. More organizations will start to use policy deployment as the means to align all efforts in the organization towards its major goals. The role of the quality professional will need to change in response to this in both an operational and strategic sense. Williams et al. (1999) provide some details of the logic behind this and what will be required of quality managers/directors in the future. They argue that when TQM is considered by an organization to be of strategic importance then fundamental changes will be needed not only in the role of the quality manager but in the type of skills they possess.

There will be a greater focus on process streams linked directly to customer groups and suppliers, replacing the traditional functional orientated structure. The challenge will be to integrate these process streams owned by different business organizations and align them to satisfy the requirements of a common end-user and to exploit specific market opportunities. In relation to this, customer expectations will continue to rise as the 'excitement' or 'wow' factors of today become tomorrow's standard features. Organizations will be tasked with finding more in terms of differentiations be it cycle times, responsiveness, flexibility, cost reduction, etc.

The EFQM and MBNQA models will become increasingly recognized by business as general management models useful as a starting point which individual units then need to develop to fit their own situations. It is expected that the misuse of such models will tend to become less as managers become familiar with them, rely less on the use of management consultancies, the hype surrounding them dies away, and consultancies switch their attention to the latest money generating concept.

In the late 1980s and the 1990s was almost a clarion call that the reason why some introductions of TQM had been unsuccessful, (e.g. Wilkinson 1992) was a lack of focus on the so-called soft issues of TQM. The EFQM model, with people management and people satisfaction being the second element after customer satisfaction, in terms of the number of available points, should have changed this perception. A future challenge is to decide how much influence the model has had on these people issues, in particular, management style.

There will be a development in the direction of integrating quality into the normal management procedures and operations of a business. This will be aided by the development of integrated management systems dealing with quality management, the environment and occupational health and safety (see Wilkinson and Dale 1998).

Bridging the gap between the ISO 9000 series level of quality maturity and that of award winning companies will need to be faced in the future. A large number of companies are involved in ISO 9000 series certification. In many cases they have been changed little by the certification process and there is a failure to use the experience as a starting point for quality management development. It is predicted that these companies will come under increasing pressure from their customers to take the quality journey further. They will need to be guided and supported to develop, from the base of ISO 9000 series registration, their quality management maturity.

Small and medium sized enterprises have to join the quality journey. The larger companies have already been exposed to many different types of quality initiatives and usually have well developed contacts with other organizations which have effective quality management practices and with whom they share learning experiences and best practice. SMEs have a problem not only to bridge the gap between the ISO 9000 series and TQM, but also in understanding that there is more to do after receiving an ISO 9000 series certificate (see van der Wiele et al. 1997). The pressure of day-to-day business and the problems which this brings is much stronger than in larger companies. The fostering of continuous improvement mechanisms are more difficult in SMEs because the results might not always be visible and/or will only become evident in the longer term; SMEs are often dealing with today's problems and find it difficult planning for the future. The survival of many SMEs will depend on their continuous improvement efforts in the longer term.

Knowledge gathering and dispersal is a central part of quality management. The basic PDCA improvement cycle is a procedure that automatically leads to increases in knowledge. In addition, many of the other management tools such as empowerment, benchmarking, peer assessment and policy deployment are involved not just in knowledge creation but also in knowledge dispersion. With the rise of interest in the management of knowledge, within the context of a learning organization, as a possible source of corporate competitive advantage in the future, there will be a central role for quality management.

The link between manufacturing and service quality needs to be explored in more detail (see Dale et al. 1997). The early quality management focus of manufacturing organizations has been mainly on the ISO 9000 series, tools and techniques, reliability, process capabilities, etc. Service organizations and those engaged in public services entered the quality management arena much later. They started the process with customer care initiatives, quality circles, flexibility in relation to customer orientation, service recovery, and self-assessment. There are many simple standard statements used in the literature on the differences between manufacturing and service quality (e.g. Gronroos 1990 and Rosander 1985). However, in reality there are few pure manufacturing companies or pure service companies. There are considerable opportunities to learn from each other, much more than has currently taken place. The strengths of the manufacturing and service approaches need to be critically examined to develop new and improved routes on the quality journey.

The term 'Total Quality Management' might well become obsolete during the next decade or so as the principles, practices and models of TQM become part of the every-day fabric of the business.

Business excellence will be the hallmark of the successful organization. Today only a handful of companies can be truly described as 'excellent', 'world class' or 'superior performing'. Benchmarking will play a critical role in determining these companies. By natural evolution there will be many 'excellent' companies and these will be the maturing exponents of TQM using it as the integrative framework. Today 'excellence' is unusual in that it stands out but in the future it will be taken for granted, becoming the expected level of performance and the entry ticket without which an organization will not be able to compete.

REFERENCES

Burnes B. and Dale B. G. (ed.) 1998: *Developing Partnerships*, Gower Publishing, Hampshire.

Dale B. G., Williams R. T., Barber K. D. and van der Wiele T. 1997: 'Managing Quality in Manufacturing Versus Service: A Comparative Analysis', *Managing Service Quality* 7 (5), 242–7.

Dale B. G., van der Wiele T., Williams A. R. T. and Greatbanks R. W. 1998: 'Quality Management Prospects: the Challenges for European Businesses', *Quality World*, July, 46–9.

Gronroos C. 1990: *Services Management and Marketing: Managing the Moments of Trust in a Service Competition*, Lexington, Berkshire.

Rosander A. C. 1985: *The Quest for Quality of Services*, ASQC Quality Press, Milwaukee.

van der Wiele T. and Dale B. G. 1996: 'Total Quality Management Research and Teaching: the Latest Picture from Europe's Leading Universities and Business Schools', *Quality World Technical Supplement*, September, 108–13.

van der Wiele T., Dale B. G. and Williams R. T. 1997: 'ISO 9000 Series Registration to Total Quality Management: the Transformation Journey', *International Journal of Quality Sciences*, 2 (4), 236–52.

Wilkinson A. 1992: 'The Other Side of Quality: Soft Issues and the Human Resources Dimension', *Total Quality Management*, 3 (3), 323–9.

Wilkinson G. and Dale B. G. 1998: 'The Case for Integrated Management Systems', *Quality Engineering*. 11 (1), 249–56.

Williams R. T., Bertsch B., Dale B. G. and van der Wiele, T. 1999: 'The changing role of the quality manager: an examination', *European Quality*, 5 (1), (awaiting publication).

ACKNOWLEDGEMENTS

Barrie Dale wishes to thank Professor Roger Williams and Dr Ton van der Wiele of the Strategic Quality Management Institute, Erasmus University, Rotterdam, for their contribution to the material contained in this chapter.

Index

LIVERPOOL
JOHN MOORES UNIVERSITY
AVRIL ROBARTS LRC
TITHEBARN STREET
LIVERPOOL L2 2ER
TEL. 0151 231 4022